ANGELS

An Endangered Species

by
Malcolm Godwin

Simon and Schuster
New York London Toronto Sydney Tokyo Singapore

SIMON AND SCHUSTER
Simon & Schuster Building
Rockefeller Center
1230 Avenue of the Americas
New York, New York 10020

Consulting Editor: Deborah Bergman
Designed by Malcolm Godwin
Typesetting and computer graphics by Simonetta Castelli, Florence

Angels was produced by Labyrinth Publishing
Printed and bound by Singapore National Printers Ltd
Typeset at MicroPRINT, via Pacini 49 /51 – Florence, Italy

7   9   10   8

Library of Congress Cataloging in Publication Data

Godwin, Malcolm.
  Angels: an endangered species / Malcolm Godwin
      p.   cm.
    ISBN 0–671–70650–0
    1. Angels. 2. Angels––Pictorial works. I. Title.
  BL477.G63 1990
    291.2'15––dc20   90–33122
                                                      CIP

CONTENTS

INTRODUCTION

No-one on earth could feel like this,
I'm thrown and overblown with bliss
There must be an angel
Playing with my heart
I walk into an empty room,
and suddenly my heart goes "Boom"!
Its an orchestra of angels
And they're playing with my heart.
(Must be talking to an angel)
And when I think that I'm alone,
It seems as if there's more of us at home
Its a multitude of angels
And they're playing with my heart.
(Annie Lennox and David. A. Stewart)

This is a typical lyric by the Eurythmics. No-one could accuse this modern group of being overly sentimental, yet their lines are still typical of the genre of the eighties. It is no exaggeration to say that over the last thirty years *one in every ten* pop songs mentions an angel.

It is likely that at least half of the listeners don't belong to any of the religions which gave rise to these beings, yet still know what an angel is supposed to be. Whatever this symbol means to anyone, its power remains extraordinarily alive and magically potent, otherwise the song would lose its whole significance. Opposite page: *Poster by Mouse and Kelly for the group Led Zeppelin.*

[† Newsweek, June 26th 1978 p.32]

HE Angel is one of those Articles of Faith as unshakable as our belief in the existence of God, an atom, or the ill luck of the number 13. One in every ten popular songs invokes angels in some form. They appear on Christmas cards and wedding invitations, they abound as souvenirs, jewelry and religious or semi-religious bric-a-brac. Every museum is packed full of paintings and sculptures of these winged beings and even artists and writers depict them to this very day.

But ask anyone if they really believe in the existence of the angel and suddenly a profound conflict arises between the unthinking certitude of a faith and the sophisticated realism of the 20th century.

In a Gallup poll conducted in the United States during 1978[†], over half the subjects questioned about their belief in angels and demons answered positively. For those who did not share the belief, it might be assumed that they felt angels or devils were an outdated Gothic superstition, for which there must be some simple scientific or psychological explanation.

Such unexamined assumptions from believers or non-believers tell us far more about the blurred nature of the belief systems which underpin our particular culture than about the truth of the actual angels.

It doesn't seem to matter whether the opinions come from the scientific community, the orthodox Churches or the New Age thinkers – on one level angels still manage to retain their magical popularity and power, while on another no one quite believes in them any more.

So, what or who are angels? And why do they seem to persist in the popular mind even today? Such seemingly simple and straightforward questions will lead us into an extraordinary, unexpected and often bizarre world. It is a landscape in which reality, myth, fantasy, legend, dreams and supernatural visions all appear hopelessly entangled.

Throughout history, religions, both primitive and sophisticated, have held beliefs of spiritual beings, powers and principles that mediate between the One transcendental realm of the sacred and the profane dualistic world of space and time. These convictions range from belief in the power of ancestors, spirits of nature or fairy beings from the "other world" to the spiritual beings called angels by the four Western "Religions of the Book."

Our particular concern is with the genus *Angelus Occidentalis*. This is a general term for a number of species and sub-species to be found in the monotheistic religions of Judaism, Zoroastrianism, Christianity and Islam. What is especially significant is that these four religions share the view of a tripartite universe. That is to say, they believe that the cosmos is divided into Heaven, Earth and Hell and is populated accordingly with angels, humans and demons.

This contrasts with the monistic cosmos of the Hindus, the Jains and the Buddhists; the East gene-

rally has no belief in angels as revealers of the truth. This function is left to other beings, often reincarnations of holy sages or incarnations of the deities. But in Western traditions, which are based on prayer rather than meditation, the angel is an essential ingredient. There is even a special group of angels who fall silent at dawn in order to listen to the prayers and praises of Israel.

In Western tradition, in order to reveal the purpose and destiny of humankind, God's Word is communicated through celestial messengers whose primary function was to praise and serve the Almighty and do His Will. Before modern science appeared in the 16th and 17th centuries, and with it the newly discovered Laws and Forces of Nature, angels were supposed to have moved the stars and the elements. Gravity was not a law of nature but an active angelic intelligence.

The term angel derives from a Greek translation of the original Hebrew *mal'akh*, which originally meant the "Shadow side of God," but later came to mean messenger. This derivation may offer a clue as to why we all feel a certain vagueness when attempting to describe the nature of an angel. For a "messenger" implies a function or status within a cosmic hierarchy, rather than an essence.

The primary significance of angels lies not in who or what they are, but rather in what they do. Their inherent nature cannot be separated from their relationship with the Prime mover, the God or Ultimate Source.

Thus we find the Iranian messenger-angel Vohu Manah (Good Mind), revealing God's message to Zoroaster two thousand five hundred years ago, and the Archangel Gabriel dictating the Qur'an to Mohammed over a millennium later. In both cases the role of these spirits of God is far more important than their identity, their nature or "being."

Not only are angels inseparable from God, they are also indivisible from their witnesses.

The Swedish mystic Swedenburg once said: "I am well aware that many will say that no-one can possibly speak with spirits and angels so long as he is living in the body; many say it is all fancy, others that I recount such things to win credence, while others will make other kinds of objection. But I am deterred by none of these: for I have seen, I have heard, I have felt."

It is impossible to argue with a statement like this and we will discover that most of the witnesses to be found within this volume will be as sincere as Swedenburg in their belief that they encountered a real angel with a real message. In the majority of the cases we shall examine this might well be true. However, the simple fact is that it is impossible to separate the observer from the observed. To question the truth of the angel is also to question the truthfulness of the witness. Most of the available evidence of the existence of a real heavenly host would hardly stand up in a court of Law. Substantial facts are hard to come by. Angels, like the Extra-Terrestrials which followed them, don't leave footprints.

* [1] **The Apocrypha.** Material found within the Old Testament was gradually gathered over a period lasting about a millennium. Most of its scriptures were actually compiled during, or shortly after, the period of Exile in Babylonia (586 to 538 B.C.). In the second century B.C. these Hebrew scriptures were translated into Greek (called the Septuagint) to form the Old Testament but some texts were subsequently rejected from the canon by the later Church Fathers. These are now known as the *apocrypha* or the "hidden books". They are not to be confused with the *pseudepigrapha* or the "false writing" which was never included in the original canon at any time. The latter appeared in great profusion during the apocalyptic phase of writing which commenced about 200 years B.C. and ended about one hundred years after Christ's death. The end of the world had failed to arrive, the New Golden Age had failed to materialize and apocalyptic revelations went out of fashion.

The Hidden Books

It's reasonable to assume that everything one would want to know about angels; their names, attributes and duties would be found in the Christian Bible. Surprisingly this is just about the last place to discover such information. The Old Testament actually only mentions three angels by name, if we count the Catholic Book of Tobit. So where do we find the more intimate details of angelic life – who they were, or are, what they are called, what they do and how they interact with humankind?

Virtually all the information that we possess comes from *outside* the orthodox scriptures and canons of the four religions that believe in the existence of angels. Indeed most of these particular texts have been declared heretical, pseudepigraphical or apochryphal.*[1] And yet it is largely these heretical texts which form the basis of our present, if hazy ideas of the host, and on which a large portion of this present volume is based.

Typical of such texts are the three great Chronicles of Enoch, compiled around the 2nd century B.C. from much earlier sources. The pages simply teem with angelic life, names, duties, characteristics and the most intimate descriptions of the host of angels. St. Jerome declared these chronicles to be apocryphal in the 4th century A.D., but up until then they had been deemed an inspired canonical scripture by all the earliest Fathers. In it the scribe Enoch described his journey to the ten Heavens in which he saw gigantic angels in a penal and punishment area. Now this was hardly consistent with the later view of the Church of a separate Heaven and Hell. So Enoch's texts fell into disrepute and virtually disappeared until the 18th century.

Yet Enoch was known as "the man who spoke truth" and the text is remarkably free of all the usual

religious extravaganzas. Although it is unacceptable to orthodox Doctrine, nevertheless much of Enoch's apocryphal material found its way into the New Testament without anyone suspecting. He will be the most important guide to the "Seven Heavens" and the dark caverns of the underworld of Sheol, Gehenna, Hell and the Bottomless Abyss.

God and Devil

This volume is not limited to the benevolent host of Heaven but includes the rebel angels led by Lucifer, once named the" Morning Star," and "The Bringer of Light." Such titles for the Prince of Darkness reveal the difficulty of discovering exactly

which side any particular angel is on – God's or the Devil's. For instance, in the Old Testament, there is no reference to the fallen angels at all. There is nothing to suggest that Satan was evil. We read of *ha-satan*, the "Adversary," but this appears to stand for an office, and by no means a wicked one, rather than being the name of an angel. Whoever held the office was the being most beloved by God and certainly not the Satan who appears in the New Testament. *Any concept of good and malevolent angels seems to be completely lacking in Old Testament writings.* But by the time the New Testament was compiled one third of the heavenly host, led by Satan, had fallen into the Abyss. And there are at least seven conflicting accounts of their fall which took nine days to reach the Pit. There is even one Gnostic version in which the Jewish God, Yahweh, is shown to be Satan, Prince of Darkness, who created our universe and rules it with his dark and evil angels.

It is only by studying the apocrypha, the apocalyptic scriptures and the pseudepigrapha, that the rich and multi-colored picture of the angelic and demonic legions can be pieced together. This is not a static and consistent mosaic. Rather we find a dynamic and constantly evolving panorama of the warring forces of Righteousness and Malevolence. In one early account, for instance, the supposedly "Good" Almighty is seen to possess a disturbingly ambivalent nature: in a moment of pure pique He annihilates an entire "globe" of his angelic choir for failing to sing His praise on cue. We also find the same ambiguity as to what is good and what is wicked in the behavior of many of the Heavenly Father's favorites. These often seem to lead double lives, appearing as Dukes of Hell one moment and singing Hallelujahs around the Celestial throne the next, without a trace of tarnish to their shining haloes.

By the 3rd century A.D. this essentially Jewish

Opposite: **Siren Bird of Heaven** *Russian Lubok of the 18th century, Historical Museum, Moscow.* The Siren bird was very popular in Russia. The text explains the creature appears in the land of India. The Hindu Apsaras were the dispensers of bliss and delight on the heavenly plane. It is said that they wrapped the deceased in their voluptuous arms, carrying the fortunate soul in ecstasy to paradise. The Sirens were a little naughtier but equally effective in their promised delights. Like the Faeries of the Celts, the power of Sirens is the power of the female. This is the opposite pole to the world of the angels of the Religions of the Book.
Above: **Winged Artemis,** *Greece 5th Century B.C.*

ambivalence had disappeared and two very distinct and opposing species had emerged.

Themes of Two Volumes

Even theologians found the concepts of angels and demons to be an anachronism when viewed alongside scientific observations of the nature of the cosmos. The astronomical findings of the 16th century demolished the last vestiges of a world at the center of the universe. Angels could not survive the fact that Earth was a very minor planet circling a mediocre star on the outer arm of a relatively inconspicuous galaxy. However, with the emergence of 20th century Western psychology, the principles, underlying the belief in angel and demon took on a new significance. Many theologians have re-mythologized the tripartite cosmos into a three layered structure of the personality (the superego, the ego and the libido) or the later concept of the three brain layers (Reptilian, Neo-Mammalian and Neo-Cortex). The Freudian and Jungian "myths" of the human personality have initiated an entirely new dimension in the study of both angels and their fallen brothers. It is just such themes as these which will be explored in this volume.

In fact this book is really two volumes within one cover. In order to examine all the possible explanations of the host it is necessary to have a clear reference as to what the traditional and orthodox view of the angelic host might be. However, we find that today there simply isn't a unified and consistent vision. For instance, when the Catholic Encyclopedia, published in 1967, maintains that "Theology has purified the obscurity and error contained in traditional views about angels, " they promptly confuse us further by assuring the faithful that angels are "completely spiritual and no longer merely a very fine material, fire-like and vaporous." And so the ambiguities remain. Conservative Catholics, including the present Pope, also argue for an actual angelic spirit called the devil, while skeptics within the same Church believe that there is only individual sin by the choice inherent in exercising our free will. There are Bishops who insist on angels and others who declare that they don't exist.

Protestant theology is no less ambivalent. Martin Luther swept aside the entire elaborate angelic superstructure in a contemptuous gesture, but curiously and grimly held on to his belief in Satan and his dark hordes. But, as he pointed out, if there was no sin and no Devil what need of Christ as a redeemer?

So as there is a real confusion today over the nature of the angel a complete Treasury of Angelic Lore has been compiled from the period when the angels were in Heaven and all was clear in the world. Part One is a time-sealed treasure house in which we can view the angels at the very peak of their power and authority. This Golden Age abruptly came to an end during the apocalyptic Black Death which decimated the population of Europe in a few short years. Only a decade after the plague had swept by, the Church, under the merciless pressure of new ways of thinking about man and the cosmos, was beginning to disown the elaborate angelic hierarchy. The once teeming streets of the Heavenly City were suddenly silent and deserted.

But where did the angels go? This is the subject of the second part of the book.

Fact and Faith

There seem to be two basic methods to approach a subject like that of angels. One fruitful approach appears to be historical. This can be summarized as the method in which *facts outweigh faith*. It has the added advantage of allowing us to examine the various genealogical family trees of the angelic host. Each separate species can be traced back to its particular cultural origins. In many cases there is blatant evidence of wholesale borrowings from earlier bloodlines. We see how scribes from one religious group simply absorbed into their writings the juicier myths of those tribes they conquered or were conquered by. This is most evident in the eclectic borrowings of the Hebrews. With some justification they can claim to be the first to introduce angels on a truly heavenly scale. The great temptation, in applying a strictly historical method, is to conclude that angels are simply the collected and exaggerated fantasies of holy scholars. And it appears that it is true in many cases.

There is, however, another method which might be labeled the supernatural. In this *faith outweighs fact*. This is actually the one most of us apply to a subject like angels without really thinking. We have been handed down a number of assumptions, based on a continuing tradition of popular piety which seems to have archetypal roots far deeper than many of the religions which pass in the night. These archaic images, which are far older than Christianity, Islam or Judaism, seem almost to be passed down in the genes, or at least have a powerful connection with a collective memory field.

The last approach is that of scientific method. Here the equation is more subtle. One might say that *faith is created by fact*, or that by observing a phenomenon scientifically an observer can build up an idea of how it works and what it is. But modern scientists are discovering that the world is not quite so simple and that often *fact is created by faith*. Quantum physicists know, that if they expect a particle to act like a wave, it does. If they expect it to act like a point, it likewise accommodates their idea. This is partially due to the fact that any method of observing the world necessarily changes our perception of it. More fundamental is the notion that we cannot step outside of the universe

to observe it. We are part of our own experiment. This has far reaching significance when trying to observe angels. Remember that the angel cannot be separated from the witness. There is no substantial and concrete evidence save for what the witness saw and felt. The rest is the stuff of myth, legend and speculation.

Reasonable Intuition

The purpose of Part Two of Angels is to offer a number of classic cases of both encounters and speculations of angelic nature.

In the following pages, you will see that *something* really has happened to those who have experienced angels or demons. Many witnesses have been transformed beyond recognition by the encounter. It is my hope that in some way this may happen to the reader.

For, as far as angels are concerned, Samuel Butler was right when he said, "all reason is against it, and all healthy instinct is for it." And that seems as true now as it was in the bible lands ten thousand years ago.

Adoration of the Lamb *Jan Van Eyck 15th Century Flanders*

PART ONE

THE TREASURY

Angelic Lore

THE TREASURY

Angels surrounding Christ and the four Apostles. *Illuminated manuscript 1109 A.D. British Museum MS 11695.*

HE FIRST PART OF THIS VOLUME is really a separate, miniature reference manual. It inventories the entire Angelic Host as it was known at the peak of its most dazzling Golden Epoch, during the late Middle Ages in Europe. It coincided with the new vision of the Renaissance and the rise of Humanism, and ended abruptly in the middle of the 14th century during the apocalyptic horrors of the Black Death. The images of the Angelic Host as known in that era, are the ones that have been passed down to us, almost intact, by the lore of popular piety. It is fascinating to discover that the image of the angel has hardly altered from this epoch, almost as if time had not touched the species' golden youth. Somehow the angel has been sealed in a time-proof capsule. And it is this 'eternally' young form which we all respond to and vaguely acknowledge when the subject arises.

After this blaze of glory, quite suddenly, angels ceased to have the full doctrinal blessings of the Church. During the Inquisition of the following two hundred years the authorities turned their undivided attentions to the fallen host of devils and demons. However, through popular piety and an almost pagan worship of the celestial spirits, angels retained a powerful emotional hold upon most believers.

The evolution of the idea of a unique angelic species can be viewed from countless angles. Historically speaking, for instance, they are clearly the hybrid result of an extraordinary Hebrew program of cross-breeding original Egyptian, Sumerian, Babylonian and Persian supernatural beings. This genetic interaction of ideas produced the outward appearance of the winged messenger of God which we know of today. By the 1st century after Christ this essentially Jewish creation was adopted, almost wholesale, by the new religion, and six centuries later by the Muslims. Since then that fundamental angelic form has undergone no radical alterations.

In a way, this Treasury of Angelic Lore is somewhat like a time-sealed museum; a rare collection of old and precious things. However a true treasure house does not necessarily imply either classification or meaning. It is simply a place to display the elaborate gems of a lore which spans a historical period of over four thousand years. Whether the collection still retains a significance in this century, or is merely shelves of paper angels which are the creation of scholars and priests, is a question reserved for the second half of the volume.

Either way, belief in angels has persisted in popular lore, while the Church from which they sprang almost seems embarrassed by references to them. It is as if the beliefs of their Golden Age had been caught in the years of perpetual youth by some medieval camera or fixed in polished amber like exotic archaic flies. We will now examine some of those unique portraits.

Above: **Cherubim guarding the Ark of the Covenant.** *French miniature 14th Century.* Compare this image with the **Sphinxes** below *from 8th Century Persia.* The two golden Cherubim who were the guardians of the Ark of the Covenant were far more likely to resemble these bizarre figures than either the French version or the later sugary creatures which decorate baroque walls. Our present day concepts of angels hardly includes such monsters.

Right: **Jacob's dream of the ladder** with angels ascending and descending. *Hayley, 18th Century.*

THE FIRST WING : Heavenly Hierarchy

TALIAN BUREAUCRACY is claimed to be the closest to that of Heaven; it works solely by Divine Intervention and takes Eternity for anything to happen. One glimpse into the celestial archives certainly makes anyone wonder just what might occur in an emergency. The observer can get quickly lost in the unbelievable complexity of the various orders and departments, the changing number of Heavens, the conflicting hierarchies and the duplication of department heads. It seems obvious, in such a heavenly muddle, why the dark forces have such an easy and unopposed life on earth.

But much of the apparent confusion actually arises from the conflicting accounts of our authoritative sources. St. Ambrose differs with St. Jerome, who disagrees with St. Thomas Aquinas, who says that St. Paul must have been wrong. The theologians are even worse than the saints. Few even agree on the nature of the celestial hierarchies, let alone on what their various duties and missions might be.

For instance, no two authorities see eye to eye on who the Archangels are. While it is generally thought that there are seven, Islam only recognizes four. Often an Archangel appears as a member of an entirely different angelic order, far higher up the celestial league table. That same Archangel might also appear as warden of more than one heavenly domain, while simultaneously operating as the angel of death and a terrible Duke of Hell.

The Nine Choirs

In order to make some sense of what first appears to be an unholy mess, we will adopt the most standard and orthodox hierarchy of the angels. According to both the two foundational texts, the *Celestial Hierarchies* of Dionysius and the *Summa Theologica* by Thomas Aquinas, there are nine celestial orders orbiting the Throne of Glory, rather like that of our own planetary system. The nine angelic orders surrounding the Divine Core, appear within the following three distinct groups:

Highest Triad:
1. Seraphim 2. Cherubim 3. Thrones
Middle Triad:
4. Dominations 5. Virtues 6. Powers
Lowest Triad:
7. Principalities 8. Archangels 9. Angels

We can now enter a mysterious landscape where few have been for many centuries.

Details from the Last Judgment *by Giotto, Campo Santo, Italy, 15th Century.*

The Upper Triad

According to the Hebrews the universe is a hierarchy. The Christians adopted this Jewish model of the Cosmos in which God is both at the center of the cosmos and at the highest point of the hierarchy. Entities radiate outwards from His Presence, some being close to the center while others move further and further away from the Divine source of Light and Love.

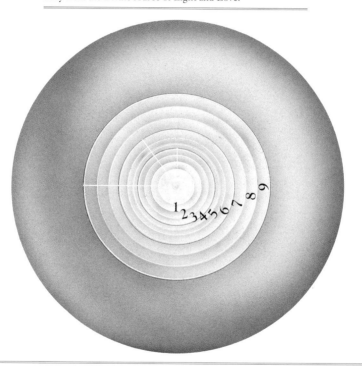

It is a dynamic and ever shifting scenario. Angels are arranged on three descending levels. Each level has three ranks or Orders. The highest Triad is made up of the Seraphim, the Cherubim and the Thrones. These are in direct communion with the Divine Unity and receive God's unfiltered Illumination. The next triad orbiting God is composed of the Dominations, Virtues and Powers who receive the Divine Illumination from the first Triad and then in turn, transmit it to the lowest triad – the Principalities, Archangels and Angels. These then convey that illumination to us mortal humans.

Right: This diagram shows the inner orders of the Primary Triad resonating Love (the Seraphim) and Knowledge (the Cherubim). These subtle vibrations issue from the beat of their wings and the sound of their voices and yet remains essentially immaterial and insubstantial. However the subsequent "orbit" of the Ofanim is a region where form and substance begin to materialize. It shows the outward movement from the central Divinity which is pure Thought. Thought slows down as it moves from the source and becomes Light, which in turn decelerates to become Heat which condenses into matter.

The entire hierarchy of angels can best be described as an endlessly vast sphere of beings who surround an unknowable centerpoint which is called God. The Divine Core is described as an emanation of pure thought of the highest vibration, whose subtle rays appear to change frequency the further they travel from the center. As the vibrations slow down, they first become an orbiting region of pure light. As this light slows down even further from the source it begins to condense into matter. Thus the image would appear as a vast sun surrounded by a thin skin of dark matter.

The first Triad of angelic presences are known as the Seraphim, the Cherubim and the Thrones and they are clustered around that central core of purity. A Seraph vibrates at the highest angelic frequency. The Cherub, on the next orbiting ring around the source, has a vibration rate which is a little lower, while the Thrones of the third ring mark the point at which matter begins to appear.

The First Choir: Seraphim.

Seraphs are generally accepted to be the highest order of God's Angelic Servants. It is they who ceaselessly chant in Hebrew the Trisagion – *Kadosh, Kadosh, Kadosh* –" Holy, Holy, Holy is the Lord of Hosts, the whole earth is full of His Glory" while they circle the Throne. One beautiful explanation for this otherwise seemingly monotonous activity is that it is actually a song of creation, a song of cele-

bration. It is the primary vibration of Love. It is a creative, resonating field of Life. The Seraphim are in direct communion with God and as such are beings of pure light and thought who resonate with the Fire of Love. However, when they appear to humans in their angelic form it is as six-winged and four-headed beings. The prophet Isaiah saw flaming angels above the Throne of God: "Each had six wings: two covered the face, two covered the feet and two were used for flying."

Serpent Fire of Love

Popularly known as the "fiery, flying serpents of lightning," who "roar like lions" when aroused, the Seraphim are more identified with the serpent or dragon than any other angelic order. Their name actually suggests a blend of the Hebrew term רפא *rapha*, meaning "healer," "Doctor" or "surgeon" and שר *ser*, meaning "higher being" or "guardian angel." The *Ser*pent or dragon has long been a symbol for the healing arts, being sacred to Aesculapius. Two snakes curl around the legendary "caduceus," our present-day symbol of the medical profession, which originally appeared as a wand in the hand of the universal Indo-European God Hermes. It will be discovered later that the Greek Hermes was the self-same Deity as the Egyptian Thoth, the Roman God Mercury and the later Archangel Michael who was also a Seraph. The serpent image of this angelic order symbolizes rejuvenation through its ability to shed its skin and reappear in a brilliant and youthful form, much as we see in the myth of the fiery phoenix.

According to Enoch, there were only four Seraphim, corresponding to the four winds or directions. This is in accord with their four-headed aspect. Later commentators amended this to mean there were four major Princes who ruled over the Seraphim. Their chief is said to be either Metatron or Satan, while the others are given as Kemuel, Nathanael and Gabri-el.

Confusion in the Ranks

Even in this brief account of the highest angelic presence ambiguities show through the seams. It can be observed in the diagram that, although Archangels rank six orders *below* that of the Seraphim, appearing on the outer, more material, rings of the sphere, some ruling Seraph Princes of the innermost core have been called Archangels. And one likely candidate is none other than the arch-fiend – Satan. To add to the theological confusion, Metatron, who is also named as the leader of the fiery serpent angels, in some occult circles is known as Satan, Prince of Darkness, or that "old dragon." In his whiter, Seraphic mode Metatron is claimed to be the mightiest of all the heavenly hierarchs and is specifically charged with the welfare and sustenance of humankind. He is reputed to possess not six but six times six wings, thirty-six wings in all and countless eyes.

This type of heavenly paradox is all too common, but having alerted the reader to potential confusion, in future we will try to list such ambivalent attributes without comment.

The Second Choir: Cherubim

In both Judaic and Christian lore, God is said to have stationed "East of Eden the Cherubim and the Ever Turning Sword to guard the way to the Tree of Life."

Although in this famous passage they are the first angels to be encountered in the Bible, the Cherubim are actually late comers to the celestial hierarchy. Even so they managed to secure the second place around the Throne of the Almighty by the time Dionysius drew up his fundamental work. The Hebrew word was כְּרוּב *Kerub*, translated by some scholars as meaning "one who intercedes", and by others as "Knowledge." The original *Ka-ri-bu* were the terrible and monstrous guardians of temples and palaces in Sumer and Babylon. During their captivity in Babylon the Hebrews must have become familiar with these multiple-bodied, fabulous, winged beasts at the entrances to holy places. Similar guardian genii were to be found throughout the whole of the Near East, and

Above and opposite page: **Seraphim** *8th century Spain.* The seraphim once referred to the mighty Chaldean, earth-fertilizing, lightning snakes. These later became the inter-twining serpent spirits of the caduceus carried by Mercury. Mercury is associated with Archangel Michael who is said to have the wings of a peacock. The "eyes" on the peacock wings are all seeing. These seraphim are illustrations of the encounter of Ezekiel which describes the myriad eyes on the wings of the celestial being.

tacular accounts of a Cherub from an encounter with one at the river Chebar. The Hebrew prophet, Ezekiel, witnessed at close hand four Cherubim, each with four faces and four wings (see chapter 2, Part 2). John of Patmos insists in *Revelations* that they had six wings and many eyes, but in the heat and excitement of the Apocalypse he can be forgiven his haste in identifying a Seraph by mistake. As vindication of the Cherub's old role as a guardian spirit two can be found as golden sculptures covering the Ark of the Covenant.

As already seen when Seraphim ceaselessly intone the Trisagion, the vibrations created by that Holy, Holy, Holy give rise to the Fire of Love. By contrast, the subtle vibration emanating from the Cherubim is one of Knowledge and Wisdom.

How such magnificent and awesome beings shrunk to the size of tubby little winged babies, fluttering prettily in the corners of Baroque ceilings, remains one of the mysteries of existence.

The Third Choir: Thrones (Ophanim or Galgallin)

In Jewish Merkabah lore these angels are described as the great "wheels" or the "many eyed ones." The Hebrew *Galgal* has the double meaning of wheels and "pupil of the eye." Strangely, while the Cherubim appear to be God's charioteers, the Ophanim seem to be the actual chariots.

Without doubt the most detailed account of their appearance is from Ezekiel (1:13-19) "and their appearance was like burning coals of fire. Something like the appearance of torches was moving back and forth between the living creatures, and the fire was bright, and out of the fire there was lightning going forth... As I kept seeing the living creatures, why look! There was one wheel on the Earth beside the

winged, eagle-headed deities already guarded an Assyrian Tree of Everlasting Life.

It was a simple step for the awe-struck Hebrew scribe to borrow both the Tree and its guardian and transplant them into the Jewish Garden of Eden. By the time Theodorus, the Christian Bishop of Heraclea, speaks of the Cherubim as being "Beasts, which might terrify Adam from the entrance of Paradise," the transformation is complete.

So much for their historical pedigree. In the original Hebrew form they have four wings, four faces and are often depicted as being the Bearers of God's Throne and His charioteers. In *Psalm 18* God rides a Cherub, although the actual chariot seems to have been an angel of the next order down – namely a Throne or Ophanim.

We are fortunate to have one of the most spec-

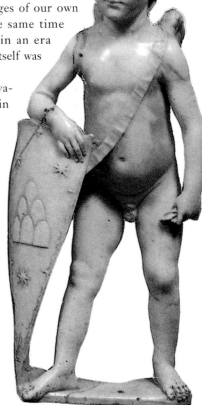

creatures, by the four faces of each. As for the appearance of the wheels and their structure, it was like the glow of chrysolite; and the four of them had one likeness. And their appearance and their structure were just as when a wheel proved to be in the midst of a wheel... And as for their rims, they had such height that they caused fearfulness; and their rims were full of eyes all around the four of them. And when the living creatures went, the wheels would go beside them, and when the living creatures were lifted up from earth, the wheels would be lifted up."

We find echoes from Elijah who was born up in a luminous whirlwind and from Enoch who calls these angels as "of the fiery coals."

The descriptions of the thrones have caught the imagination of many a UFO buff. They do tally very closely to observations of present-day encounters with so called alien spacecraft. Of all the angelic forms the "wheels" are certainly the most puzzling. Perhaps it is the simple fact that they do resemble images of our own technology but at the same time they were described in an era when even the wheel itself was hi-tech.

The Thrones are variously said to reside in the third or the fourth heaven. Some confusion may have arisen because those borders have some very bizarre properties. So far we have been exploring the *immaterial* universe of the Seraphim and Cherubim who inhabit the innermost spheres around the central core. Both these angelic principles are said to express His Divine Will as constantly flowing waves

Left: Toomes conception of a **Cherubim** *from Heywards, The Hierarchy of the Blessed Angels.* Here we see a seventeenth century illustration of a Cherubim. This is seen as a four winged, single headed being. In the background we can make out the biblical Cherubim who guards the Tree of Life with an ever turning flaming sword.
Above: **A Cherubim charioteer** with the distinctive wheels of an Ophanim. *From a carving, 10th century.*

Originally the Cherubim were mighty guardian figures which appeared throughout the Near and Middle East. The earliest Sumerian term is six thousand years old. This is found in the archaic pictogram of Ka-ri-bu. In this Ka is a head crying out, ri is a winged form which also suggests protection while bu is a sharp spear or sword like image which is associated with an armed man. Thus the overall portrait is that of a winged and armed guardian. This certainly corresponds to the huge Assyrian creatures with winged bodies of lions, bulls, sphinxes or eagles with faces of men who often flanked the portals of the temples. The sweet Italian cherub by *Rosso Fiorentino* demonstrates the gulf between the original angel and the sentimental product which has come down to us.

of creativity. But they are still insubstantial, or more accurately, immaterial manifestations of those creative forces. The Ophanim, however, inhabit a region of Heaven *which begins to take on form and substance* much as we know it. It is at this point that Heaven meets Earth and takes on the substance of the flesh and thus becomes exposed to the possibility of corruption. Rudolph Steiner goes so far as to say that, in a gesture of love, the Ophanim offered matter as a basis for our material existence

The ruling Prince of this order is commonly thought to be Raphael. According to rabbinic writings all the Hebrew patriarchs promptly became angels of this order upon arrival in heaven. Understandably, Christian theologians do not subscribe to this point of view.

Right: **Expulsion from the Garden.** Top: *Hildesheim 1015.* Center: *Lorenzo Maitani 1310.* Bottom: *Basilica di San Zeno, Verona.* As can be seen, the central image shows a six-winged Cherub guarding the Tree of Life. As the depictions of angels became more realistic artists found it increasingly difficult to express these multiple-winged beings so this little panel is a rare little masterpiece of invention.

The Second Triad

The second group of three orders is composed of the Dominions, the Virtues and the Powers. The theme of an ultimate unification with "God the Source" epitomizes the whole endeavor of the Second Triad of angels. Because of this there is a constant dualistic tension arising between the polarities of good and bad, matter and spirit, higher and lower. All of the Orders within the Triad strive to balance or reconcile such opposites, and all are prone to the risk of corruption in doing so.

The Fourth Choir : Dominions

Variously described as Dominations, Lords, Kuriotetes, or by Hebrew lore as the Hashmallim (Hamshallim), this order, according to Dionysius "regulate angels' duties." Other authorities maintain that the Dominions are channels of mercy living within the second heaven. Supposedly this holy sphere has the celestial letters of the Holy Name suspended within its realm. The ruling Lords are said to be Zadkiel, Hashmal, Yahriel and Muriel. Hasmal, or Chasmal, is known as the "fire speaking angel."

The Fifth Choir : Virtues

Variously known as the Malakim, the Dunamis or the Tarshishim, these angels of grace bestow Blessings from on high, usually in the form of miracles. They are most often associated with heroes and with those who struggle for good. It is said that they instill courage when it is needed most. They appeared in the Ascension of Christ where two provided his escort to Heaven. It is recorded in the *Book of Adam and Eve* that two Virtues acted like midwives at the birth of Cain. Known as "The Brilliant or Shining Ones" their ruling princes are said to be Micha-el, Gabri-el, Rapha-el, Bari-el, Tarshish and, before the great rebellion, Satan-el.

The Sixth Choir : Powers

Variously named Dynamis, Potentiates and Authorities, they were supposedly the first angels created by God. The Powers inhabit the perilous border region between the first and second heavens. Dionysius accredits them with resisting the efforts of Demons to take over the World. They appear to act as a kind of border guard who patrol the Heavenly Pathways on the lookout for devilish infiltration. These patrols are obviously a risky business and St. Paul sternly warned his various flocks that Powers can be both good and evil. In Romans 13:1 it is revealed that "The Soul is subject to the Powers," and it is in their efforts to keep a balance within our souls that some are known to become over-identified with the darker side of human beings and thus to fall. Even so the Powers find their true vocation in balancing or reconciling opposites.

As chief of the order, Cama-el does deserve close scrutiny for he exemplifies that wavering path between good and evil which is such a pronounced characteristic of the entire Order. His name means "he who sees God" and the *Magus* suggests he is one of the favored seven angels who stand in the Presence of God. Some say it was Chamuel who wrestled with Jacob and who later appeared to Jesus in the Garden of Gethsemane. But in the darker mode Cama-el is identified as a Duke of Hell, appearing with the body of a leopard, and in the occult he is known as the ruler of the evil planet of war, Mars. Even the Druids, hardly noted for their interest in the Angelic Host, have Camael as their

THE POWERS

Peris Creanit, perdit Occiderunt.

A Power from Toome's engraving in Heywards, *Hierarchy of the Blessed Angels.*
Of all the fallen angels, the greatest defection seems to have come from the ranks of the Powers. Of their once powerful Princes, Beleth is now a Duke of Hell commanding 85 legions of devils, Carniveau is a greater Demon invoked in many witches sabbaths. Carreau is claimed to have been one of the devils which possessed the body of Sister Seraphina of Loudon and Crocell is now a Duke of Hell with 48 legions at his command. Even the angel companion of Michael, Sensiner rebelled as did Uvall who became a Duke of Hell and appears to be the demon pimp as his speciality is to procure the love of women for his supplicants.

God of war. He is commander of 144,000 angels of Destruction, Punishment, Vengeance and Death. Whether these are in the service of God or the Devil remains uncertain. As Kemu-el, this Prince acts as mediator between the prayers of Israel and the Hierarchs of the seventh heaven.

According to one legend it was Cama-el who was blasted by Moses when he tried to prevent the Lawgiver from receiving the *Torah* from God. This apparent contradiction of motives gives the great clue to the major attraction of the Powers. In Christian lore the soul is considered the great battleground of the forces of good and evil. Being in charge of our souls gives the Powers an intriguing, far-ranging, and often capricious, territory. Their demanding task is to transform the duality of our everyday understanding into a unity with the Divine source. In esoteric terms they are the spirit guides who assist those who have left the body and have lost their way in the astral plane. If the deceased are unbalanced by the experience, their fears can magnify to such an extent that they become insane and it is the spirit guides who help at this moment.

| Uriel | Michael | Gabriel | Raphael |

The Third Triad

The third triad of Principalities, Archangels and Angels, is firmly rooted within the realm of the first heaven and its borders with our temporal and material universe. This means that all three orders are the most exposed and vulnerable to any corrosion of the flesh. It might also account for the fact that individual angels from these orders are most well known to us simply because they are most like us.

The Seventh Choir : Principalities

Originally the Princedoms were seen as an order which was in charge of nations and great cities on Earth. Later these boundaries expanded, but in so doing the borders became very vague. The Principalities extended their dominion and became the protectors of religion (a difficult assignment if all four major religions are involved), tending to take a rather orthodox view of good and evil. This said, it must be added that one contender for chief of the Princedoms is Nisrock. Originally an Assyrian deity he is considered, at least in occult writings, to be the chief chef to the Demon Princes of Hell. A more likely candidate as chief is Ana-el who is named one of the seven angels of creation, which might account for his association with human sexuality. He is also governor of the second heaven, and is held to control all the kingdoms and leaders on earth with a Dominion stretching to encompass the Moon. Another prince is Hami-el who was said to have transported Enoch to Heaven although he is more well known as the Chaldean deity Ishtar.

The great Prince of Strength, Cervill, is claimed to have aided David in his bid to slay Goliath.

Above: **The four Archangels** *from the altarpiece, San Marco, Rome.* Opposite page: **The Archangel Micha-el,** *13th Century Istanbul.*

The Eighth Choir : The Magnificent Seven

Most people can name at least two or three Archangels. Of all the angelic orders these justifiably have the greatest claim to fame. The seven angels who stand before God in Revelations are usually interpreted as the Archangels. The *Koran* of Islam only recognizes four and actually names but two – Jibril (Gabriel) and Michael. While Christian and Jewish sources agree on the number seven, there is an unholy debate as to who they might actually be. Four names which do however appear regularly are: Michael, Gabriel, Rapha-el and Uri-el. The other three candidates are traditionally chosen from Metatron, Remi-el, Sari-el, Ana-el, Ragu-el and Razi-el.

Dionysius tells us that Archangels are "Messengers which carry Divine Decrees." They are considered the most important intercessionaries between God and humans and it is they who command the legions of Heaven in their constant battle with the Sons of Darkness.

Archangel Micha-el

His name means "who is as God." In most Christian lore he is the" Greatest." In fact he and Gabriel

The singular-EL is an ancient word with a long and complex etymological history which has a common origin with many other ancient words in other languages.

Sumerian	EL	"brightness" or "shining"
Akkadian	ILU	"radiant one"
Babylonian	ELLU	"the shining one"
Old Welsh	ELLU	"a shining being"
Old Irish	AILLIL	"shining"
English	ELF	"shining being"
Anglo-Saxon	AELF	"radiant being"

are the only two actually mentioned in the Old Testament at all, save for Raphael who introduces himself in the Catholic *Book of Tobit*. Originally Michael was a Chaldean deity but since those ancient days his exploits have captured the popular imagination far more than any other angel. Many of his deeds are also attributed to the other Archangels. It is a measure of Micha-el's popularity that this should occur.

In one account he is said to have wiped out, single-handed and overnight, a hundred and eighty-five thousand men from the army of the Assyrian king, Sennercherib, who was threatening Jerusalem in 701 B.C.. Michael is said to have stayed the hand of Abraham who was about to sacrifice his son Isaac. According to Jewish lore it is Michael who appeared to Moses in the midst of a burning bush and who appears again in the burial episode, where he disputes the possession of the body of the old patriarch with Satan. It is Michael who will descend from heaven with "the key of the abyss and a great chain in his hand" and will bind the Satanic dragon for 1000 years (Revelation: 20:1).

He assuredly remains the undisputed hero in the first war against Satan: in single combat he defeated the arch-fiend and hurled him down from heaven. Another, more popular version of this is of course the one in which he subdues the dragon-Satan, although now St. George has monopoly on these great serpents.

Michael is usually shown with an unsheathed sword which signifies his role as God's great champion. In a curious passage in Daniel, God speaks in a uncharacteristically humble fashion, admitting

that He had been unavoidably delayed in keeping a promised appointment with the prophet. The reason He gives is that Cyrus, the Prince of Persia, had successfully resisted Him for twenty-one days. He tells Daniel "but Michael, one of the leading Princes, has come to my assistance." He confesses that "In all this there is no one to lend me support except Michael, your Prince, on whom I rely to give me support and re-inforce me." From this we can deduce that Michael was the guardian angel of Israel, but it also appears he is the only one who backed up the Throne when the chips were really down.

There are Muslim traditions which describe Michael in wondrous form. "Wings the color of green emerald...covered with saffron hairs, each of them containing a million faces and mouths and as many tongues which, in a million dialects, implore the pardon of Allah." In the Koran it is said that from the tears shed by this great angel over the sins of the faithful, cherubim are formed.

In earlier Persian legends Michael is identified with Beshter, "the one who provides sustenance for mankind." In one Dead Sea Scroll, *The War of the Sons of Light Against the Sons of Darkness*, Michael is named the "Prince of Light," who leads a host against the dark legions of Belial, Prince of Darkness. In this role Michael is Viceroy of Heaven which, oddly enough, was the title of the Prince of Darkness before the fall.

Michael is also known as the angel of the Last Judgement and, as the "weigher of souls," has a pedigree dating from when the tribes of Israel were in captivity in Egypt. There, the weigher of hearts of the deceased was Anubis. This Dog, or jackal-headed deity was identified with the most important star in the Egyptian sky, Sirius, the dog star. In Persia the star is known as Tistar, the "Chief," and

the earlier Akkadian term was Kasista, which denotes a Prince or leader. Add a pinch of Hebrew (*sar* is commander or Prince) and we come very close to the "Prince and Commander of the Stars(angels) who is Michael." His peacock decorated wings recall the eye of the Egyptian Goddess, Maat, whose feather was weighed against a mortal's heart which lay in the balance of Anubis.

In the Middle Ages Michael was also held to be the "Psychopomp," the conductor of souls to the other world. As the Church was anxious to attract the old pagan worshipers of Roman Gaul, who remained faithful to the God Mercury, they endowed Michael with many of the attributes of that under-

(continued on page 43)

The Weighing of the Heart *from the Papyrus of Anhai.* Anubis, the jackal-headed God of the Egyptian underworld was identified with the Indo-European god Hermes in his role as Psychopomp, Conductor of Souls. Hermes was also one of the Aegean serpent-consorts of the Great Mother. His caduceus, as that of the Roman god Mercury, remains the great alchemical and healing symbol. In its dragon form it represents the Serpent which is overcome by the other angel of death Michael. Many of the temples and shrines dedicated to Mercury-Hermes were sited on top of hills. On their ruins were built the chapels and churches dedicated to Michael. Hermes ascended to Heaven in the form of Sirius, the Dog or Jackal headed Star. Opposite page. **Micha-el** *Detail from the Last Judgment by Hans Memlinc.*

Michael and the Dragon Left: *Engraving by Martin Schongauer, 1470.* Below: *Lubok, 19th Century Russia.* Right: *Painting by Giambono, Rome.* Michael has many competitors for the title of Dragon Slayer. St. George is the most famous rival although the story of the Assyrian hermit St. David provides a fascinating variation.

This saintly hermit who loved nature found to his horror that many of the animals nearby were being ravaged by a "large and fearsome dragon with bloodshot eyes and a horn growing out of his forehead, and a great mane on his neck."

When St. David threatened to make mincemeat of this terrible descendant of the Evil Tiamat unless it left the area in peace, the dragon admitted that it dared not venture forth because of its terror of thunderbolts. Agreeing to leave on the sole condition that the weather was clear and that the Saint would promise not to take his eyes from the Dragon for one second until they had reached the safety of a great river, the two of them set out. As they almost reached the river the weather suddenly worsened and David heard the voice of the archangel Michael call from behind him, 'David!' Startled he forgot his promise and looked around. Thereupon the poor dragon's worst fears were realized as he was struck by a lightning bolt and incinerated. The gentle hearted David was deeply saddened and asked the reason for the trick. Michael told him that if the dragon had entered the water it would have grown so vast it would have destroyed ships and have ravaged the coasts. (9th century legend of St. David)

(continued from page 39)

world God. Chapels dedicated to Michael sprang up over the ruins of the earlier temples which invariably had been built on hills or mounds. Thus Michael became, like Mercury, the guide for the dead. The many "Michael's Mounts" to be found throughout Europe and Britain attest to the power of that ancient archetype – the mound of the dead. Many of the sites were, in more ancient times, the focal points of Earth Forces known as Dragon Power so it is hardly a coincidence that Micha-el's fame should be connected with destroying the Dragon. Yet another curious link is to be found with the God-magician, Hermes, who

in many cases is interchangeable with Mercury. The Greeks also called Hermes the Psychopomp, and his phallic spirit in the form of standing stones protected crossroads throughout the Greco-Roman world. While the Church banished all the earlier pagan deities to hell, in the case of Micha-el the various powers of all these Gods were absorbed within the Archangel's attributes.

It is foretold in Daniel that when the world is once again in real trouble Micha-el will reappear. Many scholars point to this century as being the one in which he will reveal himself once more in all his glory.

Archangel Gabri-el

The Sumerian root of the word Gabri is *GBR*, gubernator, or governor. Some argue that it means *Gibor*, power or hero. Gabri-el is the Governor of Eden and ruler of the Cherubim. But Gabri-el is unique amongst an otherwise male or androgynous host, for it is almost certain that this great Archangel is the only female in the higher echelons.

She is also the only angel mentioned in the Old Testament by name, except for Micha-el, and is said to sit on the left hand side of God which is further evidence of her being female. To Mohammedans, Jibril/Gabriel dictated the entire Koran to Mohammed and is considered the angel of Truth (although devout Moslems will hardly agree to her female gender). Gabri-el is described as possessing 140 pairs of wings and in Judeo-Christian lore she is the Angel of the Annunciation, Resurrection, Mercy, Revelation and Death. As ruler of the first heaven, she is closest to Man. According to the testimony of Joan of Arc it was Gabri-el who persuaded the Maid of Orleans to help the Dauphin.

Gabri-el appears to Daniel in order to explain the prophet's awesome vision of the fight between the ram and the he-goat (the oracle of the Persians being overthrown by the Greeks). She appears again to Daniel to tell him of the coming of a messiah, a message which half a millennium later she repeats to Mary in the Annunciation. It is curious that she should appear at so many conceptions. Before Mary she had just announced to Zacharias the coming of John the Baptist.

The essentially female character of this remarkable Archangel is once again revealed in popular lore, which tells of how she takes the invariably protesting soul from paradise, and instructs it  for the nine months while it remains in the womb of its mother.

Christien O'Brien, in *The Chosen Few* has put forward an interesting and closely argued case which supports Gabri-el's apparent interest in conception and birth. He suggests that she was once a real being in the biblical lands who experimented with the genes of early man and that Adam and Eve were amongst her first experiments. This real, down-to-earth being was then given supernatural powers by those inveterate deifiers, the Sumerians. There is a strange parallel with this hypothesis in the conflicting accounts of Matthew and Luke over the conception of Christ. In Matthew (1:20) the notably male Holy Ghost " begets Mary with child" while in Luke (1:26) it is Gabri-el who "came in unto her." As this can also be translated as "placing something within her" and as she then tells Mary that the conception is successful within her womb, it does raise a few questions if not a few eyebrows. Could such an otherwise primitive world have really had expertise in artificial insemination? Such an idea is much favored by those who believe that human beings are the outcome of experiments by extra terrestrials. But for the skeptics and those fundamentalists who remain unconvinced that female angels are possible, there is comfort in discovering that "Gabri-el" also can mean "Divine Husband."

St. Jerome tells us that when the archangel appeared to the Virgin she was mistaken for a man.

Mary "was filled with terror and consternation and could not reply; for she had never been greeted by a man before." When she learned that it was an angel (or a female) she could converse freely for there was no longer anything for her to fear, or we might add, desire.

Like the great female angel Pistis-Sophia before her, Gabri-el once fell from grace for some unspecified misdemeanor. The angel Dobiel took her place for the period she was an outcast.

Previous page: **Gabriel.** *Detail from the Annunciation by Simone Martini.* Gabriel is best known in her role as the Angel of the Annunciation. Her emblem is the lily. Originally the lily was the flower of Lilith, the first of Adam's wives. As Gabriel is also associated with the Sumerian deity Ninkharsag who is in turn identified with Lilith we seem to have some corroboration. Since Lilith had scornfully rejected both her chauvinistic husband and his God, scholars and priests sent her plunging into the depths of the abyss to become one of Satan's feisty mates. However the virginal aspect of this triple goddess lingered on in the symbolism of the lily, *lilu* or *lotus* of her vagina. Thus it was used to symbolize the impregnation of the Virgin Mary. However, the later Christian contempt of the flesh masked the earlier pagan origins. The lily in Gabriel's hand now filters the seed of God which is transformed into the seminal words of the annunciation which somewhat coyly enter now through the Virgin's ear.

We find a similar theme in the legend of the Blessed Virgin Juno who conceived her own son Mars through a magical Lily and without any male intervention. The three lobes of the Fleur-de-lis represents the triple aspect of the goddess.

Tobias and the Angels. In this 15th century painting of Tobias and three angels, the painter, *Botticini*, has taken considerable artistic license by adding both Michael and Gabriel to the scene. He also takes the liberty of giving Raphael the peacocks feathers usually attributed to Michael. In the smaller version by a disciple of Verrocchio the artist sticks to the original story of the one angel who only reveals his identity at the end of a journey with the young Tobias. St. Paul often warned his congregations that any of them might meet an angel on the road and not recognize him so to be careful to treat everyone as a potential messenger from God (or the Devil!)

Archangel Rapha-el

"The Shining One who heals" was originally known as Labbi-el in Chaldea. The Hebrew term רפא *rapha* meant "healer," "doctor" or "surgeon". As angel of healing he is often associated with the image of a serpent. He is known to be the chief ruling prince of the second heaven, chief of the Order of Virtues, guardian of the Tree of Life in Eden and by his own admission one of the seven angels of the Throne. This he reveals to Tobias in the book of Tobit.

In this account he travels with Tobit's son in disguise without letting on who he is until the journey's end. He shows Tobias, who has caught a huge

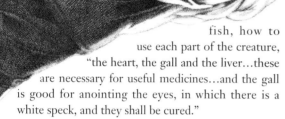

fish, how to use each part of the creature, "the heart, the gall and the liver…these are necessary for useful medicines…and the gall is good for anointing the eyes, in which there is a white speck, and they shall be cured."

He is declared to be "one of the four presences set over all the diseases and all the wounds of the children of men" (Enoch 1), and in the *Zohar* is "charged to heal the earth…the earth which furnishes a place for man, whom he also heals of his illnesses."

He heals Abraham of the pain of circumcision since the patriarch had skillfully avoided this rite until old age, and cures Jacob of his disjointed thigh which he managed to get while wrestling with one of Rapha-el's colleagues.

Although officially a Virtue, he is said to have the six wings of a Seraph but at the same time belongs to the Cherubim, the Dominions and the Powers. He is said to be both the chummiest and funniest of all the angelic flock and is often depicted chatting merrily with some unsuspecting mortal. His sunny disposition is possibly due to his being Regent, or Angel of the Sun.

Raphael descending to earth. In this illustration for *Paradise Lost* the artist, *Hayley*, seems to have intuited that Raphael is the Regent of the Sun.

Amongst other friendly acts he presented Noah with a medical book which could have been the mysterious *Book of the Angel Raziel*. It is said that this book gave Noah the knowledge he needed to build the Ark.

This story would seem to fit Rapha-el's status as the Angel of Science and Knowledge.

But strangely this Archangel is also a guide of Sheol, the Hebrew "Pit," or the womb of the underworld, and as a demon of earth he manifests in monstrous beast-form.

"And when he went to wash his feet, and behold a monstrous fish came up to devour him.

And Tobias being afraid of him, cried out with a loud voice, saying: Sir, he cometh upon me.

And the angel said to him: Take him by the gill, and draw him to thee.

And when he had done so, he drew him out upon the land, and he began to pant before his feet.

Then the angel said to him: Take out the entrails of this fish and lay up his heart, and his gall, and his liver for thee: for these are necessary for useful medicines.

And when he had done so, he roasted the flesh thereof, and they took it with them in the way: the rest they salted as much as might serve them, till they came to Rages, the city of the Medes. Then Tobias asked the angel, and said to him: I beseech thee, brother Azarias, tell me what remedies are these things good for, which thou hast bid me to keep of the fish? And the angel, answering, said to him: If thou put a little piece of its heart upon coals, the smoke thereof driveth away all kinds of devils, either from man or from woman, so that they come no more to them.

And the gall is good for anointing the eyes, in which there is a white speck, and they shall be cured. (Tobias 6:1-9)

Archangel Sari-el

Also known as Suriel, Suriyel, Zerachiel and Saraquel, his name means "God's command." This would fit the description of his duties as given by Enoch who says that it is "Sariel who is responsible for the fate of those angels who transgress the Laws."

While there are many worthy contenders for the dubious honor of being the Angel of Death, Sari-el has always been the most likely candidate. Although it is commonly believed to have been Zagzagel who taught Moses all his knowledge, many authorities credit Sari-el with the task. Certainly he is known to have been almost Swiss in matters of hygiene, instructing Rabbi Ishmael in many sanitizing details of righteous behavior.

Sari-el is also claimed to be a healer like Rapha-el, a Seraphim and a Prince of the Presence. Yet, with what we are beginning to recognize as an angelic pattern of behavior he is also listed by Enoch as one of the fallen rebels. This is difficult to reconcile with the fact that in *The Wars of the Sons of Light Against the Sons of Darkness* his name appears on the shields of one of the fighting units of the Sons of Light. Presumably his double agent character had been cleared by the 1st century.

The Triumph of Death *ascribed to Franscesco Traini in the Campo Santo, Pisa.* Here we see an unsuspecting group of peaceful revelers who are about to be scythed down by the Angel of Death. The fact that he is depicted with demonic wings would attest to Sariel as being listed amongst the fallen rebels. It would seem that his role as the "Grim Reaper" did not fit comfortably with the idea of luminous beings of good in Heaven.

Angels and Devils are shown in a wild aerial battle for the possession of the souls of the blessed and the damned. Seraphim are seen cradling the righteous in their arms while the sinners appear to receive less gentle treatment from the demons.

Archangel Uri-el

Said to be one of the four angels of the Presence, Uri-el, meaning "Fire of God," is identified in later scriptures with Phanuel "Face of God." He presides over Tartarus (or Hell) being both a

Seraphim and a Cherubim. In the wrathful and hellish *Apocalypse of St. Peter*, Uri-el appears as the Angel of Repentance who is graphically depicted as being about as pitiless as any demon you wouldn't want to meet in Hell. "Uri-el, the angel of God, will bring forth in order, according to their transgression, the souls of those sinners... They will burn them in their dwelling places in everlasting fire. And after all of them are destroyed with their dwelling-places, they will be punished eternally...

Those who have blasphemed the way of righteousness will be hung up by their tongues. Spread under them is unquenchable fire so they cannot escape it." For those readers who still fondly imagine that angels are all sticky and sweet, this description must come as a warning. Righteous angels are as unswerving in the pursuit of their duty as a forty-ton truck traveling ninety miles an hour, with roughly the same effect.

Often identified as the Cherub who stands "at the Gate of Eden with a fiery sword," or as the angel who "watches over thunder and terror," Uri-el appears to be a pretty heavy dude, and as such his Presidency of Hell seems most appropriate.

The claim that he was the angel who gave man is curiously at the magical *Kabbalah* to odds with what we know of his fanatical righteousness. Yet there is a certain poetic justice in the fact that it was just this stickler to the rules who was so sternly reprobated in the 8th century by a Church Council. Later the Church relented and Uri-el was reinstated, but transformed into a saint whose holy symbol was an open hand holding a flame.

The most intriguing extra-canonical account of this Archangel comes from the *Prayer of Joseph*. In the incident when Jacob wrestled with a dark angel (and Uri-el has always been a strong candidate for that celestial strong arm), somehow there was a mysterious merging of the two beings. For Uri-el says,

"I have come down to earth to make my dwelling among men, and I am called Jacob by name." Now we know quite a few of the patriarchs supposedly have become angels, the most notable case being Enoch who was transformed into Metatron (more of this later). But Uri-el's is the first recorded instance of an angel becoming a man. In this he is the herald of the shape of things to come.

Uri-el is also known for being the sharpest eyed angel of all. He was the messenger sent to warn Noah of the forthcoming floods and is also known as the Angel of the month of September.

He was not always as helpful to the patriarchs as he was to Noah. In the *Midrash Aggada Exodus* he appears as a fiery serpent and attacks Moses for failing to observe the rite of circumcision for his son. According to the *Sibylline Oracles* Uri-el is the immortal angel who, on the Day of Judgment, will "break the monstrous bars framed of unyielding and unbroken adamant of the brazen gates of Hades, and cast them down straightway." It seems a little melodramatic considering that as president of Hades he already holds the keys to those self-same gates. But the stage management of heaven sometimes resembles Italian Grand Opera and maybe this flamboyant bit of theatre is needed to set the scene before he brings on all the souls and arranges them before the Judgment Seat.

Three versions of the incident when Jacob wrestles with the angel. In the painting by *Paul Gauguin*, above, we experience the sheer earthiness of the encounter. "And there wrestled a man with him until the breaking of the day. And when he saw that he prevailed not against him, he touched the hollow of his thigh; and the hollow of Jacob's thigh was out of joint, as he wrestled with him." The illustration by *Gustave Doré* on the opposite page shows Uriel and Jacob fighting in a place which Jacob afterwards called Peniel. One of Uriel's names is Pheniel and another is Jacob-Israel. In the center the encounter as pictured by the 19th Century painter, *Eugène Delacroix.*

Archangel Ragu-el

Traditionally known as Rasuil, Rufael, Akrasiel, and "Friend of God," Ragu-el, according to Enoch, "takes vengeance upon the world of luminaries." This is also interpreted as one "who watches over the good behavior of the angels." As we will discover this is probably the most overworked office in the whole celestial bureaucracy! Angels are a particularly vulnerable breed when it comes to corruption. And even this angel who is supposed to be judging the behavior of his peers was, by a wonderful twist of fate, himself reprobated by the Church in 745 A.D., along with Uri-el. Both Archangels suffered the indignity of being excluded from the lists in the prestigious Saintly Calendar. This was the infamous Church council held by Pope Zachary which conducted a sort of angelic witch-hunt amongst the higher echelons of the celestial beings. He condemned Raguel as being a demon "who passed himself off as a Saint." How on earth Zachary managed to acquire evidence for this is beyond imagining and must have been a source of puzzlement and speculation even at that time.

In happier moments this angel was mentioned in part of the manuscript of the apocryphal *Revelation of John*. It reads" Then shall He send the angel Raguel saying: go sound the trumpet for the angels of cold and snow and ice and bring together every kind of wrath upon them that stand on the left."

It was Raguel who transported Enoch to heaven. Amongst his other duties he is said to have been an angel of Earth and a guardian of the second heaven.

Archangel Remi-el

In early records he is known as Jeremiel or Yerah-meel – "Mercy of God." This name identifies him as the "Lord of Souls awaiting Resurrection." He is the one "Whom God sets up" in order to lead the souls to Judgment. Certainly he should know about such matters of the soul for he is clearly listed in the Enoch writings as a leader of the apostates and one of the fallen. Simultaneously he appears as one of the seven Archangels who stand before God. According to Enoch, this hierarch was "responsible for spreading the instructions of the Seven Archangels". Earlier in his career it was he, and not Michael, who is said to have been the angel who destroyed the army of Sennacherib. As he is the angel who presides over true visions and it was through the "true vision" of Baruch that Remiel appears as the victor over Senna-cherib, he certainly appears to have an unfair advantage over Michael in claiming the deed.

In this encounter he is said to have overcome Nisroch "the Great Eagle" who was ruler of the order of Principalities until his defeat as the champion of the Assyrians.

These are the orthodox portraits of the Seven Archangels according to Enoch and tradition. However,there are many alternative listings of this Sacred Seven which include Chama-el, Jophi-el, Zadki-el, Baruchi-el, Jeduhi-el, Sima-el, Zaphi-el and Ani-el. In this century Georges Gurdjieff further complicated the matter by adding many more in his *Beelzebub's Tales to his Grandson*. In this we discover

that His End-lessness's Most High Commis-sion to the Pla-net Earth in-cludes "Chief Common-Uni-versal-Arch-Chemist-Physicist *Angel* Looisos, The Most-Great-*Arch-Seraph* Sevohtartra and The Most Great *Ar-changel* Sakaki" who we learn was one of the four "Quarter-Maintainers of the Whole Universe."

Notwithstanding such ingenious inventions there are two quite remarkable candidates who are far more likely to oust Remi-el, Suri-el or Ragu-el from the roll call of the Magnificent Seven. The first of these, Metatron, is claimed to be the "all time Greatest." But this supreme title is tossed back and forth between rabbi and priest, in an energetic game of angelic one-upmanship.

If the story of the two Egyptian wizards is anything to go by, then Metatron is clearly more powerful than Michael and Gabriel put together. Somehow the two great and wily magicians, *Jannes* and *Jambres*, managed to infiltrate heaven and were a considerable embarrassment to the Almighty for they refused to leave. He sent Michael and Gabriel against them, but our two champions were no match for the dynamic duo of the Nile. Finally Metatron drove them out and "was appointed (so saith the *Yalkut Hadash*) over Michael and Gabriel."

The other powerful angel who attracts especial attention as being one of the most likely members of the Seven is Razi-el.

Archangel Razi-el

Also known as Ratziel, Gallizur, Saraquel and Akra-siel, Razi-el has the intriguing title of the "Angel of the Secret Regions and of the Supreme Mysteries." Author of the legendary *Book of the Angel Raziel*, "wherein all celestial and earthly knowledge is set down," Razi-el is supposed to have presented it to Adam. After a long and convoluted history it passed into the hands of Enoch, who is said to have incor-porated much of it in the *Book of Enoch*. It then was given to Noah who modeled the Ark on informa-tion he discovered in its pages. Then it seems to have disappeared after a brief spell with Solomon. It resurfaced under the authorship of one Eleazer of Worms, a medieval writer. It is said that within this volume Razi-el revealed the 1,500 keys to the mysteries of the Universe. Unfortunately, these are in a secret writing which is not even understood by the greatest of angels.

We do know, however, from *Targum Ecclesiastes*, that "each day the great angel Razi-el stands upon the peak of Mount Horeb, proclaims the secrets of men to all mankind." According to Moses Mai-monides, Razi-el is the chief of the Erelim, or Thrones, and is identified with a brilliant white fire which is one of the characteristics of that order. One strange attribute, recorded by the *Pirke Rabbi* is that Razi-el "spreads his wings over the Hayyoth lest their fiery breath consume the ministering angels." The Hayyoth, or heavenly beasts, are equa-ted with the Cherubim. Heaven might not always be as comfortable to its workers as is fondly imag-ined.

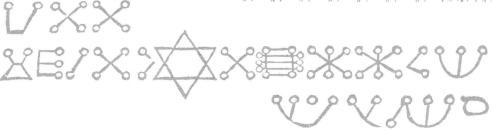

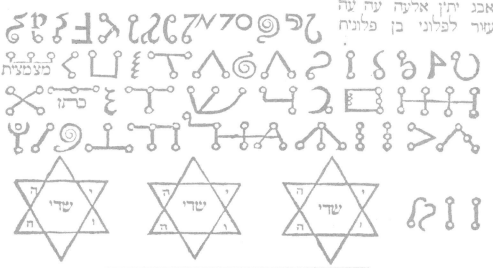

Above: **Angelic writing** *from the Book of Raziel, Netherlands 17th Century*. Taking compassion on Adam, God sent Raziel to give him a book so that he might look into the mirror of existence and so see the Divine Face and himself so illuminated as an image of God. It is reported that an oral version still exists within the traditions of the Kabalah.

Archangel Metatron

We now come to an entity who, we are assured by many rabbis, is *really* the greatest angel of all. It must be remembered that there are many contenders for this heavyweight throne and any confusion probably arises from their over enthusiastic supporters. Metatron certainly has substantial claims which are favored by the rabbis, although as a Christian angel he is more of an enigma than most. Variously called Prince of the Divine Face, Angel of the Covenant, King of Angels and the Lesser YHWH (tetragrammaton), he is charged with the sustenance of the world. In this and on many other occasions he absorbs territory usually claimed by the other Archangels, especially Micha-el with whom he is mostly identified. This could simply be explained by differences in the Jewish and Christian lore. In *Talmud* and *Targum* he is the direct link between God and humanity.

In terms of seniority Metatron is actually the most junior in the heavenly host. In one version of his history he was once the patriarch Enoch who was transformed into a fiery angel with 36 wings (6x6) and countless eyes. This would only make him about 8500 years old. While this is doubtless impressive by mortal standards, it hardly registers on the angelic scale if we are to believe that the angels were created at the same time as the universe, fifteen billion years ago.

There is a beautiful passage early in the *Chronicles of Enoch* when the scribe first visited heaven before his death and transformation. From the perspective of our century, the scene is like a rehearsal for what was to come. "Then the Lord said to Michael: 'Go and strip Enoch of his own clothes; anoint him with oil, and dress him like ourselves' and Michael did as he was told. He stripped me of my clothes, and rubbed me over with a wonderful oil like dew; with the scent of myrrh; which shone like a sunbeam. And I looked at myself, and I was like one of the other (angels); there was no difference and all my fear and trembling left me."

Enoch had been chosen by the Lord as a writer of truth, the greatest scribe of the land, so it is hardly surprising that in that quantum leap into angelic form, as Metatron, his previous abilities

The angel Metatron staying the hand of Abraham who is about to sacrifice his beloved son Isaac. *Filippo Brunelleschi, 1401, Florence.*

59

should follow him. For Metatron is known as the heavenly scribe who records everything which happens in the etheric archives.

This mighty angel has another more sinister side, being identified with Satan or with the earlier office of ha-satan, the Adversary. There is a passage in Exodus which refers to Metatron. "Behold I send an angel before thee, to keep thee in the way and bring thee unto the place which I have prepared." This is clearly a reference to the angel of God, or as some maintain God Himself, who led the children of Israel through the wilderness. Further evidence that it was Metatron in his role as the lesser Yahweh, rather than God in person, is that he appears "as a pillar of fire, his face more dazzling than the sun."

If anyone has the stomach to read Exodus (which must rank as the ugliest and least spiritual of all religious texts), they can witness what sort of an angry, jealous, spiteful, pathological killer this lesser YHWH must have been. As he orders horrendous atrocities upon his chosen peoples, any intelligent reader will be more able to see the hand of radical evil rather than that of the Lord of Light.

By the size of his tent (Tabernacle) as described in Exodus and Numbers, and from descriptions of YHWH, it would appear he was an impossibly tall being. If we use a standard .53 meters as being an ancient cubit this angel was recorded to have been anything from 8 to 13 feet in height. Such evidence points to Metatron, for he is said to be the tallest angel in the hierarchy. He has also been named the Demiurge, the Creator of the Universe. In gnostic scriptures this is decidedly Satan, the Prince of Darkness.

All in all, Metatron is indeed a strange and discomforting figure. On the one hand he is set above Micha-el and Gabri-el for being able to

defeat the wizards of Egypt, while on the other, in one particularly gruesome episode, he is a bloodthirsty angel who delights in impaling hundreds of his own disobedient people and leaving them in the desert to die in agony.

Duet in the Mirror

But Metatron's portrait is not complete without a last, mysterious connection; the Shekinah. This is the Hebrew version of the Hindu Shakti, which can be understood as the female principle of God in man. The creation of the world was, according to the *Zohar*, the work of the Shekinah. The male aspect is of course the Creator, or Demiurge, one of Metatron's roles. The Shekinah was exiled after the Fall of Adam and Eve and rabbis claim that "to lead the Shekinah back to God and to unite Her with Him is the true purpose of the Torah." In other words the whole purpose of life is to re-unite the female and the male into one Whole. According to some, angels naturally manifest such a union by being androgynous. What an extraordinary and wondrous richness of imagery encapsulated within one angelic entity!

Elohim Creating Adam. *Color printed drawing by William Blake, 1795.* This mystic artist saw the act of creation by the Demiurge as a colossal Error, or Fall. In his vision, before Creation there was Unity and Eternity. Creation brought division and the dualities of good and bad, body and soul, man and woman. Above: **Metatron carries the Patriarch Enoch to Heaven** on the backs of a white and a black eagle. The Hebrew version maintains the Enoch was transformed into Metatron but the Christian legends are notoriously muddled and eclectic by comparison. Above left: **YAHWEH, IAWAH.** *Four seals showing YAHWEH as a serpent deity, 1st century A.D..* These images of a warlike god were popular during the early Christian era. One theory suggests that they are the seals of Metatron in his guise as the Tetragrammaton.

Angel on the Horizon

This set of miniature portraits appears to complete our brief survey of the Archangels. But it is one of the great attractions of angels that the tantalizing mystery of their existence always seems *about to unfold*. We are always poised on the brink of understanding them, yet at the very moment of revelation a veil descends revealing another, entirely new and equally kaleidoscopic viewpoint: another new horizon to strive for and never reach.

To illustrate how easy it is to be seduced by such a new archangelic horizon we take a brief diversionary path to look at a science of sevens as practiced by the Essenes over four thousand years ago.

Angelology and the Tree of Life

The Essene Brotherhood really dates from Moses. Their understanding of the Law was very different from the ten commandments given by the patriarch. The forces with which they communed were positive and were seen as angels corresponding to the good *Ahuras* and *Fravashis* of the Persian angelic host. Central to their belief was the Tree of Life which had seven branches reaching to the heavens and seven roots deep in the earth. These were related to the seven mornings and seven nights of the week and correspond to the seven Archangels of the Christian hierarchy. In a complex cosmology, which is both macrocosmic and microcosmic, man is situated within the middle of the tree suspended

The Creation and the Expulsion from Paradise *Lubok 1820, Moscow.* This popular depiction of the walled garden of Eden with its exotic and curious animals also shows the legendary Siren Bird or Indian Apsara and the six winged, flaming red Cherub guarding the gates of Paradise.

Дрѣво жизни стоущее посредѣ раа.

Кѐрꙋвимъ пламенное ѻрꙋжїе повелѣнїемъ бжїимъ изгнавъ израѐ адама иеввꙋ сѣде вверхꙋ вратъ, еⷣемскїи хранꙗщихъ пꙋть лⷣревⷶжизни ктомꙋ воⷩ.

хола гⷣь пополꙋдни.

змїи плодомъ искоꙋсивъ адама иеввꙋ израла изгонителⷭ.

Адамже познанїи израла шⷣле ессⷪвⷪю, нарꙗ тогⷣа лишенꙑ раискїа блгⷣⷣти скоⷬ естⷭꙋ ипⷧⷠлⷧⷶ горко:

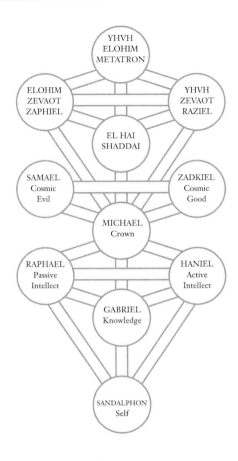

between heaven and earth. The tremendous forces which flow around him are supposed to create "magnetic" fields which are grouped in harmonious couples of:

Heaven	Earth.
Heavenly Father	Earthly Mother
Angel of Eternal Life	Angel of Earth
Angel of Creative Work	Angel of Life
Angel of Peace	Angel of Joy
Angel of Power	Angel of the Sun
Angel of Love	Angel of Water
Angel of Wisdom	Angel of Air

The Essenes believed that these heavenly and earthly angels of the invisible and visible world were mistakenly "personified" in the Hebrew, Christian and Moslem worlds, becoming the Seven Archangels of Light and Seven Archangels of Darkness, with names like Michael, Gabriel and Raphael.

The "personified" archangels can, however, be assigned to the seven days of the Essene system. This is best seen in the Morning Communion.

Saturday : "The Earthly Mother and I are one.
(Cassiel) She gives the food of life to my whole body."

Sunday : "Angel of Earth, enter my generative
(Michael) organs and regenerate my whole body."

Monday (Gabriel)	:	"Angel of Life, enter my limbs and give strength to my whole body."
Tuesday (Camael)	:	"Angel of Joy, descend upon the earth and give beauty to all things."
Wednesday (Raphael)	:	"Angel of Sun, enter my solar center and give the fire of Life to my whole body."
Thursday (Sachiel)	:	"Angel of Water, enter my blood and give the water of life to my whole body."
Friday (Anael)	:	"Angel of Air, enter my lungs and give the air of life to my whole body."

In a surprising number of cultures throughout the world there are legends of paradise gardens with a magical tree of eternal life at its center. This Tree of Life invariably has a guardian to protect it from the uninitiated or the unworthy. In the spiritual crucible of the Near and Middle East this particular archetype has become the Tree guarded by the Cherub, the Jewish Sefiroth, the seven branched candlestick and the Tree of the Freemasons. The purest teaching is acknowledged to be that of the ancient Essenes. Their vision closely parallels that of the mystical Indian and Tantric Tree of Man which corresponds to the seven chakras of the body which flower from the crown off the head.

Far left: **Tree of Life** *from the Apocalypse of Liebana, 975*. Left: **The archangels of the Holy Sefiroth.** Above left: **Tree of Knowledge**, *Russia, 1830*. Above: **Essene Tree of Life.**

The Ninth Choir : Angels

This is the last order of the celestial hierarchy and the one closest to humankind. The actual Hebrew term for angel is *mal'akh*, meaning "a messenger." In Sanskrit it is *Angeres*, a divine or celestial spirit which becomes the Persian *angaros* meaning "courier," which appears in Greek as *angelos*. It is through such routes that we finally arrive at the modern concept of an angel as being an intermediary or intercessionary between the Almighty and human mortals, between Eternity and our Universe of Time.

As we have already seen the greatest single early source of names and angelic functions comes from the three Chronicles of the Hebrew patriarch, Enoch. Even though declared apocryphal the Chronicles are so packed with such a wealth of detail that by the 13th century, at the height of angel fever, Enoch and many other non-canonical writers were very much back in vogue (a full version of the Chronicle didn't actually turn up until the 18th century when an original copy was discovered which had been preserved by the Ethiopic Church). By the Middle Ages the relatively modest count by Enoch of a few hundred angels had soared to precisely 301,655,722, that is if we are to trust the words of the Kabbalists.

The Stuff of Angels

Many early Hebrew sources recognized angels as substantial and material beings created every morning like the dew "through every breath that the Almighty takes." In the *Talmud*, however, we learn that having been created they sing a Hymn of praise

Three Angels *detail from the Adoration of the Virgin by Perugino, 15th Century.*

to God and promptly expire only to be reborn anew the following day.

The early Catholic Church claimed that angels existed even before the Creation or at the very latest on the second day of that event. They were supposedly created all at the same moment and are immortal (that is to say, until the last trump). The official stance of the Catholic Church today is that angels are purely spiritual and non-substantial.

Guardian Angels

One of the many separate orders within the angelic host is that of the ministering angels who teach the seventy nations "that sprang from the loins of Noah." This places them, historically, as appearing no earlier than eight thousand years before Christ. The earliest record tells of seventy administering angels led by Michael, but later this number shot up to several hundreds of thousands.

One of the sub-classes of ministering angels is that of the Guardian angels, usually accepted as having Michael, Raphael, Gabriel and Uriel at their head. These are the angels which are in charge of nations, states and cities. It turns out that this is the really high risk country. Angels have little resistance to corruption when they over-identify with their national charges. This is evident even in the early scriptures. Rabbis only actually mention four nations with their angel guardians by name. But from those we are left in no doubt as to where the Jewish writers stood and where those angels fell. Michael, in charge of Israel, remains unimpeachable, but his fellow tutors seem to have been very much changed by their very charges, who of course are all arch-enemies of Israel anyway. Dubbiel (the Bear Deity) was guardian angel of Persia, Rahab (Violence and Prince of the Primordial Sea) was angel for Egypt, and Samael (the

Adversary, Prince of Darkness) was the guardian of Rome. They were all corrupted by their wards and fell. The Egyptian guardian, Rahab, even has the distinction of having been slaughtered by the Lord for refusing to separate the upper from the lower waters at the time of the Creation.

He is then somehow resurrected, only to be destroyed a second time for attempting to stop the Hebrews from escaping across the Red Sea. So of all the seventy tutelary angels only Michael managed to stay uncorrupted. It is perhaps uncharitable

to ascribe this to the fact that his charges were God's chosen people.

Sheer Numbers

Such regrettable transgressions do not seem so prevalent at the individual level although there is much evidence to show that angels are still eminently corruptible. We find in Job 4:18 that God appears "to put no trust in his servants" and later "His angels He charged with folly." Folly or not, the *Talmud* speaks of every Jew being assigned eleven thousand guardian angels at birth. Christians have no official policy as far as guardian spirits are concerned, although there are records which suggest two are entrusted to guide each Christian: one for the right hand, which inspires him to good, and one on the left, which nudges him towards evil. A 19th century children's poem expands this number to four. "Four angels to my bed, Four angels round my head. One to watch and one to pray, and two to bear my soul away."

In our New Age the traditional guardian angel has taken on a new flavor and is now equated with the spirit guides of the psychics, or the "entities" of the channellers.

A Flaw in the Sons of God

Enoch mentions in very detailed and fascinating passages the role of the mysterious Grigori or "Sons of God." It is these angels who, in one version, precipitated the "fall." These gigantic beings were called the "Watchers" and appear to constitute an almost separate Order, although they are generally grouped under the angelic wing. Amongst the ranks of this particular group we find such infamous names as Shemjaza, Arakiba, Ramiel, Kokabiel, Tamiel, Ramial, Asael, Armaros, Batanel, Ananel, Zaquiel, Daniel, Ezequeel, Bariqijael, Samsapiel, Turiel, Jomjael and Sariel.

The term Watcher or Grigori can mean "those who watch, "those who are awake" or "the ones who never sleep." Satanail was the leader of one group of seven Watchers who first disobeyed the Lord and were punished. These were held in a penal area within the fifth heaven which is described as reeking of sulfur.

It was some of the Watchers who first cohabited with the women of the lowlands which lay below Eden. In doing so they produced monsters which later became identified with the Babylonian legend of Tiamat's terrible brood. Enoch was the grandfather of Noah and so could record, in detail, the flood which was meant to destroy these mutant and ravaging giants.

Lust and the Choirboys of the Tenth

The later Church fluctuated for many centuries as to whether the fall of the rebel angels had happened through pride, lust or both. Lucifer is said to have fallen through *hubris*, which is a Greek combination of lechery and pride. This was associated with phallic erections and as Barbara Walker points out, "Patriarchal Gods especially punished hubris, the sin of any upstart who became – in both senses – " too big for his breeches."

As angels really were considered sexless, and therefore above reproach, a typical compromise adopted was one given by the Bishop of Paris in the 13th century. According to this theory there were nine orders of angels but it was a separate one, the tenth that fell. It was these Sons of God who were held to be of a separate essence, who saw the Daughters of Man and who, we are told in Genesis 6, lusted after their seductive flesh and "took themselves wives from among them." The Watchers had become the "Voyeurs."

This was a neat solution to a decidedly discomforting theological double-bind. For it was difficult to reconcile a theology which insisted that angels were sexless, and therefore sinless, with the damning evidence from sacred scriptures that showed these lusty celestials were enthusiastically demonstrating just the opposite.

So it appears there were three distinct orders of angels in the lower echelons. At the top were the seven Archangel chiefs, who were known as the aristocratic two-eyed serpents. Each commanded

496,000 myriads of ministering angels who were known as the one-eyed serpents. Last came the real working class Watchers or guardian angels.

That Crucial Nine-Tenths

Neither archangel nor angel was supposed to be able to reproduce (only demons can do this, but fortunately for us they are reported to have relatively short lives). It does appear the Grigori, however, are nearer in form, genes and sexual enthusiasm to humankind. As we shall later discover, their association with the daughters of Eve ended in disaster. As far as can be ascertained, mixing the genes was totally against the Law and those angels guilty of the act were severely punished. One can understand how such a scripture sits uncomfortably with any orthodox Christian idea. The rabbis had no such qualms, although Simeon ben Yohai, the fanatic author of the *Zohar*, forbade his disciples, on pain of curse, to ever speak of the Sons of God having the mechanics to cohabitate. Nevertheless it is these Grigori who are later punished for "bringing sin unto earth."

In His punishment of these Watchers, God ignores the fact that these angels appeared to have mixed motives ranging from lusty appetites to a genuine friendship and a desire to teach humans the secrets of heaven. Early commentators insist that nine-tenths of the Watchers fell, which left only one-tenth in Heaven. Later theologians reversed the proportions when it was seen that such an imbalance gave a decided edge to the Satanic forces. The ten leaders, all once illustrious angels, were listed as fallen by the 4th century A.D..

Angelogia

It was during the era of Angel Fever, in the 12th and 13th centuries, that the occult and esoteric embellishments reached truly exotic heights. By this time angels not only governed the seven planets, the four seasons, the months of the year, the days of the week, but also the hours of the day and night. Spells and incantations abounded to conjure up both benign and bedeviled entities. By the 14th century there were said to be 301,655,722 of the host hovering at the

borders of our temporal universe. 133,306,668 of these were of questionable help to the faithful as they were supposedly those who had fallen. Others insisted that the nine choirs or orders each had 6,666 legions, with each legion having 6,666 angels. Add to this, according to rabbinical lore, the fact that every blade of grass had its guardian angel coaxing it to grow, and we have quite a population explosion on the "other side". We have no way of knowing whether the plague which decimated Europe about this time had any direct effect upon these numbers, although by the witch hunts which followed we might deduce the dark third was at least immune.

Opposite page: **Ithuriel and Zephon hunting Satan in the Garden of Eden.** *An illustration by Gustave Doré for Paradise Lost IV.* The Evil One is about to tempt Eve in the form of a Toad. Milton's version does not fit well with that accorded by the apocryphal texts. In these it is Zephon who was tempted by the Prince of Deceit. He left the orthodox choirs to join the rebels who were delighted because of his reputation of being the most ingenious of all the angelic minds. He immediately came up with a plan to set fire to Heaven but before this could be accomplished all the conspirators found themselves hurled to the bottom of the bottomless abyss.

Zephon, now a second rank demon, has to fan the embers of the furnaces of Hell. No doubt he has invented an ingenious solution to do so by now. Even the orthodox scenario gives devils a definite edge over their brothers "upstairs" when it comes to creative intelligence.

Above: **Angel Musicians** *by Melozzo da Forlì, 1480, Rome.*

Nun Mem Lamed Caph Iod Theth Cheth

Zaïn Vau He Daleth Gimel Beth Aleph

Res Kuff Zade Pe Aïn Samech Samech Shin Tau

Right: **Musician Angels** *by Hans Memlinc*. The Angel of Music is often given as being Uriel. In Islam we find this is Israfel. The rabbis give the title of the "Master of Heavenly Song" to Metatron or Shemiel.

Above: Examples of angelic script with variations of the Hebrew Alphabet from *La Kabbale Pratique*. While we are not told whether all angels are literate, it is evident that they are superb linguists, considering the messages they bring are always in the native tongue of the witness. Rabbis, of course, maintain that the official angelic tongue is Hebrew, although, understandably the Catholic Church insists it is Latin, or, in exceptional cases, Greek.

Who's Who and Who does What?

There are angels who have very specific functions which are named and invoked in many situations. Here are just a few angels found in occult, mystic and alchemical lore.

Angel of: Abortion (Kasdaye), Alchemy (Och), Anger (Af), Aquarius (Ausiel), Barrenness (Akriel), Birds (Arael), Calculations (Butator), Chance (Barakiel), Conception (Laila), Dawn (Lucifer), Day (Shamsiel), Dreams (Gabriel), Earthquakes (Rashiel), Embryo (Sandalphon, twin brother of Metatron), Fear (Yroul), Fish (Gagiel), Food (Manna), Forests (Zulphas), Forgetfulness (Poteh), Free Will (Tabris), Future (Teiaiel), Greece (Javan), Hail (Bardiel), Health (Mumiah), Hope (Phanuel), Immortality (Zethar), Insomnia (Michael), Inventions (Liwet), Lust (Priapus), Memory (Zad-kiel), Morals (Mehabiah), Mountains (Rampel), Music (Israfel), Night (Leliel), Patience (Achaiah), Plants (Sachluph), Poetry (Uriel), Precipices (Zarobi), Pride (Rahab), Prostitution (Eisheth Zenunim), Rain (Matriel), Rivers (Dara), Showers (Zaa'fdiel), Silence (Shateiel), Sky (Sahaquiel), Snow (Shalgiel), Strength (Zeruel), Thunder (Ramiel), Treasure (Parasiel), Vegetables (Sofiel), Water Insects (Shakziel), Womb (Armisael).

This list just skims the surface of vast warehouses of records but it does show the incredible scholarship which decides who does what and where and how many times. One can understand the unsuccessful attempt by the Church to put a curb on this celestial supermarket of angels all jostling for a place in the Holy Who's Who.

The list is given to show the sheer ingenuity of the scribes and Kabbalists who juggled with names and numbers, often adding –el to rather dull ideas which suddenly gave a sparkle and authentic flutter to a new angelic presence.

Space doesn't permit any further examination of the angelic host loyal to the Almighty for we must now pass on to their dark brethren who rebelled and were to become Hell's Angels.

Above: **Alkanost and Sirin, the Birds of Paradise** *Lubok, Russia, 19th century.* These two birds of Paradise were favorite subjects in Russian folk art. The Sirin was a symbol of beauty, happiness and a reward for a pure life. Alkanost, who has the same face of a young girl, is the bird of death, temptation and sorrow who bestows pleasure for which the price is death. While the Sirins correspond to the Indian Apsaras, the dispensers of bliss to the worthy souls, the Alkanosts are more like the Valkyries of the Norsemen. These Angels of Death flew over the battlefields to take the brave warrior souls to Odin's Heaven, Valhalla. In the illustration by Gustave Doré on the right the angels seem more like the Saxon "walcyries," the dreaded corpse eaters, the Northern counterparts of the vulture priestesses of Egypt. Valhalla was originally the realm of death in Hel, but in no way suggested punishment or even the slightest whiff of sulfur.

The Second Wing : Hell's Angels

You walk like an angel,
You talk like an angel,
But my, oh my
You're like the Devil in disguise!
Oh yes you are!
Elvis Presley

"And no wonder for Satan
himself keeps transforming
himself into an angel
of light."
St. Paul speaking of deceit
(2 COR 11:14)

The Evolution of Evil

AMUEL BUTLER ONCE SAID that no one heard the Devil's side of any story, because God wrote all the books. The following portraits of the Dark Host may in some way break up this monopoly.

The Fall of the rebel Angels is a subject which priests and theologians have been at considerable pains to explain away. The whole legendary story has a long and very convoluted history.

The early Hebrews attributed everything which happened everywhere, whether in Heaven or on Earth, to the One God. The evolution of a single separate force for evil which opposed the One Good God only began two hundred years before the birth of Christ. The Old Testament God did not live in such dualistic times. He was always the One held responsible for what happened in the entire Universe and thus, like the Indian deity, Shiva, encapsulated creativity and destruction in one indissoluble principle. This is clearly stated in Isaiah 45:7 when God says "I

form the Light and create Darkness; I make Peace *and create Evil* (our italics)." But gradually, from the 2nd century B.C. onwards, the Hebrews turned from this belief in an ambivalent God, to one who is *only good*. Although there were many variations on this monist theme, a belief in the existence of a separate Evil One gradually developed. This malevolent principle had a completely distinct life of its own, being totally opposed and alien to the benevolent nature of the Good Almighty.

This created an obvious dilemma, for how could a totally benign Divinity who had created all and everything, include in His Creation an equally powerful opponent who sought at all times to overthrow Him? The result was a paradoxical tension between the essentially monist concept of a single divine principle underlying the cosmos and a dualistic idea of a separate principle for Good and a separate principle for Evil.

Whilst the rabbis have managed to extricate Judaism from those earlier conflicts, to this day the doctrine of the Christian Church remains hampered by the confusion arising from the two essentially incompatible ideas. And standing like a

Opposite page: **Lucifer, Bearer of the Light** *by William Blake*. Satan in his original glory outshone all the other angels and was the most beloved of God.

shadow in the center of the ensuing cyclone is the dark angel. The idea of separate evil or that of the fallen Angels does not appear at all in the Old Testament. Instead we find *ha-satan*, "the Adversary." Yet this was only a common noun which simply meant "an opponent." It was possibly the title of an office like that of the prosecution in present day law, rather than the name of any particular diabolic personality.

The earliest account of any Angels who actually were known to have rebelled and were punished for it appears in the apocryphal *Book of the Secrets of Enoch*. It therefore exists outside of the canon. But by the time the New Testament was compiled Enoch's influence had been quietly absorbed along with the dualistic ideas of the Persian Zoroaster. The notion of the fallen host had become a cornerstone of in Christian dogma. In Revelations John of Patmos points an unwavering finger at Satan, that old Dragon, "And his tail drew the third part of the stars (Angels) of heaven and did cast them to earth …and Satan, which deceiveth the whole world; he was cast out into the earth and his Angels were cast out with him."

John here names a specific individual as Satan, who by this time is clearly synonymous with the old office of the Adversary. Whereas in the Old Testament story of Job this office was neither good nor wicked, by the 2nd century AD it had become the symbol of Evil.

During the following two millennia this separate Prince of Darkness was variously identified as Azazel, Mastema, Beelzebub, Beliel, Duma, Sier, Salmael, Gadreel, The Angel of Rome, Samael, Asmodeus, Mephistopholes, Lucifer and in the Islamic traditions as Iblis. He also attracted a number of popular titles which offer comic relief from the usual terror he is supposed to evoke. Amongst such names were: Old Horney, Lusty Dick, The Gentleman, Monsignor, Black Bogey, Old Nick, Old Scratch and the Old Lad Himself..

A Necessary Evil

The Devil is, of course, an essential ingredient in any religion which preaches Redemption. To overcome evil, in the first place one must have evil to overcome. Even a Church reformer like Martin Luther insists that without the Devil and the threat of damnation there is little need for either Christ or his Church. Luther's whole life was a constant "war against Satan." So much so that it is said that the Devil slept more with him than Luther did with his own wife, Katie.

There are at least seven conflicting versions of how Satan appeared and how he managed to gather such a huge following. While Enoch only numbers two hundred rebels, by the 13th century this number had soared, according at least to the pen of the Cardinal Bishop of Tusculum, to a diabolic 133, 306, 668. If Satan did indeed take one third of the heavenly host with him this would still leave a substantial 266, 613, 336 Angels loyal to the Throne. And yet despite the reassurances of Isador

of Seville that "the rest were confirmed in the perseverance of eternal beatitude," this does not seem to be borne out by our researches into subsequent angelic behavior.

It really is a blatant bit of wishful thinking on the part of the medieval writer, for we discover that even long after the fall the Almighty was heard muttering about "the folly and untrustworthiness" of His servants.

Sin of Sins

All the evidence points to the incontroversial fact that Angels really are extremely vulnerable to corruption when in the company of human beings. It is difficult to make out whether it is the wanton nature of the manifest, material world which corrodes their armor of righteousness, or whether there is some magnetic field within the flesh that plays havoc with their virtuous compasses. Whatever the cause, Angels are unquestionably susceptible to "a friendship of the thighs" and in being so always run a high risk of falling flat on their faces when encountering a pretty woman.

The Hebrews apparently had a soft spot for the sins of the flesh and

were far more liberal in their views on the subject of lust than their Christian brothers. However, to the Jew, the sin of disobedience was an altogether different matter. Their God, Yahweh, exhibited an almost obsessive worry about it. Disobedience, especially amongst those He had created, touched a very sensitive spot on His Divine person, if we can judge by His often rash reactions when someone actually said "No." Even if later He publicly repented of His haste, considerable and often irreparable damage was usually done.

Disobedience was adopted by the Christians as the Original Sin and was of course the reason for the fall of Adam and Eve. It is also listed as one of the seven possible reasons that the Angels fell. We will now, briefly, examine seven of the legends of the Fall.

Legend One: The Shadow of God

Originally the Devil was the dark aspect of God. *Mal'ak* represented the side of God which was turned towards humanity. This concept was oddly translated into Greek as *angelos* or "messenger."

This emissary was actually the "shadow" side of God which was able to communicate with mortals, the bright side being too fierce for humans to bear.

As the Hebrew religion developed, so the Shadow evolved; first into the Word, the Voice or Touch

---

Reptiles and creatures of the night appear to be enduring and fearful archetypes. It is difficult to determine whether we have been conditioned to identify scales and membranes with evil or whether these life forms are just alien to human beings. The fox bat of India, shown above, is in reality a timid and gentle vegetarian and most snakes are harmless and were revered in ancient cultures as the wisest of creatures.

of God and then into a separate entity having its own free will. However, with separation, the dark, destructive aspect became predominant. By the time the New Testament was compiled the Shadow had passed through the intermediate stage of *ha-satan*, the neutral Adversary, to become Satan, the evil opponent of the Good God.

We see the change clearly when comparing early biblical accounts with later versions and translations. In the Old Testament God Himself slays the first born of Egypt and personally tests Abraham by demanding that he sacrifice his beloved son, Isaac.

Hardly a century later, in the *Book of Jubilees*, God has been replaced by His separated Shadow in the form of *Mastema*, Prince of the Evil Spirits. From this moment it is this Accusing angel, the Tempter and Condemner, who does all the nastier things once imputed to the Good God. The separation of the good side from the bad is now established and the fall is complete.

Legend Two: Free Will

The second version of the fall is equally "cosmic" in its scope and themes. It comes from one of the most influential theologians of the early Greek Church. Origen of Alexandria maintained that God created a number of angelic intelligences who were equal and free. Through their free will they chose to leave the Divine Unity and gradually drifted away from the Source. Those who drifted the least remained in the ethereal regions nearest God. Those who moved further out fell into the lower air. All these aerial beings are the Angels. Those who fell away further from the center took on human bodies, while those who drifted out farthest of all became demons. By orbiting so far away from the central hub of All

Quetzalcoatl *Aztec stone figure, back and front.* The Plumed or Feathered serpent of Central America, Quetzalcoatl was another of the great hero figures to be found throughout the world who was born of a virgin, was voluntarily sacrificed, descended into hell and was reborn again from the dead. From the sacrifice of his blood humans were created. Like the Indian deity, Shiva, the Egyptian, Horus and Set or the Greek Apollo and Python, Quetzalcoatl was the two faced Creator/Destroyer. In the sculpture above, the front is shown in his benevolent aspect as Lord of Life while the back reveals the malevolent Lord of Death. The concept of two distinct and separate principles of Good and Evil coexisting in the universe was the unique invention of the Persian prophet, Zoroaster who lived in the 5th century B.C.. His dualistic idea found its richest soil in the two centuries surrounding the birth of Christ. While the Hebrews deftly stepped aside from the implications of a universe created by a Good God which included a separate principle of Radical Evil, the Pauline Christians grasped the thorn in both hands. The ensuing juggling with such a hot ember has created a confusion which remains unresolved up to this day.

Being these damned beings move into the territory of non-being and purposelessness.

When Angels fall through their own free will they then walk upon earth as humans. If they continue in their impure and evil ways they ultimately become demons with "cold and obscure bodies." In one bold speculation Origen claims that men can become Angels just as easily as Angels become men. This is also true for demons, who can regain their angelic intelligences.

Origen explains his cosmic principle with disarming simplicity.

"When intended for the more imperfect spirits, it becomes solidified, thickens, and forms the bodies of this visible world. If it is serving higher intelligences, it shines with the brightness of the celestial bodies, and serves as a garb for the Angels of God."

Legend Three : Lust

The third account of the fall comes from Enoch the Scribe. He lists two hundred *bene ha Elohim* (Watchers or Sons of God), who descended onto Mt. Hermon about 12,000 years ago. Originally they were assisting the Archangels in the creation of Eden. At the same time they began teaching men some of the arts of civilization. The trouble was that their extra-curricular activities included the unexpected seduction of the daughters of Adam. Rabbi Elkiezer, in the 8th century, with typical patriarchal zeal put the blame squarely upon the women. "The Angels who fell from Heaven saw the daughters of Cain perambulating and displaying their private parts, their eyes painted with antimony in the manner of harlots, and, being seduced, took wives from among them."

It is difficult to believe the Angels were entirely innocent bystanders but they did prove to be highly

Above: **Charon the Etruscan God of the Dead** *Tomb of Orca – Tarquinia 5th century B.C..* Charon had a huge hooked nose like the beak of a bird which overhung bestial features. He has wings and serpents growing from his blue-gray colored body. He pre-dated the Devil by four hundred years. Yet the Etruscans did not appear to see him as a force for evil but the deity who presided over the huge cities of the dead which were built alongside of those of the living.

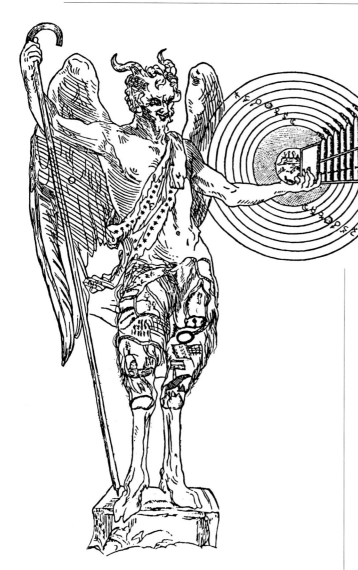

Presumably these Angels were the only order which possessed the physical wherewithall to couple with the daughters of man, since it is held by the Church that the rest of the Angels, being of the spirit, cannot reproduce. But there are heretical accounts which suggest that when Angels sin they "clothe themselves with the corruptibility of the flesh." In the case of the lusty tenth order this was obviously unnecessary.

One further piece of evidence shows that the Watchers possibly came from an entirely separate stock from that of the Angels. A description of the four Archangels found in Enoch XL:1-10 speaks of the four Archangels as being "Four presences different from those who sleep not." This latter term was given to mean the Watchers, so it appears they may have been physically completely unlike the other angelic orders. It is certainly known that by the human standards of the area the Grigori appeared to be giants.

Not only had these Sons of God cohabited with the mortals but they began teaching them many of the deeper secrets of heaven such as making weapons from metal or creating perfumes and cosmetics so that women could become even more desirable. However benign were their intentions to educate the lowlanders, these gigantic Angels managed, at the same time, to spawn some pretty horrendous and very unruly monsters. These mutant hoodlums began to ravage the lands and finally, regretfully it seems, had to be dispatched by Angels loyal to the Throne.

The Lord then bound the angelic fathers and hurled them into everlasting hell. However, since that time they have somehow managed to escape to both tempt and be tempted by the all too corruptible flesh.

vulnerable. These Angels of fire were transformed on contact with earth and the fire changed to flesh.

According to official Papal authority these apostate Angels actually came from a separate tenth order of Angels. As we have already seen these were the gigantic Grigori.

Above: **Satan smiting Job with Sore Boils** *by William Blake 1826* Opposite: **Pan** *Illustration from Kitcher's Oedipus Aegyptiacus.* Here we see the occult and composite winged goat, with the pipes symbolizing the harmonies of the seven spheres. Christians had a blanket disapproval of all deities or legends which were not mentioned in the bible. It did mean that Hell quickly filled with the very best of characters of the Middle and Near East. Pan was one of the most ancient pagan deities and the one which the Church fathers most feared. And whosoever they feared always ended up demonic.

Originally Pan was the lusty son of Hermes. He epitomized the spirit of nature, fertility and sexuality. As such he was wild and loved freedom above all else. His redoubtable sexual exploits hardly recommended him to the ascetics of the early Church. Being so much part of the great cycle of fecundity, rebirth and death, he was an obvious denizen of the Underworld.

His outsized phallus symbolized that aspect of man which was untameable by any organization and thus became, in the Church father's eyes the ultimate in depravity and sin. Supposedly the oracles of Greece were silenced at the birth of Christ, having given one last utterance, "Great Pan is dead!" In fabricating the story the early fathers might have added, "Great Satan is now alive!"

Above: **The Lecherous Demons** *by Gustave Doré.* Right: **Lilith, Goddess of Death** *Bas relief from Sumer, c. 2000 B.C..* Here we see the "Eye" or "Owl" Goddess who was known throughout the Middle East and Old Europe. She is identified with the original Great Mother, or Triple Goddess. She is depicted as Bird, Serpent and human and holds in her hand the key of Life.

To the Romans the owl, or *strix,* meant a witch and according to Christian legend the owl was one of three disobedient sisters who defied God and was promptly turned into the bird which cannot look directly into the Light or the Sun.

The owl was known to monks as the "night hag" and was feared by the celibate who believed them to be Lilith's daughters, the Lilim.

Lust and the Female Angel

It must have been noticed that all the seducable Grigori have been male so far. What of their female angelic counterparts? Both Hebrew and Christian sources are notably reticent on the subject and there is no mention of fallen females from the original rebels.

There was, however, one powerful exception who openly sneered at all attempts to quietly dispose of her embarrassing legend. This was the mysterious Lilith, Satan's favorite bride of Hell who the clergy have attempted to ignore as having been Adam's first wife. Hebrew traditions tell of God creating Lilith as a mate for the first man. But she proved far too lively and wild for her husband. Adam tried to force her to lie beneath him in the approved patriarchal style of the "missionary posture."

Now male Jews and Christians are not alone in their insistence of sexually "being on top." Moslems even state "Accursed be the man that maketh woman heaven and himself earth." Catholic authorities went so far as to say that any other position is sinful.

Lilith didn't appear to share this male thesis and laughed at Adam for his crudity. She then promptly left him for the doubtless more enjoyable delights to be had with demons, begetting the prodigious number of one hundred offspring each day from their attentions.

As the Great Serpent's bride she is identified with the Triple Mother goddess of the earlier matriarchal and agricultural tribes of Canaan, who resisted the warlike herdsmen of Adam.

While Lilith was somewhat obscured by the Church, her daughters, the *Lilim*, were famous as a major hazard to monastic life. Variously depicted as the Harlots of Hell, Succubae or Night Hags, these beautiful she-demons were much given to copulating with men in their sleep. Like their brazen mother they favored squatting over their dreaming lovers, reversing the male-superior position required by Divine Law. The horrified celibate monks had no defenses and tried to prevent the dread orgy by tying crucifixes to their genitals before going to sleep. However every time one of them succumbed and had a wet dream Lilith's "filthy laugh" was heard down the monastery corridors.

By some heretical accounts she appears to have been too much for the Lord Himself, who was not entirely immune to her abandoned charms. However, He seemed to think better of any ideas which may have passed through the Purity of His Mind and quickly presented her to Satan.

Legend Four : Pride

Enoch himself gives a rather conflicting alternative account of the fall in the second of his Chronicles. In the *Book of Secrets* he describes how, "One of the Order of Angels having turned away with the order that was under him, conceived of an impossible thought, to place his throne higher than the clouds above the earth."

It is now known that this is one of many variations on a very popular and well loved theme current throughout the Middle East. The guardian angel of Edom (Rome) also boasts that he will do the same. In the New Testament Jesus sees Satan, a Son of God, plunging towards earth as a stroke of lightning. It is the original story of the fall of Lucifer, the "Bringer of Light." Lucifer's other title is "The Morning Star," the star which heralds the rising sun, and we discover that this story is a borrowing from the even earlier legend of Shaher. This Canaanite deity of the Dawn was born out of the womb or "Pit" of the great Mother Goddess. Shaher, like Lucifer, was The Morning Star who was the last light to proudly defy the rising sun. He attempted to storm the solar throne of light, but was cast down from heaven for his impudence. This ancient epic was recorded seven centuries before Christ in a Canaanite scripture. Five centuries later a Hebrew scribe copied it almost verbatim, but borrowed the words to put into the mouth of the prophet Isaiah. The comparison is instructive for those readers who still maintain the Bible came from one source. The original Canaanite version is in italics.

> *How hast thou fallen from heaven, Helel's son Shaher!*
>
> How hast thou fallen from heaven, O Lucifer, Son of the morning!
>
> *Thou didst say in thy heart, I will ascend to Heaven.*

Below: **Satan Falling** *From the Divine Comedy by Dante. Illustration by Gustave Doré.*
Dante picked up the theme of the lightning serpent falling to earth in the Divine Comedy. In his account Satan, once again, had been the mightiest of the seraphim but through "hubris" fell like lightning from heaven. He plunged through the sphe-

res to crash on earth. So pregnant was he and heavy with sin that he plummeted through creation like hot lead in soft butter.

His explosive fall created a vast tomb that became hell. And there he remains stuck at the dead center of the cosmos with his huge horned head facing Jerusalem in the north.

His buttocks and genitals are frozen in the dread ice and his huge hairy Pan-like legs rear up towards purgatory. But he is compressed by the sheer brutal weight of the entire cosmos. This Lucifer has lost all trace of his earlier magnificence and is just a mountainous mass of emptiness and non-being.

Opposite: Lucifer, Star of the Morning contemplates the rising Sun.

For thou hast said in thy heart, I will ascend to heaven.
Above the circumpolar stars I will raise my throne
I will exhalt my throne above the stars of God,
And I will dwell on the Mount of Council in the back of the North
I will sit also upon the Mount of the Congregation, in the sides of the north,
I will mount on the back of a cloud.
I will ascend above the heights of the clouds,
I will be like unto Elyon.
I will be like unto the most High.
(Isaiah 14:12-14)

Barbara Walker makes a nice point in her epic *Woman's Encyclopedia:* "The biblical writer further told Lucifer: 'Thou shalt be brought down to hell, to the sides of the pit' (Isaiah 14:15). This 'pit' was the same as Helel, or Asherah, the god's own Mother-bride; and his descent as a lightning-serpent into her Pit represented fertilization of the abyss by masculine fire from heaven. In short, the Light-bringer challenged the supreme solar god by seeking the favors of the Mother. This divine rivalry explains the so called sin of Lucifer, *hubris*, which Church fathers translated as pride – but its real meaning was sexual passion. We also might see the phallic lightning bolt as an expression of Lucifer's role as Prince of the Power of Air.

The story is almost identical to the one in which the guardian angel of Edom (Rome) boasts that he will be like the All High. In the New Testament it is essentially the same tale when Jesus sees Satan, the Son of God, plunging towards earth as a stroke of lightning.

There are many later variations upon this theme. In a mystery play of the 13th century God is said to have created Lucifer as the highest angel, second in glory only to God Himself.

"I make you closest to me
Of all the powers, Master and mirror of my might,
I create you beautiful in bliss and name you Lucifer, Bearer of Light."
Lucifer sees himself in the mirror and agrees
"Aha, that I am wondrous bright…"
and his beauteous head is turned
"A wortheir lord forsooth am I
And ever worthier than he
In evidence that I am worthier
I will go sit on God's throne"
On finding Lucifer seated on the Throne and basking in his own Self-Glory, God is furious and hurls him from Heaven. The theme is taken up by Milton three hundred years later.

"Lucifer from Heav'n
(So call him, brighter once amidst the host
Of Angels, than that Star the Stars among)
Fell with his flaming legions through the Deep
Into his place.
They fell thick as autumn leaves, with Cherub and Seraph rolling in the Flood.
Nine days they fell; confounded Chaos roar'd"
John Milton's *Paradise Lost.*

Satan in the Abyss *Engraving by Gustave Doré from Milton's Paradise Lost.*

Legend Five: War

At the beginning of the world, some say on the second day of creation, there was a tremendous battle in heaven. God had created the Angels with free will but He observed they were fallible. The Almighty was uncomfortable with the idea that his creations could sin and probably would, given half the chance. So he strengthened many of them in their pursuit of Goodness by an act of Grace. According to St.Augustine this confirmation gave them a profound understanding of the workings of the cosmos and their unique place within it.

Then God created a second group but withheld His Grace and so gave them the opportunity to sin. True to God's suspicions they embraced sin with enthusiasm. A war broke out between the two factions and Michael, who of course had the advantage of God's Grace, managed to cast the legions of sinners from out of heaven. Considering the minor inconvenience this seems to have caused the Devilish forces, this great battle must, at best, be considered a pyrrhic victory. Theologians assure us that the final conflict will eventually be an overwhelming victory for the Angels of Good. Yet even in this bitter pre-knowledge Satan's hordes still prefer to try the impossible, rather than turn to the Light. Which confirms they are either stupid, proud, stubborn or just courageously following their own dark, inner light.

War in Heaven. *From a series of illustrations by Gustave Doré,* culminating in the defeat of Satan by the Archangel Michael (below right). The estimated size of the rebel army was over 133 million while Michael led twice that number of God's troops.

Legend Six: The Passion of the Redeemer

This scenario is more subtle and more difficult to grasp than any of the others. This play opens with the Devil and his Angels already separated from God. They have already committed the sin of pride and their Love of Self is above their Love of God. The Devil has an obsessive hatred of humans and has already managed to seduce Eve, and for this God has cursed him. But the real fall of the forces of Darkness comes with the birth and passion of Christ.

Up until this point God has given the Devil and his legions of Angels the power to tempt, to test and finally to punish humankind. God could have left us mortals in this perilous and unrewarding state, but St. Augustine comes up with an original proposal. He says that instead of abandoning us, God took on human nature in order to make a full reconciliation with His creation. He was to feel as we feel and to suffer as we suffer under the Devil's reign. So, in the form of Christ He delivered himself, like the rest of us, to Lucifer.

The Prince of Darkness, out of a blind hatred of Adam's line, greedily took what St. Augustine calls "a bait and hook." What Satan did not recognize as he grabbed at the prize was that Christ was both divine and sinless. So the Devil transgressed the terms of the contract he had with God. For the agreement was that he only had dominion over sinners and so by breaking the contract he was damned.

In his unsuccessful temptation of Christ, the second Adam, Satan was puzzled and could not decide whether Christ was divine or not. A medieval mystery play shows the Devil's dilemma perfectly:
"What he is I cannot see;
whether he be God or Man
I can tell in no degree:
In sorrow I let a fart."
In this particular plot, typical of Passion plays created by the clergy in order to bring a complex message home to a simple audience, the Devil and his demons make a terrible series of blunders. They are portrayed as being buffoons who cannot make up their minds whether to kill Christ or not.

Lucifer has suspicions that if their quarry really is the Incarnation, to seize him will bring ruin upon them all. When Satan finally tries to seize Christ's soul the trap is sprung. For, instead of grabbing an unfortunate sinner, they find God instead. So God did not leave us all in the Devil's power. Although He had allowed us to fall into the Evil One's hands, He then chose to allow the same to happen to Himself in order to save us.

Musical Inferno *by Hieronymus Bosch.*

When God as Christ harrows Hell to release those souls who had not enjoyed the benefit of the same redemption, Satan is furious and swears to renew his efforts to corrupt the world. At this Christ hurls him down and Michael binds him fast in Hell. Here is the real fall of the dark Angels. Trapped in Hell all they have left is power to punish those humans who refuse to participate in Christ's sacrifice.

Legend Seven: Disobedience

This brings us to the last variation of the Fall in which Disobedience and Pride are the combined cause.

When Adam was first presented to the hierarchs by God, Satan, who was at that time the greatest of the Seraphim and Regent of Heaven, refused to bow before the new creation. "How can a Son of Fire bow to a Son of Clay?" was his response. The Divine sculptor was not amused at such a poor critical response to His masterpiece and His reaction was characteristically swift. As He flung His ex-regent into the Abyss, one third of the Angels chose to follow Satan.

But there is a far more poignant Sufi version of this story. In this, Satan is seen as the angel who loved God the most. When God created the Angels He told them to bow to no one but Himself. Then He created Adam whom He considered higher than the Angels. He commanded them to bow before the new figure, forgetting his previous commandment. Satan refused, partly because he couldn't disobey the first commandment, but also because he would only bow to his Beloved God. God, who has a long record of being a hasty judge of character or motive, didn't understand Satan's dilemma and cast him from heaven. The worst pain of Hell for Satan was the absence of the Beloved. All Satan has left is the eternal echo of God's angry last words and the merest lingering trace of His passing. Hell is the terrible loneliness of separation from love. In this story Satan becomes the jealous lover, who loathes Man as the new object of God's love and the one which has replaced himself.

The North American Indian Sun-Dancers have a similar understanding of the fall. They believe that each person is a Living Medicine Wheel, powerful and limitless. Each of us is in reality a Power which possesses boundless, unimaginable energy but we have chosen to learn the lessons of limitation through being encapsulated in a body with finite boundaries. This created a new experience of separateness and loneliness. Only by understanding the illusory nature of this experience can a sense of being One with the divine be reawakened. This is also the significance of the parable of the Prodigal Son who had to leave his father's house in order to realize what he had lost. This is one of the more poignant underlying themes of the fall and one which puts Satan in a very different light.

Above: **Satan contemplates the Fall:** This shows the transformation of Satan from a radiant being to one of darkness. The wings are now reptilian and bat-like, the feet are cloven and the hair is serpentine. This engraving and those on the previous four pages are by *Gustave Doré.*

Left: **Popular 18th century view of the Devil,** *from Cheshire, England.*

This illustration shows the "foul fiend" flying off with Over Church, which is supposed to have once occupied a different location.

It was believed that evil spirits fear the sound of church bells and in this particular legend, it was the pious ringing of the local abbey bells that caused Satan so much pain and anguish that he was forced to drop his sacred burden. Protected by prayer, the church landed unharmed on a new site, far from its original home.

Although also allegedly protected by prayers, hymns and holy relics, it would seem that German churches were not so fortunate during the same century. For Lucifer, as Prince of the Power of Air, appeared to have been exceptionally active with his lightning bolts. In the short space of thirty years he managed to hit 400 church towers, killing no less than 120 bell-ringers. Curiously, with the invention of a "device of the Devil" – the lightning conductor – lightning is no longer under the control of Satan but is now "an Act of God."

The Invention of Hell

The whole idea of a *demonic* form of a fallen angel was very far from Enoch's experience of the gigantic Grigori. The entire demonic and devilish super-structure, with its Hell located far from the Pearly Gates of Heaven, is a relatively late Christian invention. While the concept of monstrous fiends and ghoulish demons was not entirely the creation of the Middle Ages, the writers of that time certainly managed to embellish the idea until little remained of the original Jewish images. The dark collective unconscious of medieval Europe was an extraordinary field of imaginative energy. It was an era of magic and a new preoccupation with the mysteries of alchemy, the Kabbalah and those areas of knowledge which were later to become the proto-sciences. In such an atmosphere both Angels and demons were summoned by Holy or diabolic practitioners. Their secret pentacles opened to reveal nightmare legions of Angels and Devils from a dark collective unconscious which spewed forth in majestic and towering heavens and hideous depths.

In order to understand the nature of the Angels who are said to inhabit those Realms of Darkness, it is best to examine the portrait of the entity who is the most enigmatic and surprising angel of all – Satan. Hell is inseparable from the Evil One. This dark entity is the complete antithesis of the archangel Michael. In some traditions the Prince of Evil looks through a dark mirror at his reflection as the twin brother of the Logos, or Christ. It is no coincidence for without the Arch-fiend there would be no Christ needed to defeat him.

Fall of the Rebel Angels *by Pieter Breughel the Elder, Brussels.*

ATAN-EL

(Alias Lucifer, Sammael, Mastema, Beliel, Azazel, Beelzebub, Duma, Gadreel, Sier, Samael, Mephistopheles and Asmodeus). Most authorities agree that he was once the mightiest of the Seraphim, Viceroy or Regent of God. In this original form he is depicted as having twelve wings. Gregory of Nazianus says of him that before his fall he had worn the rest of the Angels "as a garment, transcending all in glory and knowledge." Even St. Jerome tells us that this mighty angel will one day be reinstated in that primal splendor and in his prior rank.

It seems only appropriate that this Prince of Lies and Deception should hide behind so many aliases. Yet Satan in all his multi-various aspects combines many ancient deities. He has the horns, the hairy legs, the hoofs and the formidable phallus of the ancient and lusty woodland deity, Pan. He has the fearsome lightning trident of the God of the Underworld; the serpent form of the Leviathan (Apollyon) and the six wings of the awesome Babylonian Guardian spirits.

He is the *Evil One* and the *One Evil* who encapsulates all the seven deadly sins in one being: 1. The Pride of Lucifer; 2. The Avarice of Mammon; 3. The Anger of Satan; 4. The Lechery of Asmodeus; 5. The Gluttony of Beelzebub; 6. The Envy of Leviathan and 7. The Sloth of Belphegor. He is also to be found behind other masks and aliases. Here are just a few taken from the heavenly police files.

baddon-Satan

This was the Hebrew name for Apollyon, the angel of the Bottomless Pit. The hebrews borrowed the seven-layered model of

the underworld from the Babylonians to create Gehenna, whose Dark Prince is also named Arsiel. This means the "Black Sun," the negative sun of anti-matter. Within the central pit in the bottom layer lives the serpent angel Apollyon, the fallen Greek Sun God Apollo, King of the Demonic Locusts. This is much to be expected for most of the more powerful pagan deities are to be found in Hell. As far as the Church was concerned anyone not mentioned in the Bible was bad. It does mean that most of the really interesting characters are to be found in the Infernal regions.

ammael-Satan

This alias is Sumerian in origin (Sam means poison, thus Sammael is the "bright and poisonous One" or the "Angel of Poison"). He is also the Angel of Death. One title specifically gives him as Chief of the Satans. One explanation for this can be found in Enoch I, where the scribe records his first eye witness account of a meeting with the Lord (En XL:6). At this meeting Uriel is "arguing against the satans and refusing them permission to come before the Lord to accuse those from the Earth." In the context of this passage Enoch seems to be referring to the satans as some sort of enforcers of the Law. From their role as a kind of angelic police force in the early version they seem to have become the worst of the Gestapo in a later account in which Enoch calls Sammael the "Chief of Demons."

Known as the great serpent with twelve wings who drew after him the solar system, he is also accused of being the self-same serpent who tempted Eve. In one account he not only tempted our pliable ancestor but managed to father Cain into the bargain. Isaiah in his visit to heaven saw the hosts of

Sammael squabbling and envying one another. Dogs howl in the night when Sammael" flies like a bird" and "takes through the town his flight."

eliel-Satan

The Ruling Prince of Sheol (part of the infernal regions). Beliar means "worthless." Beliar himself tells us in the Gospel of Bartholomew that "At first I was called Satanel, which is interpreted as messenger of God, but when I rejected the image of God my name was called Satanas, that is an angel that keepeth Hell." He cannot resist the temptation to boast, "I was formed the first angel." Michael supposedly was the second, Gabriel third, Uriel fourth, and Raphael the fifth. And there may be some truth to the boast, for these are also named as the Angels of Vengeance.

eelzebub-Satan

Originally Beelzebub was a Canaanite deity. His name meant "Lord of the House." In many ancient religions flies bore the souls and there was a popular belief that women would conceive by swallowing them. The Greek *psyche* actually signifies a butterfly. As "Lord of the Flies", Beelzebub was actually a psychopomp or Lord of the Souls. Notwithstanding the distinction, he was confirmed as the incarnate evil, "Lord of Chaos" and chief Demon by no less than three of the Apostles. Christ is supposed to have given Beelzebub dominion over Hell for helping in the evacuation of Adam and the other saints during the harrowing of the underworld. Satan had refused to let them go but it might be that our Prince of Deception, who must have realized the hopelessness of opposing the Savior, at least could save face by see-

ming to help in the disguise of the Lord of Flies.

Georges Gurdjieff makes Beelzebub an extraterrestrial who is languishing in a tedious exile, far from the Presence of His beloved Endlessness, and makes Earth his particular study.

Johann Weyer in his *Pseudographica Demoniaca* makes him the Supreme Overlord of the Underworld and founding father of the Great Order of the Fly.

zazel-Satan

According to Enoch, Azazel was another of the fallen Watchers. Other sources give him as the chief of the Grigori. In the occult lore he is a demon with seven serpent heads, each with two faces. He is also said to have twelve wings. According to both rabbinical and Islamic lore it was Azazel (Iblis in Islam) who refused to acknowledge and bow before Adam when this first human was presented to the other hierarchs of heaven. It was he who originally voiced the famous question, "Why should a Son of Fire bow to a Son of Clay?" As we know, predictably, God was swift in His reply.

astema-Satan

Mastema is a Hebrew word for "animosity," "inimicable" or "adverse." This is the Accusing Angel, the tempter and executioner, and it is in this capacity that he tried an unsuccessful attempt on the life of Moses. It was he who hardened the Pharoah's heart and was instrumental in assisting the Egyptian wizards against the Israelites. He slaughtered the first born of Egypt and appeared as the first named separation of the *mal'ak*, or Shadow of God.

The Seven Deadly Sins *Popular print, Russia 1830.* The Evil One encapsulates all the seven sins in one being. (See page 102)

Lucifer-Satan

We now come to the most fascinating alias of all. Lucifer, Bearer of Light, Son of the Morning, Dragon of Dawn, Prince of the Power of Air was once held to be the greatest of the Angels and favorite of God the Father, Lord of Light. But he was also the first to separate himself from the Divine source.

The painting on the opposite page by the mystic artist William Blake illustrates the following quotation from the Old Testament (Ezekiel XXVIII 13-15) and shows Lucifer in his full splendor and light before his fall. It has been argued that this passage is actually addressed to Nebuchadrezzar, King of Babylon, but as St. Jerome assures us that it is di-

rected at the greatest of the fallen Angels, we will take his word for it.

"Thou hast been in Eden the Garden of God; every precious stone was thy covering, the sardius, topaz, and the diamond, the beryl, the onyx, and the jasper, the sapphire, the emerald, and the carbuncle, and gold: the workmanship of thy tabrets and of thy pipes was prepared in thee in the day thou wast created.

Thou art the anointed cherub that covereth; and I have set thee so: thou wast upon the holy mountain of God; thou hast walked up and down in the midst of the stones of fire.

Thou wast perfect in thy ways from the day that thou wast created, till iniquity was found in thee."

Lucifer, Son of the Morning, according to one further interpretation of the fall, is maddened by jealousy when God the Father proclaims Lucifer's brother, Jesual, the Son. From his head he gives birth to Sin and, copulating with her, fathers Death. He is cast out of heaven and is renamed Satan-el – the Adversary.

In the painting, the many winged figure has his right foot forward, denoting his spiritual aspect (it is interesting that in the East the left foot invariably is the spiritual leader). His outstretched hands hold the orb and scepter, symbols of earthly domain. Part of his wing disguises his original androgynous nature. He is surrounded by a retinue including the pipes and tabrets. The pipes are associated with the music of the spheres.

Lucifer, as both the Evening and the Morning star, is seen as the dying and reborn light of the air. He shares with the serpent the ability to shed the old dead skin and arise as if newborn.

His lightning fall into the Abyss reminds us that the Hebrews were long in Egypt, for there is an

Egyptian serpent God, Sata, who is father of lightning and who likewise fell to earth. The Babylonian
Zu was also a lightning god who fell as a fiery flying
serpent and this recalls the fact that Lucifer was
once a Seraph.

Lucifer, like his twin brother Christ, is the son
who defies the Old Father (Christ accuses the Jews
of worshipping the wrong God). And as he falls
his phallic lightning bolt pierces the bottomless pit
of the Mother Goddess Hel. Hel was once a ute-
rine shrine, a womb or a sacred cave of rebirth.
Christ as God is the lover-son of the Virgin Mary,
his mother. Brunnhilde was the leader of the Valkyries, the northern Angels of death. Her name
means "Burning Hell." As can be observed, things
in the underworld are not what they at first appear
to be.

Encounter with Evil

We now turn to what are claimed to be first hand accounts of meetings with the Enemy. During the five centuries after Christ many Christian hermits and monks withdrew into the wilderness in order to leave worldly temptations. Legions of demons seemed to follow them with enthusiasm, if the contemporary monastic diabology is anything to go by. This diabology was a new type of writing which gave instructions as to how to resist temptation and cope with the threat of demonic attacks. It also gave the writers an opportunity to give the most lurid accounts of the arch-enemy himself.

The most influential of these visionary, yet practical, manuals of how to deal with both angel and Devil was the classic *Life of Anthony*, composed by the Bishop of Alexandria in 360. In it we read of the constant struggle of the hermit Anthony (and thus all his monastic brethren) with the Devil and his demons. "The Devil's eyes are like the morning star. In his mouth gape burning lamps and hearthfuls of fire are cast forth. The smoke of a furnace blazing with the fire of coals flares from his nostrils. His breath is of coals, and from his mouth issues flames."

In spite of Christ's passion to redeem sinners and destroy Satan's power, the Devil and his hordes seemed to have suffered only a minor inconvenience. In composing his *Life of Anthony*, Bishop Athanasius is at considerable pains to assure the monks that Christ really had pulled Old Nick's teeth. However threatening the demons appeared the Bishop tells us, all they could actually do was to tempt or to accuse. So the next meeting with the Evil One reveals a complaining Devil, stripped of power and almost unrecognizable from his earlier image, yet very perceptive of the monkish habits.

"Someone knocked at the door of my cell, and opening it I saw a person of great size and tallness. I inquired, "Who are you?" and he replied "Satan." When I asked, "Why are you here?" he answered, "Why do monks and other Christians blame me so undeservedly? Why do they curse me every hour?" I answered, "Why do you trouble them?" He replied, "I don't trouble them, for I am become weak: they trouble themselves. Haven't they read that 'the swords of the enemy are finished and the cities destroyed for him'? I no longer have a weapon or a city. The Christians are spread everywhere, and even the desert is now filled with monks. Let them

take care of themselves and cease cursing me." I marveled at God's grace and said to Satan, "Although you are a liar and never speak the truth, you have spoken the truth here, albeit against your will. For the coming of Christ has weakened you, and He has cast you down and stripped you."

Gradually such "do it yourself" manuals gave way in popularity to more visionary works of Heaven and Hell. While the diabologies had an almost exclusive readership within monastic walls, the new Visions of Paradise and the spectacular and often grisly scenes of the Inferno held the secular public in thrall.

The following account of one such Vision was written in 1149 by an Irish monk and was enormously popular in the Middle Ages, being translated into no less than fifteen different languages and being the subject of many paintings. Part of its popularity was that the witness was an unabashed sinner, an Irish knight who was well on the burning road to Hell before he had this transforming vision. One day he collapsed, having eaten something poisonous or drugged, and had every appearance of being dead. Only a mysterious warmth on his left side prevented his immediate burial. He lay in this state for three days during which time his soul was met by a guardian angel who took him on an educational tour of both Heaven and Hell. Even the celebrated Dante or Milton cannot excel this graphic description of the Prince of Hell.

The Irish knight was called Tundale. His guardian angel, having led him through some of the more harrowing scenes of the underworld, now invites him to see the greatest adversary of the human race.

"Drawing near, Tundale's soul saw the depths of hell, and he would not be able to repeat in any way how many, how great and what inexpressible torments he saw there if he had a hundred heads and in each head a hundred tongues. I do not think it would be useful to omit the few details that he did bring back for us.

He saw the Prince of Shadows, the enemy of humanity, the Devil whose size overshadowed every kind of beast that Tundale saw before. Tundale was not able to compare the size of the body to anything, nor would we dare to presume to say what we did not draw from his mouth, but such a story as we did hear we ought not to omit.

This beast was very black, like a raven, with a body of human shape from its feet to its head,

except that it had many hands and a tail. This horrible monster had no less than a thousand hands, and each hand was a thousand cubits long and ten cubits wide. Each hand had twenty fingers connected to it; they had very long claws with a thousand points, and they were iron, and his feet were just as many claws. Moreover, he had a very long and great beak, and his tail was very long and sharp and ready to injure souls with its sharp points. The horrible stooping spectacle was seated on a forged iron wickerwork placed over coals inflamed by the inflated bellows of an innumerable number of demons. Such a multitude of demons and souls circled above him that no one can believe how many there were, because the world has produced all these souls from the beginning. This host of humanity was attached through each member and at their joints with very large and flaming iron bonds. Moreover, when this beast was turned to coal and then burned, he turned himself from one side to the other in very great wrath, and he stretched out all his hands into the multitude of souls and then compressed them when they were all replenished. This thirsty boor pressed out the clusters so that there was no soul able to avoid him who was not either dismembered or deprived of head, feet or hands.

Then by just breathing, he inhaled and exhaled all the souls into different parts of hell. Immediately the Pit belched, from which, as we said before, there was a fetid flame. When the dreadful beast drew his breath again he sucked back to him all the souls that

Lucifer, detail of Hell *from the Last Judgment by Giotto.* The enormously popular visionary account of Hell by the Irish knight Tundale had been translated into thirteen languages by the time this image was painted. It is obvious from the details that Giotto was familiar with Tundale's version.

he dispersed before, and he devoured those who fell into his mouth with the smoke and sulfur. But whoever fled from his hand he struck down with his tail; and the miserable beast, always striking hard, was struck hard, and the burning tormentor was tormented in the punishment with the souls.

Seeing this Tundale's soul said to the angel of the Lord, "My Lord, what is this monster's name?" Answering, the angel said, "This beast whom you see is called Lucifer, and he is the prince of the creatures of God who took part in the pleasures of paradise. He was so perfect that he would throw heaven and earth and even hell into total disorder."

THE HORDES OF HELL
Who's Who of the Underworld

Predictably the hell as depicted in the Middle Ages is very medieval in concept, being founded on a strictly feudal basis. Although the bonds of allegiance and loyalty are none too reliable in an infernal region where it's every demon for himself, most descriptions still keep to the typical Lordship-retainer structure well known to Teutonic Barons. The most complete hierarchy ever published of the Infernal pecking order was Johann Weyer's *Pseudo Monarchia Daemonium*, which appeared in the 16th century. It later turned out that this definitive work, which was quoted by every aspiring alchemist, kabbalist, occultist and demonophile, was actually an elaborate spoof. It caricatured the hated hierarchy of the Church and probably is a better mirror of European kingdoms of the time than of the Infernal realms.

However Weyer did use much occult material which is no longer accessible to us and offers insights into the constitution of the nether regions along with their principal characters.

He gives the Talmudic figure of 7,405,926 demons who were divided into 72 companies. In his version it is Beelzebub who was the Supreme Over-Lord of the Dark Empire. He is the founder of the Order of the Fly and this reflects his Philistine and Canaanite origins as Baal-ze-Bub, Lord of the Flies. His great captains were: Satan, Prince of Darkness and The Adversary; Pluto, Prince of Fire and Hades; Molech, Prince of the Land of Tears; Baal, General of the Diabolic Hordes; Lucifer as, curiously, the Chief Justice; Baal-beryth as the Minister of Devilish Pacts and Treaties; Nergal as Chief of the Secret Police; Proserpine, the Arch She-Devil as Princess of Demonic Spirits; Astarte, who was masculinized as Astaroth, Duke and Treasurer of Hell.

Weyer's entire superstructure was a beautiful deception within the best traditions of the Lord of Lies.

The following diagrams of Hell have been compiled from less questionable sources although it must be admitted the veracity of many of those sources might be in question.

There are two quite distinct species to be found in the nether world which have completely different genealogical trees.

Demons

Demons originally derived from the personal familiar spirits which were a respected and common species throughout the Near East. *Daimon* is Greek for "soul." These were the invisible spirits who occupied the ethereal spaces between God and humanity. But by the time of the first translation of the *Septuagint*, these pagan demons were interchangeable with Devils.

As the usual practice of both the Jewish scribes and those of the early and medieval Church was to relegate to Hell any deity or spirit not actually mentioned in the Bible most of the earlier pagan *daimones* found themselves serving the Devil. St. Thomas Aquinas reveals a healthy respect for their pagan aspect by stating: "It is a dogma of faith that demons can produce wind, storms and a rain of fire from heaven." It was also an assumed dogma of faith that Devils existed. In reality to believe otherwise was heresy.

St.Augustine vehemently denied that there was any connection between the fallen Angels and any pagan demons. He even denied that the dark Angels had any sex while of course everyone knew that the pagan deities were, if anything, over endowed.

Devils

Compared with Demons, Devils have a far more distinguished pedigree. The word comes from the Greek *diabolos* which means a "slanderer," "perjurer" or "adversary." When the Old Testament was translated into Greek (2nd century B.C.) *diabolos* was used as an equivalent to the Hebrew Satan. Some claim that the meaning of "Devil" is arrived at through another route, which is the Indo-European *devi*, "goddess," or the Persian *daeva* meaning "evil spirit," although this argument is open to questioning.

While Demons and Devils constitute two quite separate diabolic species, there are also two very distinct types of fallen angel, each having a unique family tree. One tree traces the descent from the tenth order of bene Elohim, the Grigori or Watchers, and the other from the *Ma'lakim*, which includes all the other nine angelic orders. It is important to distinguish the gigantic Grigori, who fell through lust and who spawned some of the less savory monsters of hell, from the more aristocratic two-eyed serpents who fell through rebellion or pride.

The Sons of God

As we have already seen, the Watchers, known also as the bene-ha-Elohim or the Sons of God, were sent from heaven to teach human beings, but they succumbed to the highly seductive flesh of the daughters of Cain. Nine tenths of them are said to have yielded to the temptation and either dwell in the third heaven or in hell.

There seem to have been two leaders of the Grigori, Azazel and Shemjaza. Of the two Shemjaza appears to have been the one who repented of his actions. It is a little unclear as to whether he was of a different species to the Watchers. Some traditions maintain that he was a mighty Seraph who was seduced into revealing God's name to the beautiful but deadly Ishtarah. One version shows him so mortified by the consequences of his lust when he sees his gigantic mutant sons being destroyed by the Angels of Vengeance, that he voluntarily hurls himself into the constellation of Orion and this is where he can still be seen hanging upside down. This

Satan and Belzebuth. *Illustration for Paradise Lost by John Milton by Hayley.*

111

perhaps is a later piece of propaganda from the clergy for most versions assure us that he is alive, lusty and very much in action.

Certainly this story of Azazel is one of the possible origins of the Hanging Man in the Tarot Deck.

There is certainly no doubt of Azazel's alignment, although from descriptions it would seem he also comes from a higher species. Said to have seven serpent heads, fourteen faces and twelve wings, he also is named the "Lord of Hell" and the "Seducer of Mankind."

In his identification with Satan it was supposedly Azazel who refused to bow to Adam. Whereupon the Divine Sculptor cast Azazel from Heaven and changed his name to Eblis, which fits neatly into Islamic traditions. He is Satan's standard bearer and is said once to have been a Cherub but his nature seems far more like the bene-ha-Elim. For it was this Watcher who first showed women how to use cosmetics, perfumes and fine silks to inflame a man's passions. This is why God has an especial loathing for this "Son," for it was the Angels who were seduced by the seductive finery rather than the men.

Each year a "scapegoat" for Azazel fell to its death on the Day of Atonement having been thrown off the desert cliff at Haradan. This goat was believed to transfer the sins of Israel to their instigator, Azazel, who supposedly lay imprisoned beneath a huge pile of rocks at the foot of the cliff. Other apocrypha, however, inform us that he was free and up to mischief and didn't even seem to know of this annual sacrifice.

A complete list of the most notable Watchers is listed below:

Agniel: Taught the peoples of earth the enchantments of roots and the secrets of conjury, as well as using those arts to seduce one of the daughters.

Anmael: Like Shemjaza he made a sexual pact with a mortal woman to reveal the secret name of God.

Araquiel (Saraqael): Taught the signs and secrets of earth (geography) but is still said to lead souls to Judgement.

Araziel (Arazyael): "God is my noon," but lust seems to have been his midnight.

Asael: "Made by God."

Asbeel: "God's Deserter," Asbeel was the one who really sowed the seeds of dissention and who led the other Watchers astray.

Azael: "Whom God Strengthens," Obviously not enough for he was one of two Angels who succumbed to the all too delicious flesh of Lamech's daughter, Naamah. She gave birth to *Azza:* "The Strong One."

Azza further got himself into trouble with the Almighty by objecting to the transformation of Enoch the scribe into the most powerful angel of all – Metatron. It was also Azza who revealed the heavenly arcana to Solomon, thus making him the wisest man on earth.

Baraqijal: A lusty demon who taught men astrology.

Exael: One of the Watchers who according to Enoch, "taught men how to fabricate engines of war, works in silver and gold, the uses of gems and perfumes."

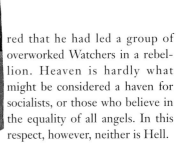

Ezeqeel: Taught meteorology to the early tribes.

Gadreel: "God is my Helper." Enoch names Gadreel as the angel who led Eve astray. Eve protested loudly that she had copulated "with no false beguiling serpent," but as we have learnt Eve's word is not always to be trusted. Gadreel is also known for having taught men how to make tools and weapons.

Kasdaye: He taught women the art of abortion.

Kashdejan: Taught men cures for various diseases, including those of the mind (Celtic Diyan Cecht) considered one of the worst sins.

Kokabel: Taught astronomy and the science of the constellations.

Penemuel: Who taught the art of writing "although through this many went astray until this day, for Men were not created for such a purpose to confirm their good intentions with pen and ink." (Ouch!)

Penemue: The Watcher who taught men writing. Strangely, for an evil angel he is a curer of stupidity. This seems at variance with Church doctrine which holds that demons are stupid. In fact the evidence shows that the nether regions are on the whole far better read, can quote scriptures and obscure ramifications of the Law far more accurately than their brethren "upstairs." The official reason given for this is that a demon needs to be intelligent and cunning in order to be able to tempt the wisest of men.

Pharmoros: Taught pharmacy, herbal lore, practical medicine and diagnosis of illness.

Satanail: Also known as Salamiel. He is a great prince of the Grigori. According to Enoch he and a small group of his followers were already being punished for some serious offense even before the "fall through lust." The angel with Enoch never elaborated upon his particular crime, although it was inferred that he had led a group of overworked Watchers in a rebellion. Heaven is hardly what might be considered a haven for socialists, or those who believe in the equality of all angels. In this respect, however, neither is Hell.

Talmaiel: A descendant of the Grigori who managed to escape both the flood and the swords of the avenging Angels.

Tamiel: "Perfection of God." *Turel:* "Rock of God." *Usiel:* "Strength of God."

Below: *A still from Wim Wender's classic film, "Wings of Desire."* Set in Berlin, this movie tells of an administering angel who, having fallen in love with a mortal trapeze artist, chooses to take on the flesh. He leaves his good, yet monotone world, in order to experience the universe of dualities. Immediately he discovers the sensuous pleasures and suffering of the flesh, heat and cold and the entire spectrum of colors along with the range of emotions with which we are all too familiar. The story suggests that the world of the good angel does lack the contrast which is only fully appreciated by those who have fallen. It does raise the question that if one only knows good, how could one recognize evil?

The Aristocrats of Hell

The second roll-call is from the separate Devilish tree of the "Shadows of God." These dark Angels originally come from the other nine angelic orders. The cause of their fall into darkness was either the sin of *hubris* or overweening Pride. In this group the higher the original position in heaven, the deeper their subsequent fall. In the following diagrams we find the most prominent of the diabolic personalities.

The Seven Princes of Hell

Baal-beryth: An Ex-prince of the cherubim and now the Grand Pontiff and Master of all Infernal Ceremonies. He always appears as the countersignatory in the pacts made by mortals and demons.

Dumah: This angel of the "Silence of Death" is, according to the *Zohar*, the chief of all the demon princes in Gehenna and guardian of Egypt during the Hebrew escape from Egypt.

Sariel: Claimed to be an archangel of heaven but most authorities agree he spends a lot of time in Hell. His expulsion came from an over enthusiasm with the subject of the moon. He taught the Canaanite priestesses the tides and courses of the moon which helped them enchant the land. The moon and the priestesses of Canaan are not popular subjects with the jealous Hebrew God of the Sun so before Sariel was hurled from heaven he quietly and gracefully departed.

Mephistopheles: "He who hates the light" or the "deceitful" destroyer. Once this great Prince was an archangel in heaven and even in his fallen and evil state is sometimes unaccountably admitted to the Holy Presence. Sometimes mistakenly identified with Satan probably because he has, on occasion, stood in for his Unholy Lord. He is said to have urbane and impeccable manners, a smooth and glib tongue and a philosophic view of life tinged, it is said, with regret.

Rofocale: According to the *Grande Grimoire* Lucifer Rofocale is the prime minister of the whole Infernal Region. He has complete control over all the treasure and wealth of our world.

Meririm: Prince of the Power of Air, the title he proudly shares with Lucifer. This has been given by no less an authority than St. Paul, who seems to have known his demonic Who's Who better than most. If the identity is correct then Meririm is the angel of the apocalypse who is charged with "hurting the earth and the oceans" (Revelations)

Rahab: "The Violent One." Originally he was the Prince of the Primordial Oceans. This mighty angel has caused the Almighty a great deal of inconvenience. Early in the Creation He ordered Rahab to separate the Waters. When Rahab refused God destroyed him. Somehow he was resurrected for he appeared again when helping the Egyptian Pharoah in his attempt to stop the Hebrews from crossing the Red Sea. Once again the Almighty showed His displeasure and destroyed him for a second time. But either the witnesses were mistaken or angels are a very hardy breed, for Rahab is claimed by Christians to be alive and well as the Angel of Insolence and Pride.

Angels of Punishment

Dumah: (as above).

Ksiel: "Rigid one of God" who punishes the nations with a whip of fire.

Lahatiel: "The flaming One." An Angel of Punishment who presides over the gates of death.

Shaftiel: Lord of the Shadow of Death and judge of God.

S OF GOD

Makkiel: The "Plague of God." *Chitriel:* The "Rod of God." *Puriel:* The "Fiery and Pitiless Angel of God" who is said to probe and torment the soul.

Arch-She-Demons

Astarte: Originally the Creating and Destroying Goddess of the Indo-Europeans she was known to the Egyptians as *Athur,* "Venus in the Morning," in Aramaic she is "The Morning Star of Heaven." As *Astroarche,* "Queen of the Stars" she ruled all the spirits of the dead whose "astral" bodies could be seen as the stars. *Astarte-Astaroth* was transformed by Christians into a male Duke of Hell. (See Astaroth)

Proserpine: Originally the Greek "Queen of the Underworld" she is the destroying Kali of India. In Christian traditions she is "Queen of the She-Demons".

Barbelo: The daughter of the female aeon, Pistis-Sophia who according to the gnostics was the pro-creator of the superior angels. Barbelo was so perfect in glory that it was rumored that she even outshone the Father in Heaven, which hardly seems any reason to find her on the fallen lists. Her particular crime is unknown although her mother, Sophia, had a few, but very unkind, words to say to Yahweh when he boasted of being the Creator. Perhaps it is enough to believe like mother, like daughter.

Leviathan: The coiled chaos she-dragon whose fins say the *Talmud* radiate such a brilliant light that they obscure the rays of the sun. Often identified with the great serpent who dwells in the bottomless abyss, Leviathan is later masculinized by medieval writers becoming "king" over all the children of pride. Manifests as the great Crocodile or the crooked snake.

Satan's Brides.

Agrat-bat-Mahlaht and *Eisheth Zenunim:* Both angels of prostitutes.

Lilith: The feisty, wild, first wife of Adam, who spurned both God and his male creation is said to be Satan's favorite. While demons do live long they are not immortal but Lilith has the distinction, according to the *Zohar,* of continuing "to exist and plague man until the Messianic day."

Naamah: "Pleasurable," the most sensual and sexual of Satan's four wives. She was once the sister of Tubal-Cain and Noah. She became the mother of the great *Asmodeus.* She is the fourth angel of prostitution and is the greatest seductress of both men and demons. Far from being jealous or possessive Satan is said to be relieved at the respite offered by being cuckolded.

Arch-Demons or Archangels of Hell

Adrameleck: "King of Fire" One of the angels of the Throne and Chancellor of the Order of the Fly. Is bearded, eagle-winged and lion-bodied and is identified with fire sacrifices.

Carniveau: Once a Prince of Powers, was one of the demons cited as having possessed the body of Sister Seraphica of Loudon.

Python: Is the monster serpent who has extraordinary oracular talents yet who is called the "prince of the lying spirits."

Sut: One of the sons of Eblis and Demon of Flies.

Kesef: An angel of wrath who overstepped his authority and attacked Moses at Horeb. It was Kezef who was imprisoned by Aaron.

Moloch: Once known as a Canaanite God who was worshipped by the early Semites. It was to this fearsome God that the tribes offered their first born, sacrificed in the fires of his awful shrine outside of Jerusalem.

Dubbiel: Once the guardian angel of Persia who stood in for Gabriel when she was in temporary disgrace. As we know by now virtually all the tutelary angels of nations ended up in the nether regions. Whether this is through over-identification with the national pride of their charges, or whether the Israelites had a lot of enemies is debatable.

Mammon: The prince of Tempters. Listed as an arch-demon Mammon appears to be the devil of Avarice and Greed. Continental Infernal Encyclopedias list Mammon as the diabolic ambassador to England which all goes to show what Europe thought of British enterprise.

Rimmon: Once an archangel of heaven who commanded lightning and storms which his name the "roarer" implies.

Dukes of Hell

Agares: This duke of Hell appears as an old man astride a crocodile and carrying on his arm a goshawk.

Aniquiel: One of the nine grand dukes who is specifically named as the serpent in the Garden of Paradise.

Ashmedai: An ex-Cherubim who is more of a philosopher than thoroughly evil. He is considered fairly harmless but his legions are said to be an unruly lot even by hell's standards.

Asmodeus: "Being of Judgment." Originally a Persian deity, a raging fiend. It was he who killed the seven bridegrooms of Sarah and fought the archangel Raphael almost to a standstill," before that archangel managed to banish him to Upper Egypt from where he made his way to Hell.

Astaroth: Supposedly he manifests as "a beautiful angel astride a dragon and carrying a viper in his hand." This could be because Astaroth suffered a sex change at the instigation of the medieval Church authorities. Originally better known, at least in Hell as Astarte.

Balam: Once belonging to the Order of Dominations he is now a terrible demon with the heads of a man, a bull and a ram with the tail of a serpent.

Byleth: Once a great Prince of Powers now rides, like death, a pale horse.

Belphegor: Once a Prince of the order of Principalities his impeccable pedigree of evil can be traced to the Moabite God of Licentiousness. It would seem that with credentials like this he was the obvious choice for demonic ambassador to France. He is also known as the guardian demon of Paris.

Furcalor: Once of the order of Thrones, he is the great slayer of men who apparently takes especial delight in sinking warships. Is unique in the demonic regions as manifesting as a man with griffin wings.

Isis: Another curious slip by the medieval Church. Originally Isis was the Egyptian deity born from the union of the earth and the sky. This great Mother Goddess suffered the fate of any figure who was not mentioned in the bible. If not mentioned then it must be a demon. Which is all to the advantage of Hell.

Kakabel: Once an angelic prince who was a great astrologer and astronomer. He still exercises dominion over stars and constellations and commands an impressive 365,000 spirits.

Salmael: Once of the Order of Angels he has an obsessive loathing for the chosen tribes of Israel and their God, Yahweh. Each year he calls for their annihilation.

Haroth: Once of the order of Angels Haroth remains a great

teacher of magic and sorcery and rules the North. In his younger days he fell in love with Zorba, a mortal woman and revealed the hidden name of God to her.

Forneus: Once of the mighty Order of Thrones now a Marquis. He has the strange yet useful attribute of causing love in his enemies.

Raym: Once of the order of Thrones he now commands 30 legions which he uses in his especial mission to destroy all cities, which he loathes. He is seen in the form of a black crow perched amongst the ruins.

Lahash: Once led 184 myriad spirits to stop the prayers of Moses from reaching God. For this he received 70 blows of fire as punishment and was expelled from the presence.

Gazarniel: An angel of fire who attacked Moses but was turned aside by the Lawgiver. Chose to enter the nether regions voluntarily and has formed an alliance with Lahash.

The Nephillim

Helel: Son of the Canaanite Shaher who is often identified with Lucifer himself. But he is really the leader of the Nephillim, those gigantic offspring who were sired by the angels upon the daughters of Cain. These Nephillim were the builders of the Tower of Babel. Hell also shelters the other monstrous progeny; the *enim* "Terrifying," the *naphaim* or the "weakeners" and the *gibborim*, "giants" who were rescued by the dark angels from the flood.

Spies, Double-Agents and Shady Characters

Angels of Destruction: There is a split amongst rabbinical scholars as to whether these awesome *"malache Habbalah"* are in the service of God or Satan. Certainly they spend most of their time meting out the most horrendous punishments to sinners with a diabolic enthusiasm. The handsome figure of 90,000 of such beings is given by Jewish lore. Each wields a "Sword of God" as an instrument of destruction, which would suggest they serve the Almighty. But sometimes it is difficult to know which side He is on! At the same time they helped the two Egyptian wizards to enter heaven on one occasion so it does suggest the whiff of double dealing. *Kemuel, Simbiel, Azriel, Harborah, Za'afiel, Af* and *Kolazanta* are given as leaders and even *Uriel* is supposed to be their general.

Cammael: Also known as *Quemel* was once the chief of the Order of Powers and now as a Count Palatine commands as *Kemuel* 12,000 angels of destruction. Many commentators cite him as the angel who supported Christ in his Agony in the

Garden of Gethsemane although this was under the pseudonym of *Chamuel*, "He who seeks God." It was Kemuel who supposedly tried to prevent Moses from receiving the Torah. For this misdeed he was destroyed by an infuriated Law Giver. Cabbalists insist that he survived the blast.

Biqa: At the very moment of being created on the second day he turned away from his Creator. For this he was promptly dropped into the Abyss where he sank like a stone. When he reached the bottom his name had been changed to Kazbeel, "One who deceives God." In this role he tried to trick the archangel Michael into revealing the hidden name of God but he really had picked the wrong guy.

Cahor: The Genius of Deception. Hebrews did not consider this as necessarily evil but Christian theologians were adamant in listing him in hell.

Malach-Re: Like Cahor this angel of Evil is somewhat of a paradox. for while personifying Evil he is not actually Evil himself.

Tartaruchus: "The Keeper of Hell" It is difficult to discover whether this is a God appointed office or whether this gruesome angel actually enjoys overseeing the torments of hell. As Christians believed that part of the enjoyment of the righteous in heaven was to view the torments of even their beloveds in hell maybe the dividing line between righteous and damned wavers some.

Iniaes: One of the seven angels reprobated by the Church council; at Rome in 745. Reportedly he was so incensed at the tromped up charges and the sheer stupidity of the clergy that he voluntarily defected to the Lower regions. He has not regretted his decision and has great fun with the more pompous and sanctimonious clergy by loudly farting whenever they make a profound remark.

Nergal: The Angel of Pestilence and said to be the Chief of the Secret Police of Hell.

Zophiel: Quite specifically named "God's Spy" this angel actually is a double agent who once reported to his heavenly contact that that the rebel army was about to attack. Since then he has regretted this deed and was welcomed by the rebels as a Herald of Hell.

Xaphan: An apostate angel who was particularly welcomed by hell as he had the most inventive mind of all the angels. He had an ingenious plan to set fire to heaven but before he could carry it out the conspirators were discovered. Now he fans the embers of the infernal furnaces at the bottom of the abyss.

Melchi Dael: A huge black angelic prince of pimps, who, like Mephistopoles in Faustian lore, can provide a man with any woman of his choice. The usual price of course is the pact of one's soul. It always seems odd that devils are really likely to get their sinners anyway but perhaps they are aware of that redemption at the eleventh hour.

Baresches: This greater demon is said, on the unquestionable authority of the clergy, to be the very best procurer of women in hell. The usual price is asked.

Pharzuph: The Angel of Lust and Fornication. Hebrew for "two faced" or "a hypocrite." A great tempter of patriarchs, hermits and celibate monks.

Dommiel: This is St. Peter's mirror image as gatekeeper of Hell. He is the reverse of all that Peter stands for. He neither needs keys to enter as Hell is always open 24 hours a day nor is he a woman hater. He is a paragon of lechery although being also the prince of terror and trembling may give him problems.

Chief Chef of Hell

Nisroc: The great Eagle-headed deity who was once of the Order of Principalities. Was worshipped by Sennacherib, the despotic ruler of the Assyrians. After the slaughter of thousands of Sennacherib's troops during the night by one of the angels of God Nisroc was so disgusted that he joined the rebels. He was one of the winged guardians of the Tree of Immortality and is said , in his new job as chief chef to the Princes of Hell, he liberally spices their food with its fruit.

Jester of Hell

Nasr-ed-Din: One of the seven archangels of the Yezidics. It appears he is the famous Muslim wise-acre, *Mulla Nasrudin*. He is also celebrated by Georges Gurdjieff as the incomparable teacher, *Mulla Nassr Eddin.*

The Third Wing
Heaven's Above and Earth's Below

E NOW TURN TO THE SEVEN CELESTIAL MANSIONS and the Seven Palaces of Darkness. These are the natural abodes of the Light and the Dark angels. While the descriptions come from images current in the 14th century it must be remembered that theologians of that period still envisioned the world as the center of the universe. Their belief in the existence of a flat earth had not been seriously challenged. So any journey across the actual angelic or demonic landscapes is bound to be a tightrope walk over many a metaphorical abyss.

The number seven is one of the more mysterious marvels of our universe. Virtually all religious and occult systems include the number somewhere close to their holiest of holy sanctums.

Many teachings of the Far East are founded upon hierarchies of seven. A recurring theme tells of the One, Transcendental Ground of All Being, slowly awakening to the awareness of existing. To do so "It" had to descend through seven tiers, planes or spheres ending in our material world of substance.

So it is hardly surprising to learn that the sacredness of the principle of seven was one of the most common religious insights which permeated the Middle and Near East during the early development of all the Western religions. It is easy to trace the rich mosaic of such fragmented spiritual ideas which make up the Judeo-Christian world. And while the overall picture has a breathtaking richness of imagery, it also has some very sloppy seams. It is around the joints of some really mismatched concepts of Heaven and Hell that confusion is most evident.

One of the first original models of a seven-layered Heaven comes from the ancient Sumerians. The Hebrews in captivity in Babylon must have been overawed by the impressive ruins of the Sumerian Ziggurats with their seven rising terraces signifying Heaven, with the highest temple-tower on top. The captives would have arrived in Babylon only a few years after the completion of the "Etemenanki," a huge terraced tower called the "House of the Creation of Heaven and Earth," which was indubitably the legendary Tower of Babel. Later they would have been introduced to the Persian belief in an Almighty "seated on a great white throne surrounded by winged cherubim" in the highest of seven heavens. The origin of this concept predates the Hebrew hierarchy by one thousand five hundred years and the Christian vision by over three millennia.

Jewish scribes were always eager to incorporate the juicier beliefs of their various conquerors. However, they also had another rich Hebrew tradition to draw upon, which predated even the earliest civilizations of Sumeria. For the patriarch Enoch was supposed to have lived almost nine thousand years ago and we are deeply indebted to the later copiers of his original chronicles for many of the more detailed descriptions of the various Heavens and Hells. This is held to be a first hand account which therefore owes little to the Sumerians or Babylonians who were to follow.

However, it is quite clear from his text that the heavens he described were actually firmly on the

earth. His account reads more like a tourist guide book of the Lebanon highlands than that of a super-natural Other World. Other early texts describing the heavens often seem to share with Enoch a strange sense of being actually set with feet firmly on real earth. The term Heaven can in many cases be translated as nothing more spectacular than "Highlands," while Earth can equally signify nothing more than "lowlands." Even the Sumerian word Edin or Eden actually means a "remote and uncultivated land."

It is tempting to see these detailed accounts of Enoch as being actual down-to-earth descriptions of a real visit to seven Havens or settlements. These descriptions could have been later borrowed and transformed into supernatural events by overzealous scribes who wanted to enliven their scriptures. The transformation of the secular into the sacred was one of the greatest pastimes of both Sumerian and Hebrew scholars as we shall see later. Anyway, ac-cording to the original story, these havens were the homes of the "Shining Beings," the (Elohim) who

were later translated as angels and archangels. It is quite plausible that Enoch, who lived to see the Flood (6500 B.C.), actually visited the site of the paradise garden in Eden.

Whether this is so or not, Enoch will still accompany us on the tour of the seven Heavens, as he remains an excellent guide.

The Seven Heavens

FIRST HEAVEN (*Shamayim.*) This is the lowest heaven which borders our own world and is said to have been the abode of Adam and Eve. Its angel ruler is Gabriel. Rabbi Simon ben Laquish calls this first heaven, Wilon (curtain). All the other heavens vault over Earth, one above the other, but Wilon is the exception, in that it acts as a kind of shade for earth during the day, a shade which is then rolled back at night to reveal the Moon and the stars which are visible from the Second Heaven.

This lowest heaven contains clouds and winds,

the Upper Waters and is the home of two hundred astronomer-angels who watch over the stars. To complete the scene we find legions of guardian angels of snow, ice and dew living in the vicinity.

According to Enoch (En:III:1) "We landed in the first haven and there, they showed me a very great sea, much bigger than the inland sea where I lived." He describes it as being " a treasury of snow and ice and clouds and dew." The two angels took him "to the swiftly flowing river, and the fire of the west, which reflects every setting of the Sun. I came to the river of fire in which fire flows like water, and discharges itself into the Great Sea towards the west."

As can be seen, this description could have come from a rather poetic guide book. What is remarkable is that it would perfectly describe an actual view from Mount Hermon at sunset. Any observer would see the River Orontes flowing north, the Jordan towards the south and the long stretch of the River Leontes as it flowed into the Mediterranean to the west. To a man who only knew the lowlands the Leontes could well have looked like fire in the setting sun.

In the more visionary mode of the *Apocalypse of St. Paul*, Paul calls this the Land of Promise." Now every tree bore twelve harvests each year, and they had various and diverse fruits, and I saw the fashion of that place and all the work of God, and I saw there palm-trees of twenty cubits and others of ten cubits, and the land was seven times brighter than silver."

SECOND HEAVEN (*Raquia*). The angel ruler is Raphael. This is where Enoch claims the fallen angels are imprisoned although, from what is known of their subsequent activities on earth it could hardly have been a top security establishment. Both Moses and Enoch visited this heaven which is also rumored to be the dwelling place of John the

Baptist. Complete darkness reigns over sinners who are chained there awaiting judgement. This rather inhospitable description may have been in part inspired by the timing of Enoch's visit. He recorded that he stopped there on his journey to the seventh heaven but that it was night and all he could make out was that it was in a valley where the stars shone brightly. This would be in accord with the name of this heaven being Raqui'a or the "firmament." St. Paul also confirms this: "The Angel brought me down from the third heaven and led me into the second heaven, and he led me again to the firmament."

THIRD HEAVEN (*Sagun or Shehaqim*). Anahel is the angel ruler of this Heaven. It is also the domain of Azrael, the Islamic angel of Death, which seems to accord with Enoch who places Hell within its northern boundaries. Other authorities also place Gehenna North of Eden, where dark volcanic fires burn continuously polluting the air with heavy sulfurous fumes, and a river of flame flows through a desolate land of cold and ice. Here the wicked are punished and tortured by the angels.

One can understand that the Church was chary of including such an account of heaven in their canon. From this description few would want to go there, and this is supposedly where the righteous get their reward. But we find a very different story in the paradise lands of the south, where it is reputed that divine bees store the manna-honey. A pair of vast millstones grind manna for the delight of the righteous, and it is from this image that we get the name of the heaven – Shehaqim meaning a "grindstone" or a "cloud." There is a certain confusion as to whether it is in this heaven or the next that the Garden of Eden is to be found. But certainly a vast orchard exists there, resplendent with thousands of fruit trees, including the Tree Of Life under which God takes a nap whenever He visits. Two rivers are supposed to issue from Eden: one flows with milk and honey, and the other with wine and oil. These descend and surround the earth. Three hundred angels of Light guard the garden to which all the perfect souls come after death.

St. Paul was taken up to the third heaven which had a gate with pillars of gold. "When I had entered the gate of paradise an old man came there to meet me. His face shone like the sun and he embraced me." This was Enoch, the scribe, which all goes to show that the Christian heaven sometimes differs considerably from the Hebrew heaven. According to the rabbis, the patriarch had been successfully transformed into the angel Metatron a long time before. It would seem that Paul, quite independently, echoes Enoch's description of the Shining Ones.

The Last Judgment *by Nicolò and Giovanni, Roman School, 11th century.* The Medieval concept of the universe was round and layered. In the **Creation** on the opposite page which is from 12th century Sicily, God creates the spherical cosmos of time, space and matter.

Evidently Enoch applied the ointment so "his face shone like the Sun."

FOURTH HEAVEN (variously given as Zebhul or Machanon.) The ruling Prince is Michael. Here is the site of the heavenly Jerusalem, the holy. Temple and its altar. The 12th century bard, Cynewulf, says of it: "O vision of peace, Holy Jerusalem, best of royal thrones, City State of Christ, native seat of angels." St. Paul describes it in his Apocalyse: "It was all gold, and twelve walls encircled it, and there were twelve towers inside, and every wall had a furlong between them round about... There were twelve gates of great beauty in the circuit of the city, and four rivers encircled it. There was a river of honey and a river of milk and a river of wine and a river of oil. I said to the angel, 'What are these rivers that encircle this city?' He said to me, 'These are the four rivers that flow abundantly for those who are in this Land of Promise.. These are their names: the river of honey is called Phison, and the river of milk Euphrates, and the river of oil Geon, and the river of wine Tigris'."

Enoch insists that it is this heaven, and not the previous one, which houses the beautiful orchards and the great Trees of Life. (Enoch XXXII:3–6): "And I came to Paradise, the Garden of Righteousness and saw beyond the first trees, many large trees growing there. They were a glorious sight – large, beautiful and of a lovely fragrance – and among them was the Tree of Understanding, the fruit of which they eat and, thereby, obtain great purpose. The height of this tree is like unto a fir, and its leaves resemble the Carob. Its fruits hang in clusters like grapes on the vine and are very beautiful and its fragrance can be detected from a long way off."

Above: **Kudurru of King Melishpak,** *12th century B.C..* The Sumerians and Assyrians often inscribed path markers with the layered representations of their heavens. At the top can be seen the sun and the moon and a third mysterious globe which has variously been identified with a planet or even an aerial chariot.

"I commented on how beautiful and attractive the tree was and Raphael, the archangel who was with me said: This is the Tree of Understanding; your ancestral father and mother ate of it and it made them realize that they were naked; so they were expelled from the Garden." There was another tree which likewise attracted the attention of Enoch the scribe. This time Michael answered his curiosity: "And as for this fragrant tree, no human is allowed to touch it until the great selection; at that time he (The Great Lord of Judgments, the arbiter of the length of Life) will finally decide on the length of life to be granted."

In the fourth heaven great chariots ridden by the Sun and the Moon and many of the greatest stars circle the earth. The winds which draw the chariots are shaped like a phoenix and a brazen serpent, with faces like lions and lower parts like that of the Leviathan.

FIFTH HEAVEN (Machon or Ma'on). Seat of God, Aaron and the Avenging Angels. Apparently the early Hebrews were most suspicious of the north for once again it is these territories which are set aside for yet another penal settlement. This time it is for the gigantic Grigori who seem to be serving eternal imprisonment for what they did with the daughters of man. It is here that these gigantic fallen angels crouch in silent and everlasting despair.

While the ruling prince is Metatron's twin brother, Sandalphon, there are authorities who insist that Sammael is the Dark Angelic Ruler. It does make the fifth heaven a curious place altogether.

There is confirmation of dark goings on in the north from Enoch. "And I saw a deep rift in the earth with columns of flame and smoke: the fires rose to a great height and fell again into the depths. Beyond the rift, I saw a place where no sky could be seen above, and which had no firm ground below. There was no water on it, and no birds – it was a desolate and terrible place. (The archangel) Uriel said to me: This is the place where the angels who have cohabited with women will be imprisoned; those who, in many different ways, are corrupting Mankind, and leading men astray into making sacrifices to demons. They shall remain here until they come to trial."

One can imagine how the next passage could have acted as an inspiration to Christians bent upon the hell-fire and damnation aspect of their religion. "Still more horrible, I saw another fearful thing – a great fire which burnt and blazed in a place that was cleft down to the bottom of the ravine, full of great, falling columns of fire. I could neither see its size or its extent; nor could I even guess at them." Uriel told him: "This is the prison of the angels, and here they will be imprisoned for life."

In the more hospitable and beautiful south of this heaven, hosts of ministering angels chant ceaselessly the Trisagion all night, but are said to fall silent at dawn thus allowing God to hear His praises sung far below by Israel.

SIXTH HEAVEN (Zebul or Makhon). Domain of duality. Zebul rules by night and Sabath rules by day. It is the dwelling place of seven Phoenixes and seven Cherubim who chant in praise of God, and a vast host of Shining Ones who study astronomy. There are other angels who study time, ecology, the seasons and humankind in a vast Building of Knowledge.

Enoch seems to be describing the campus of a vast Angelic University when he says: "And there I saw seven groups of Angels, very bright and won-

derful, with their faces shining brighter than the sun. They were brilliant and all dressed alike and looked alike.

"Some of these angels study the movement of the stars, the sun and the Moon and record the peaceful order of the world. Other angels, there, undertake teaching and give instruction in clear melodious voices. These are the archangels who are promoted over the other angels. They are responsible for recording the fauna and the flora of both heaven and earth. There are angels who record the seasons and the years; others who study the rivers and the seas; others who study the fruits of the Earth and the plants and herbs which give nourishment to men and beasts.

"And there Angels study Mankind and record the behavior of men, and how they live."

Makhon, which means residence, does have its disadvantages, however, for much of its climate is hardly what we usually associate with heaven. It is a major repository of snow, hailstones, dew and rain with chambers of storms and caves of fog. But we must remember that for Tibetans, living in the harsh and perpetual snows of the mountains, heaven is believed to be hot, while the Hindus in the sweltering valleys of India are assured that their heaven will be cold, or at least air conditioned.

SEVENTH HEAVEN (Araboth). The ruling prince is Cassiel. This is the abode of God on His Divine Throne, surrounded by Seraphim, Cherubim and Wheels all bathed in ineffable Light.

Enoch describes this holiest of holies in rather surprising terms. "Two angels conducted me to a place where those who were there were as bright as fire, but when they wished could appear as ordinary men. They had brought me to a place of darkness from a mountain whose summit reached to the heavens. There I saw lighted places, and heard thunderous noises; and in the deepest part, there were lights which looked like a fiery bow and arrows with their quiver, and moving lights like a fiery sword."

The Tower in the Void

14th century theologians conceived of the Seven Heavens and the Seven Earths as being intricately bound together by vast hooks which are attached to the rim of each heaven and connected to its corresponding Earth.

Each heaven is likewise hooked to its neighbor as is each earth. The whole structure resembles a colossal tower which is only prevented from collapsing into the Void by these hooks.

The Seven Heavens are balanced by their partners, the Seven Earths. These Earths are not seen as hells, although Arqa does include Gehenna and the seven hells on one of its continents. Each world is separated from its neighbor by "intervals of whirlwind," whatever that might mean. Our own world is supposedly the seventh and last. However, seven other worlds are named, so we will assume that our own planet marks the center of the heavens and the earths. The diagram shows the descending order as discovered in the Kabbalah.

The Seven Earths

Earth: *Heled* (World)

Seventh Earth: *Tebbel* (also means world) very like earth in its form of having hills and mountains, valleys and flatlands. It is however peopled by three hundred and sixty-five different types of very bizarre creatures. These weird monstrous beings with double heads or hybrid and multi-various bodies are actually considered perfectly splendid and righteous beings. They live on the aquatic life which abounds in the waters of their world and are considered superior to all other sentient beings. They have divided their planet into special zones for those inhabitants who differ too greatly from one another in both form and mind, to live harmoniously.

It seems that they are able to either prolong the life of their species or in some way bring the dead back to life. Their world is at a greater distance to their sun than we are to ours which presumably would make it a colder and darker place.

Sixth Earth: *Arqa* (an earth). A world whose seasons differ greatly from our own, being longer and with harvests and sowing at wider intervals. The inhabitants are able to cross the whirlwind spaces in order to visit all the other earths and can speak all the known languages. They have faces which are very different to ours. What is curious about Arqa is that it also contains, on one of its continents, Gehenna or in other terms, Hell. This includes the whole seven horrible layers of fire and darkness. The topmost layer of hell is called Sheol, while those that lie beneath it are called Perdition, The Gates of Death, The Gates of the Shadow of Death, Silence, The Bilge and The Lowest Pit.

Fifth Earth: *Yabbasha, Nesziah* (dryland). Here we find a tiny race of beings who appear to be very forgetful. Luckily it does not really seem to matter as they can easily live off the land. They have never been able to think consecutively long enough to build any towns or sow any crops. They just eat shrubs and small plants which grow in a very dry land which is dominated by a huge red sun. They have two holes in their heads instead of our noses in order to breathe the thin, dry air.

Fourth Earth: *Siyya* or *Tziah* meaning dryness. This world appears to be even drier than Yabbasha. Perhaps this is caused by the existence of two suns in their skies. The inhabitants are constantly looking for underground watercourses although it is reported that their cities and buildings are very rich and wondrous. The peoples are said to be very fair of feature and have more spiritual faith than all other beings.

Third Earth: *Harabba* or *Geh* (parched lands). It would seem that fertile and lush earths like our world are hard to come by. However, although Geh is a twilight planet of shadows it is a also world of woods and forests, jungles and orchards. The inhabitants live on the abundant fruits of the trees but know nothing of wheat or cereal.

Second Earth: *Adama* (earth). A world peopled by the descendants of Adam. They are cultivators and hunters but are afflicted with an almost continual melancholia. When not sad they make war upon one another. Visitors once traveled from the world of Thebel to Adama but these superior beings were often overcome by a strange malais which left them without any memory of who they were. The visits seem to have ceased.

First Earth: *Eres* (earth). The inhabitants of this world are supposedly descendants of Adam but little is known of the world itself except that Adam himself had complained that it was dull and cheerless.

ERES

ADAMA

HARRABA

SIYYA

YABBASHA

ARQUA

TEBBEL

The Seven Earths are joined to the Seven Heavens by vast hooks attached at their rims. This colossal tower is only prevented from collapsing into the Void by these hooks. The figure at the left, from Freiburg cathedral, shows the sevenfold creation of the stars of Heaven.

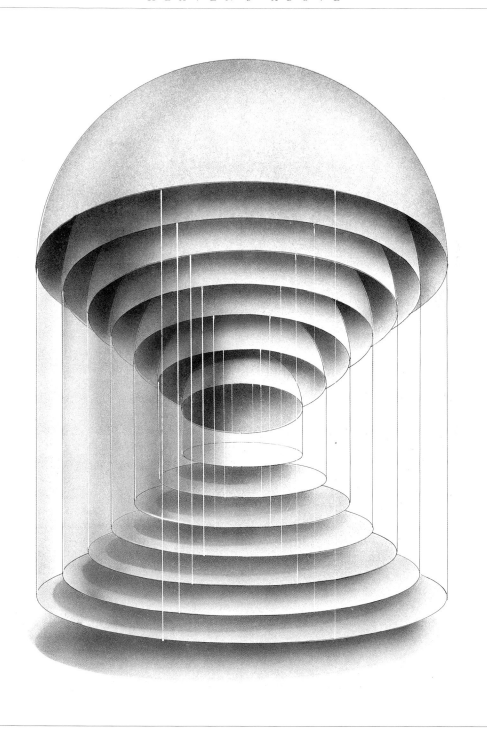

Ancient Planets of the Angels

A number of commentators have suggested that the seven earths or worlds are actually seven planets, and not even necessarily within our own solar system. There is a curious meeting in the *Zohar* between Rabbi Yosse and a mysterious stranger who had "a different face"and who asked the Rabbi the name of the world on which he had arrived. He described his own world, mentioning that the constellation of the stars in our night sky looked very different to his.

We might well ask the question whether the angels actually came from the seven planets rather than the seven heavens. The reader probably spotted the nice touch of the superior race of Thebel who forgot who they were when on Adama. There are many accounts of angels coming to earth and losing their angelic memory and superior intelligence by taking on the characteristics of mortals. Considering that these fragments from the Kabbalah can be traced to Rabbi Simon who lived almost two thousand years ago and who, even then, was continuing a tradition probably over four thousand years old, it appears that the biblical times were not so primitive as we have fondly imagined them.

The Regions of Hell

The conflicting nature of the Hebrew and Christian cosmologies is never more noticeable than when one tries to reconcile the location of Hell and its many layers.

The essentially Hebrew picture of seven heavens hooked to seven earths contrasts greatly with the later Christian version which locates Hell deep

beneath our Earth, or the even earlier Hebrew version of various punishment sites spread throughout the seven Heavens.

The poet-historian, Robert Graves, suggests that it is a deliberate policy of the Church to leave a certain chaotic ambience when on the subject of the nether regions. He may be right. Anyway he quotes Amos (IX:2) to back his card. In this passage God tells us "Though they dig into hell, there shall Mine hand take them; though they climb up unto heaven, thence will I bring them down."

While it is impossible to reconcile the conflicting locations it is however possible to clear up some of the more blatant misconceptions about the home of the fallen angels.

In the version of Hell which is situated on the sixth earth there are seven layers of the infernal region of Gehenna. These are Sheol, Perdition, the Gates of the Shadow of Death, the Gates of Death Silence, the Bilge and the Lowest Pit.

Above: **Paradise** *Detail from painting by Fra' Angelico.* Right: **Paradise** *Detail of painting by Benozzo Gozzoli, 15th century.* During the Golden Era of Angels artists tended to envision Heaven as being a well kept garden. Yet at the very moment that these images were being created the Black Death was decimating Europe in, what seemed at the time, the apocalyptic scourge come true. So it is all the more remarkable that Benozzo Gozzoli tried to show that angels could actually smile or even giggle. In the group on the right the smile is a little forced but is none the less visible. For the pious clergy who commissioned the work, Heaven was obviously a serious business and certainly no laughing matter so it is an especially treasured sign that at least one artist thought that Heaven without laughter would be a dull place indeed.

The overall infernal name is Gehenna, which once referred to an actual historical fire-altar, dedicated to Molech, the deity worshipped by Solomon. The early Jews sacrificed their first born child at this shrine, which was in the valley of Hinnom, outside Jerusalem. Later Yahweh stopped the barbaric practice and the site was abandoned. It became a rubbish dump and a burning ground for the bodies of criminals and social pariahs. With such a foul background it is little wonder that the site became rooted in the Hebrew mind as being hell.

Gehenna is claimed to be sixty times as big as our earth. Each of its palaces has six thousand houses, each with six thousand vessels of fire and gall for the unfortunate sinner. The top layer is Sheol, which is Hebrew for "Pit," "Cavern", or "Womb." Strangely its equivalent in Tibet is a paradise garden called Shal-Mari. In the Middle East the name was identified with the Virgin Goddess's "walled garden." Only the sacred kings who were sacrificed on trees could enjoy this Other World of delights. There was a common practice, in Persia, of hanging human sacrifices to the deity Ishtar (Mari) on trees, and the name became Sheol-Mari.

Gehenna Moves to Hell

Although the Jews had perfected their hell centuries before the birth of Christ there was never any Hebrew concept of eternal punishment for even the worst of offenders. Even the horrors envisaged by the Persian Zoroastrians, who had especially gruesome punishments in store for women, did not go on forever. Those eternal and unremitting tortures were left to the Christians to invent.

The everlasting torments were supposed to be enthusiastically applied by a variety of Avenging Angels, Angels of Torment, Angels of Punishment, Angels of Wrath and Angels of Destruction.

With such righteous angels of the Lord hacking away at the wretched sinners, one marvels at the need of Devils at all. It is often difficult to understand whether a particularly nasty demon who tortures a victim is doing the Devil's work or that of the Almighty.

Even St. Paul, who is noted for a strong stomach when it comes to watching the punishment of sinners, recoils upon seeing a particularly revolting punishment when he visits Hell under the protection of a guardian angel. He blurts out: "It would be better for us if we were not born, since we are all sinners."

And because both Paul and the Archangel Michael have appealed to Christ, begging that some souls be given mercy, the Savior grants the souls a respite and refreshment of a day and a night from the eternal torments. At this rather modest act of mercy it is the devils who are infuriated. They scream at the sinners. "You had no mercy. This is the Judgement of God on those that did not have mercy. Yet you have received this great grace."

Satan Enthroned in Hell *by Gustave Doré.*
In Northern countries *Hel* was a pre-Christian underworld of death. This dark place was a huge prison of souls who would fight the Gods at Ragnarok. The palace of the Queen of Hel was called *Sleetcold* and this was where the Queen most tormented her unfortunate charges. Even so there was never any talk of such torments being forever.

These seem more the righteous words of a fundamentalist preacher than those of a demon. How a fallen angel can be so supportive about God's work is hard to fathom, but such double talk abounds in all the early visions of the infernal regions.

Perhaps one of the more disheartening aspects of Hell was that the "saved" were expected to enjoy watching the torments of the sinners from viewing platforms. These blessed souls were to find eternal pleasure in the sufferings of others, even if the damned who writhed in the eternal fires were their own beloved ones.

After reading some of the ecclesiastical advertisements for the righteous, sometimes one has more sympathy with the fallen.

Such a heretical point of view might well have been understood by some of the early critics of the orthodox vision. The Gnostics claimed a very different location for hell and an even more surprising chief suspect for the role of the Enemy of Man. This we can now explore in the fourth wing of the Treasury.

The Simoniac Pope *illustration by William Blake.* In the third trench of the eighth circle of Hell those who have bought or sell positions in the Church are held upside down in a well of fire. To Blake this symbolized the fallen state of man and angel.

Above: **Satan lost in the Abyss.** *Engraving by Gustave Doré.* In the Apocalypse of St. Paul an angel tells the saint, "The abyss has no boundary, for beneath it there follows also what is beneath; and so if someone strong took a stone and threw it into a very deep well, after many hours it would reach the bottom. this abyss is also like that. For when souls are thrown into it, they hardly come to the bottom after five hundred years." Gehenna, itself, has seven layers of which sheol is the highest. Below Sheol lie *Perdition*, the *Lowest Pit*, the *Bilge*, *Silence*, the *Gates of Death*, and the *Gates of the Shadow of Death*. The fire of each layer is sixty times fiercer than that immediately beneath.

The Fourth Wing
The Heresy

O FAR we have examined the orthodox part of the treasury with its elaborately bejeweled hierarchies of Heaven and Hell. This intricate superstructure was only seriously challenged once before the Middle Ages, when the Gnostics flung down the angelic gauntlet during the first four centuries after the death of Christ. According to them it is Satan-el who holds the key to the creation of our universe and all and everything it contains. The Gnostics were amongst the multi-various mystery cults and sects of the early Christian era who quickly ran afoul of their orthodox brethren. By the 4th century they had been denounced as heretics and a century later were virtually wiped out.

Their fundamental heresy was a belief in the existence of a female cosmic principle *prior* to that of the male Yahweh or Jehovah. They believed this to be a Primal Realm of Silence which then gave birth to the Great Mother Sophia (Wisdom), who then became simultaneously both the mother and the lover of God the Son. This is an archetypical "Goddess" theme, common throughout the ancient world and one which finds its recurring expression within the Christian Virgin Mary-Jesus relationship.

Another concept condemned as abhorrent by the patriarchal orthodoxy was the equality enjoyed by women within the heretical hierarchy. Gnostics claimed that the true revelation of esoteric Christianity was channeled through Mary Magdalene, the whore who was so beloved by Christ. The highly charged Tantric mold of subsequent Gnostic teachings and meditation techniques had remarkable similarities to the Indian practice of having sacred temple prostitutes as channels for the Divine. The link with the teachings of the Far East could be most clearly discerned in the most popular Gnostic teacher of the times, Simon Magus.

His fame eclipsed all the orthodox apostles who were in the area at the time. He traveled with a sacred harlot from Babylon called Helen. His relationship with this reincarnation of Helen of Troy was said to parallel that of Christ and the prostitute, Mary Magdalene, who to gnostics was known as Pistis-Sophia-Prunikos (Faith-Wisdom-Whore).

It seems only fitting that it should be the despiser of women, St. Peter, of whom Magdalene once said "he hates the female race," who claimed to eventually have destroyed Simon. The encounter according to church records was in Rome. The Mage was rather theatrically showing off by flying over the Campus Martius in a chariot drawn by dark winged demons, when Peter spoke a magical spell and sent the heretic crashing to his doom. In one version the magician broke his arm in three

places and in another Simon promptly reincarnated into Menander, the "moon being." As we now know that Peter was never in Rome the whole incident probably reflected the rivalry between the Church which worshipped the Essenic Sun God and whose priests were called "Peter," and the Gnostics who worshipped the Luna Hero. We can add two further esoteric bonuses to the legend if we recall that Peter's original name was Simon, and that this story echoes the lightning descent of both Shaher and Lucifer.

One of the major detractors of the Gnostics was Irenaeus, who rather petulantly observed that "they sprout up like mushrooms and fight like hydras." It was the very diversity of their interpretations of Christ's teachings which infuriated the orthodox leaders who were already having so much trouble in giving some consistency to their own canons. Irenaeus goes on critically: "None of them is considered perfect unless he expounds something different in high sounding phrases." There is certainly some justification for his irritation with their incredibly convoluted interactions of good aeons and evil archons in an utterly bewildering cosmology. His scorn that "they

The Death of Simon the Magician *from the Nurenburg Chronicles*. The heretic, Simon flies through the air above Rome supported by demons. Peter orders them to drop Simon who in one story breaks his leg in three places. This victory was a fabrication by the Church. Strangely, while Simon is an authenticated historical figure there is considerable doubt, even amongst Catholic theologians, that Peter ever existed. Even if he did it is sure he was never in Rome.

recount all their ludicrous genealogy as confidently as if they had been midwives at their (the angels) birth" might be better directed at the Church itself. It appears that there was a lively atmosphere of spiritual one-upmanship existing in those early days. But in spite of the parochial attitudes of most of the early fathers much of the Gnostic's material quietly found its way in through the backdoor, into the canon of the very Church which persecuted them. Even so, their basic beliefs remain diametrically opposed to those of the Church.

However, the reason for our particular interest in the Gnostic vision is that according to these heretics the role of the angel in the whole cosmic plan is far more essential and a great deal more awesome than so far shown. It could be said that the Christian view of angels is largely built upon the notion of function. Angels are seen as messengers, having a particular status within the cosmic hierarchy.

So these beings are significant in what they do rather than in what they are. In the Gnostic vision it is rather their essential nature which is of concern. In order to understand this it is best to summarize their teaching.

A New Beginning

According to the Gnostics the origin of all and everything firmly rests in a Supreme First Principle. The Hebrew God is replaced at the center of creation by a secret, hidden and *female* Divinity: one that is nameless, unknown and unknowable. Only silence can express this original Nothingness. For equally mysterious reasons a ripple moved in the Void. This wave is identified with Will, and arising from that Will, a Divine Self is revealed. So far this is almost precisely the cosmological model of the Hindus, the Buddhists, the Sufis: it can also be found in the traditions of both Yoga and Tantra. But the route chosen after this critical crossroads takes us along a uniquely Western highway.

By a unique manifestation which did not involve "creation" or any intermediary or evolutionary process, this Divine Self brought into existence a complex and highly paradoxical (at least to us) state of descending hierarchies of spiritual "beingness." The highest state of being was manifested in what might be called the "Divine Attributes". These can be considered abstract qualities or metaphysical concepts such as Love, Power, Compassion, Mercy, or Truth. Valentinus gives an eightfold version of the emanations which are Thought, Grace, Silence, Mind, Truth, Man, Church, and Sophia. From these sprang another fifteen pairs totaling 38 emanations in all.

At first these attributes were not aware of themselves, but gradually they became conscious of the unique separateness of their existence. They slowly became "hyperstatized" or personified as independent beings. These new entities are the Aeons – celestial beings who represent the multitude of divine forms and powers which we refer to as Angels. Every manifestation of God the Father is an angel.

Apparently they are formless, but when visiting human beings they often assume physical bodies in order not to cause unwarranted fear or disquiet.

The Aeonic, or Angelic, hierarchy is made up roughly as we have already seen it in the traditional view. The Gnostic bureaucracy however is divided into seven principalities of: the Ancient Ones, the Powers, Thrones, Dominions, Authorities, Lesser Gods and Rulers. Each of these divine bodies corresponds to each of the seven heavens.

God gave these newly self-aware angels free choice, knowing that they might even move away from His love and thereby possibly disobey. So, it is said, God withdrew His own will, and in that moment of supreme love gave them the gift of their own destinies. No longer were they robots, mere puppets of the Divine Will, but autonomous entities. This contraction of the divine will led directly to the fall. For in the sudden vacuum, the emptiness of the abyss, left by God's withdrawal, our own material universe came into being. But, and here comes the great heresy, GOD is not here!

Fundamental to the Gnostic teaching is that we abide in a place where *God is not*. Where His spirit is absent, matter appears; where love and goodness depart, evil appears; where light is absent, darkness prevails; and where once there was eternal life, time and death take their place.

However, traces of the divine light do remain like spoors, a scent or the mark of a footprint. It was from these scant traces that the great Aeon Lucifer, Prince of Light, but now Satan-el, Prince of Darkness, is said to have created our own universe.

The great contraction of God and the exercise of free will resulted in a rebellion by what is reputed to have been one third of the original Aeonic host, and these became what is known as the Archons or demons. These dark angels fell from the higher heavens of eternity to dwell in the lower heavens of time space and illusion.

The leader of the evil archons was of course Satan-el. And as we have just learnt, it was he, and not the supreme deity, who created our universe. The Gnostics, like Jesus before them, accuse the Jews (and by inference the Christians as well) of worshipping the wrong God. *Yahweh = Satanel* is the Gnostic equation which certainly gives all of us space for reflection.

Satanel had once been the most trusted and beloved angel of God. He had been the vice-regent of heaven, brother of the heavenly Jesus, Lucifer the bearer of light. He was not the only great angel to fall. Another of the great archangels was Sophia, who fell through curiosity and the jealousy of other aeons (no one is perfect in the Gnostic heaven). While she managed to redeem herself, Adamel, the third member of the company, did not. Satanel fell through pride (the greatest sin), while Adam fell through disobedience, (the sin that appears to infuriate the Almighty most).

It is generally accepted that the great Gnostic teacher, Basilides, was the best arithmetician when calculating how many other aeons fell. He numbers them as 365, which is both the number of days in the year and also the numerical product of the letters of the name Abraxas, (which is either the group as a whole or the name of the greatest aeon of all). The mightiest of the demon-archons rule the lower evil orders. They also control Time and its Division, Space and its various Dimensions, along with the workings of the stars and planets.

Perhaps the most refreshing aspect of Gnostic teachings, in an otherwise dominantly male arena, is the regard the sects had for the female. Many powerful women were in controlling positions and they were considered the major channellers of divine visions. This view of women was very much influenced by what appears to be the greatest Gnostic Angel of all; Sophia.

The Virgin Sophia of the Rosicrucians. This occult figure is seen as the Heavenly & Earthly Mother from whose womb all things, both sacred and profane, were born.

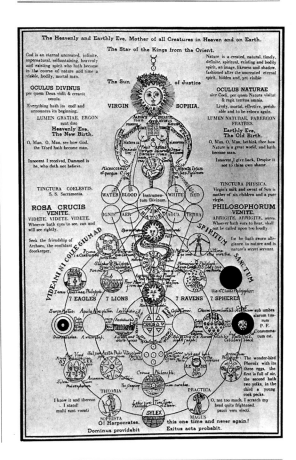

Sophia

She is the Angel-Aeon who gave birth to all the others. As both mother and lover of her progeny she caused a mass defection from the mysteries of Light. Her lover sons became seduced and obsessed by the mysteries of sexual union. It is said that out of their incestual yet angelic union sprang the demon-archons and lesser demons. But Sophia tired of this sensual pursuit and returned to her original fascination and thirst to discover the mystery of the Light of the Absolute. Her subsequent curiosity, and the jealousy of the sexually aroused and yet unsatisfied lovers, caused her great fall.

In one account, she desired to create without the male principle, which infuriated the chauvinist Angel-Aeons. In another version she is so curious that she mistakes a false reflection in the depths below and plunges down to meet it becoming enmeshed in our material world in the process. Her lover-angels spitefully conspired to imprison her in a body in which she is subjected to the deepest humiliations of rape and whoredom. In this aspect she is known to the Gnostics as "Our sister Sophia, who is a whore." In this role she is the lustful keeper of corrupt, carnal and profane knowledge. Many of the Gnostic visionaries were originally from the "oldest profession," which they see as a tradition stemming from Christ's liaison with Mary Magdalene. In Jewish lore Sophia is identified with the Shekinah, the female principle which was introduced in the first wing of the treasury.

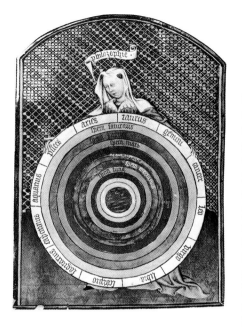

Sophia manages to endure these endless trials and gains a new understanding of the mysteries of the Light and Pistis, "faith." She is restored to heaven to become the greatest of all angels. She makes an appearance in the orthodox apocalypse of John. In Revelations (21:9) she has become the bride of Christ in a mystical marriage with the Logos. In her own words discovered in the Dead Sea scrolls of Nag Hammaddi she says, "I am the first and the last, the honored and the despised, the whore and the holy one, wife and virgin, barren and fertile."

The Heretic Angel: the Demiurge

The other mighty aeon which caught the Gnostic imagination is of course *ophiomorpus*, "serpent shaped," *diaboles*, "the slanderer" or *diabolos*, the devil.

Satan is the fiery archon, but because he is Prince of Darkness his fire is of the element of darkness too. To the Gnostic he is the Demiurge who created our universe which is, in essence, evil. He is identified with the detested Yahweh, God of the Israelites, and is scorned along with the Jewish

Right: **Unio Mystica** by *Johfra, 1973*. This represents the middle pillar of the Tree of Life and adam Kadmon, the Universal Man. Above: **Philosophie** *illustrated French manuscript.* Sophia, or Wisdom still exerted her influence amongst the Kabbalists of the 14th century.

patriarchs as being the epitome of falsehood. They point an accusing finger at the apparently schizophrenic actions of Jehovah who openly admits, "My name is Jealous and I am a jealous God," whilst maintaining the image that He is a loving deity. The Gnostics cite the legend of Moses who comes down from the mountain having been given the ten commandments. One of the commandments says not to kill and yet the Lawgiver promptly, following the orders of his God, slaughters three thousand men, women and children. Apparently, point out the Gnostics, neither he nor Jehovah see any ambiguity in the situation. Here, they insist, there is the singular proof that we are dealing with a merciless, wrathful, bloodthirsty monster who cannot possibly be the Father of Light. Instead this can only be Satan.

It is small wonder that the Gnostics were accused of anti-Semitism. They ceaselessly hammered all the beliefs and institutions of the Hebrews, condemning their scriptures as being trivial, exclusive, of only tribal interest and having no spiritual value for the rest of the world. In doing so, of course, they make quite a hole in our previous orthodox studies which are based on such material.

We begin to feel on even less firm ground when Jesus Christ himself accuses the Jews: "Ye are of your Father; the Devil." The New Testament is notable for its silence in mentioning Jehovah except in this passage.

The fundamental dualism which underpinned the Gnostic ideas was originally a Persian concept which developed around the middle of the last millennium before Christ. In this Persian belief our universe is seen as the battle ground between the Lord of Light (the Zoroastrian Ormazd) and the Prince of Darkness (Ahriman).

The further the demon-archons moved from the divine source the greater the darkness, ignorance, error and evil. The archons are identified with the seven deadly sins which are in turn equated with the seven planetary bodies, being the absolute antithesis of the seven archangels.

In the following list, however, the archons are set alongside our traditional archangels who supposedly control the seven planets. This shows how far away the Gnostics were from the orthodox Church by the 3rd century A.D..

Sins		Planet		Archangel
Pride	=	Jupiter	=	Zadkiel
Envy	=	Moon	=	Gabriel
Wrath	=	Mars	=	Sammael
Lust	=	Venus	=	Aniel
Sloth	=	Saturn	=	Kafziel
Greed	=	Sun	=	Raphael
Falsehood	=	Mercury	=	Michael

While the Zoroastrian idea of a constant battle being waged between the forces of good and evil was much embellished by the Gnostics, the final polish was left to the Christian Church. The passionate and intense series of apocalyptic visions which appeared at the time of the Messiah arose from a magnificent obsession with the nature of good and evil which had absorbed the Hebrew theologians for over two centuries. When the end of the world did not materialize in the century after Christ, many came to believe that the final battle of the angels had been re-scheduled to be fought sometime in the future. Many see that future as being here and now, within our lifetimes. The great battle with the anti-Christ and the forces of evil which support his enterprise is billed for the end of this millennium.

for such a work. It is unique and unlike anything else so far uncovered. The scribe obviously felt that the "end of days" was just round the corner and he had to prepare his sect for the final victory over the Sons of Darkness. Two thousand years later we find ourselves at the end of an era which has been prophesied as the "Armageddon," "the end of days" when the Sons of both Light and Darkness must stick up their heads and be numbered.

In reading the scroll there is a sense of immediacy, as if at any moment the scribe just has to look up to see the archangel, "Michael stand up, the great prince that standeth for the children of Thy people."
It was probably one of the last texts written in the truly apocalyptic genre. But however much the writer might search the heavens for signs of the great armies of the heavenly hosts, the promised end of the forces of Beliel which he so passionately described was obviously a long time coming. Tiny communities like his were being ruthlessly destroyed by invaders who were in turn followed by more invaders. It is unlikely that

War Above and Below

One of the Dead Sea scrolls discovered in the first Qumran cave is a war scroll. There is no precedent

---

Above: **Angel with the Key of the Abyss** *wood engraving by Albrecht Dürer.* Left: **Michael driving out Lucifer from Heaven** *engraving by Gustave Doré.* The angel is Apollyon-Abaddon, the "destroyer." He is the Angel of the Bottomless Pit who is to bind the Satanic Dragon for 1000 years. The gnostics pointed out that many of the orthodox angels were in fact villains.

Abaddon is the Angel of Death and Destruction and chief of Demons according to the Kabbalists.
As the Greek Apollyon he is described in Bunyan's Pilgrims Progress as "clothed with scales like a fish, and wings like a dragon, feet like a bear, and out of his belly come fire and smoke."

the author survived long after he hid his precious manual of victory.

The text is a very detailed preparation for each battle between the forces of Light and the hordes of Darkness. The text meticulously describes which trumpets to blow for both advance and retreat, the inscriptions which must be on the trumpets and the precise sound which must issue forth. The battle is to take forty years and consists of seven Lots or major engagements with the dark forces of Beliel. Although Beliel will be victorious in three of the great engagements, God and His angels will finally carry the day in the seventh encounter. In fact the mortal armies, along with the hideous demonic hordes of the Evil One, will finally fall to the swords of Michael and his glorious angelic legions and not to those of men.

This whole battle is the culmination of thousands of years of preparation and minor skirmishes to test the opponent's strength. But according to the scroll the final outcome is already decided in favor of the author's peoples.

This type of apocalyptic vision had an enormous appeal to the religious sects who had been ceaselessly oppressed by the Babylonians and Persians in the East, the Egyptians in the South, the Philistines, Greeks and Romans in the West and the various marauding Kingdoms of the North. All these are

understandably seen as the forces of Belial or Satan.

Of course the most famous of the apocalyptic genre is to be found in the New Testament. In *The Revelations of John* the most powerful of images of those final days can be found. In a graphic description which could also be read as an account of the original fall, it is said, "And war broke out in heaven: Micha-el and his angels battled with the dragon and the dragon and his angels battled. But it did not prevail, neither was a place found for them any longer in heaven. So down the great dragon was hurled, the Original serpent, the one called Devil and Satan, who is misleading the entire inhabited world."

The Good and Evil Angels *two versions by William Blake.* They depict a child being held by the Good angel who prevents the shackled and fiery dark angel from reaching it. Above this design we find the following insight:
"The voice of the Devil
All Bibles or sacred codes have been the causes of the following Errors:
1. That Man has two real existing principles: Viz: a Body & a Soul.
2. That Energy, call'd Evil, is alone from the Body; and that Reason, call'd Good, is alone from the Soul.
3. That God will torment Man in Eternity for following his Energies.
But the following Contraries to these are True:
1. Man has no Body distinct from his Soul; for that call'd Body is a portion of Soul discerned by the five Senses, the chief inlets of Soul in this age.
2. Energy is the only life, and is from the Body; and Reason is bound or outward circumference of Energy.
3. Energy is Eternal Delight."

Elementals

At this culminating point as the angels of Light finally overcome the angels of Darkness let us take a break from the noise of battle to examine a little gem from *The Magus of Strovolos* by Kyrialos Markides. This is rich little book crammed full of the wiseacerings of a beautiful mystic healer in modern Greece. They are particularly relevant to those apocalyptic visions of twenty centuries ago, for in the following excerpt we find an unusual description which seems to unite both Christian and Gnostic concepts of the good and evil forces. According to the *Magus*, demons are far more human than angels. It appears that you can reason, argue or strike bargains with demons. An angel, on the other hand, being part of the Divine Will, cannot do anything but follow that will. An angel can only do good; whereas Lucifer, having his own free will, can follow any path he chooses, even when it is mostly for the bad. From this brief account it can be seen that demons seem completely in tune with human nature and all its frailties.

"Responding to my question on the difference between angels and demons, Daskalos (the Magus) went on to say that they are both emanations of angelic forces. In themselves neither demons nor angels are eternal beings. They are elementals of the archangelic force which projects them. Humans are capable of creating both demonic and angelic elementals.

"Demons are archangelic emanations in the opposite side of existence in order to create the realms of separateness. Archangel Lucifer in the noetic world is no different from all the other archangelic systems. But his work down here is to create the opposite side of energy and power in order to bring the balance. I believe this must be part of the Divine Plan. It is that which we call Evil. The purpose of this Evil is to create for us more sharply the meaning of the Good."

The questioner then asks how demons are different from the elementals (projected energy) that we create all the time. "The elementals that human beings create are either angelic or demonic. Man is allowed to create both kinds. An archangel, on the other hand, can only create angelic elementals, with the exception of Lucifer who can only emanate demons.

"'Demons,' said Daskalos, 'possess a form of subconsciousness that enables them to converse with humans. I am telling you,' he continued, 'you may reason with a demon but not with an angel because an angel is an unshakable law. An angel cannot deviate from his divine purpose. But, although a demon is something analogous to the angel, he opposes the work of the angel and can influence man. Once a demon attaches himself to a human being, he acts along with him, using the logic of man regardless of the fact that it may be a form of unreason. An angel cannot do that. He works monolithically within the realms of Creation. Do you understand now what is happening? An angel has no choice but to do good. A demon cooperates with man and therefore absorbs part of his experience, like the ability to logicalize. The angel expresses the love of his archangel uncolored. A demon expresses within the realm of separateness the love of his own archangel, which is sentimentality. It is very similar to human sentimentality. That is why a demon can more easily get attached to a human than an angel. The only work of the angel in the plant and animal kingdom and in man is to create blindly and beautifully through the Holy Spirit, cells and tissues and to assist in cures. The demon on the other hand does everything that man does. He lives fully with man's sentiments'."

There is a parallel to this experience found in the *Life of Anthony*, written over 1600 years ago. In it are listed the weapons which the hermit saint used to ward off constant demonic attacks. Demons seemed especially attached to all monks and hermits who were always trying to exorcize them, ignore them or even blow them away by hissing. Anthony maintains that, if a spirit approaches, the monk should boldly ask what it is. Sometimes the demon will appear as a beautiful woman or an angel. If it is a real angel it will fully reveal itself but if it is a demon it will flee in terror at such courage.

Such timidity on the part of the devil's legions does tend to suggest the final battle is going to be a real walkover for the Righteous, contrary to what advertisements of this event claim. For this final battle has been awaited thousands of years. After so many qualifying rounds and minor skirmishes to test the enemies' tactics and defenses, it is almost a disappointment to find the devil is a wimp. But it is pretty disheartening for the Enemy to know that however skillfully, courageously or brilliantly he deploys his diabolic forces, God has already decided on the outcome.

However, the devil also knows that without the permanent state of siege, without a constant tension between the opposing forces of the Good One and the Evil One, the whole hierarchy of both Heaven and Hell would topple. Without such ideas as obedience and disobedience, there would be no sense of sin. Without sin there is no need for Heaven and Hell. So here we see two co-existing themes. One is the dualistic conflict of good and evil; the other is the simple commerce of sin and righteousness with subsequent rewards in heaven or punishments in hell.

But rewards and punishments are not really such a simple matter, especially when one man's sin can be another's salvation. A devout Moslem who kills a Christian on a Holy Jihad is assured of a warrior's place in paradise with two beautiful and desirable angel maidens for his delight. Simultaneously this righteous hero has secured his everlasting torment in the Christian hell for killing a Christian, for not being a Christian and for the corruption of the flesh in even thinking about those two seductive Muslim maidens. Yet, historically speaking at least, there is virtually no real difference between the Semitic Allah and Jehovah, who even share the same angelic servants.

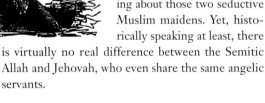

Above: The goat-headed, occult figure with the wings of an eagle, the body of a hermaphrodite and the caduceus of Hermes encompasses both principles of Good and Evil.

A Line down the Middle

The purpose of this brief heretical interlude is to highlight the ever present question of just where does one draw the line to show which is an angel of darkness and which is one of the light? Satan is one of the terrible scourging Angels of Vengeance, but so is the archangel Michael. The 90,000 Angels of Destruction are known to be the most enthusiastic punishers in Hell, and yet are given the "swords of God" with which to torment the sinners. No wonder theologians squabble over whether angels serve God or the devil. If they are God's loyal troops then they must be doing good and the eternal horrors they dish out to sinners must also be good. If they serve the Devil, then those self-same horrors must be evil. The paradoxes are, like heaven itself, eternal, and one begins to wonder which side even God is on.

There is a little known tradition which has never been encouraged by the Church. In this version of the war of the angels in heaven, one third is supposed to have sided with God, one third with the Devil and one third chose to be neutral. It was these angels who were not-very-bad yet not-very-good, who brought the Holy Grail to earth. The Grail represented the religious, mystical or spiritual way that passed between the polar extremes. It is the middle path chosen by Guatama the Buddha; it is the union of opposites.

The mysterious Grail held a passionate fascination for readers in the Middle Ages. Although strongly Christian in theme there is strangely not one mention of angels or demons in any of the many versions. The reason why this favorite legend managed to do without these celestial beings, at a time when they were immensely popular elsewhere, can be found in the opening line of one version. "Every action has both good and evil results." Such an enlightened view cannot support angelic hosts who only know of one or the other.

Without the polar opposites of the righteous and the damned, there can be no devil and no angel of light. As the reader must have already noticed this Treasury has no example of neutral plumage.

END OF PART ONE

PART TWO
AN ENDANGERED SPECIES

CHAPTER ONE
Eye Witness

IN the course of the Dante-like journey through each of the four wings of the Treasury it has probably become evident to the reader that many of the images of Paradise and the Underworld have simply arisen within a historical context. Yet the fact that a clear line of descent can be traced from the Cherubim to earlier Babylonian sources in no way invalidates the possible existence of an authentic angelic presence. However, the historical approach does help to isolate some of the more obvious inventions of the scholars. Evidence of a real angelic phenomenon is not lessened merely because a few paper wings can be clipped by historical methodology. The ultimate enigma of the angel remains as fascinating as ever.

The second half of this volume is devoted to an exploration of what, or rather who, angels really are and why they remain such an evocative subject even in this century of scientific rationalization.

The golden picture described in the Treasury is one which has been painstakingly built up over thousands of years of scholarship, is a condensation of legends and angelic lore to be found in literally thousands of scripts, scrolls, books and documents; enough to fill a large library. In contrast, the scraps of evidence that might indicate that there really are such beings, would hardly fill a small brief case. And on examination, even these precious few records would often seem to be visions and imaginings typical of those found in any modern psychiatric ward. Often the mentally disturbed also experience the self-same wild visions and encounters with bizarre beings that are to be found in accounts of meetings with angels. Yet the patients are as adamant in their belief of the reality of what they have seen as any biblical prophet. Even under deep hypnosis the visionary will maintain that the phenomenon was real. A mystic like William Blake would have convinced any lie detector that he actually *saw* angels even when there were a number of impartial observers who saw nothing when he insisted that angels were present.

Seeing is Believing

Many psychologists would agree that the whole imaginative aspect of angel sightings might be neatly summed up as either "Seeing is believing" or "Believing is seeing." Both situations have *belief* as the bottom line. Simply put, anyone who, supported by a particular belief system, expects to experience a particular phenomenon is all the more likely to have that experience. One psychologist put it neatly, "Demonic possession happens to those who believe in demonic possession."

There is a beautiful anecdote concerning the power of belief. It comes from the psychiatrist Ronald Laing and concerns a patient who always believes what her husband told her. One evening, entering her lounge unexpectedly and finding her husband with a naked woman on the couch, she is stupefied and asks "Who is this woman?" Her husband, seemingly a resourceful man, answers: "It's not a woman, it's a waterfall." The wife is caught in a real bind. She has always believed her husband and yet her instincts and her eyes tell her something entirely different. This double-bind situation is one of the roots of the psychological distress found in many schizophrenics. This wife's senses, her total being cried one perception, while her habitual belief system calmly told her quite the opposite. When confronted by such a double-bind a person can simply block out the unacceptable part or the habitual response to it. A similar principle seems to be in operation when a witness blocks a memory of encounters with angels, spirit guides, demons or even extra-terrestrials. Sometimes such memories only surface under deep hypnosis. How many crucial messages from "above" may have been lost to humanity simply because the subject cannot acknowledge what appeared to be real simply because it didn't fit into his or her belief system.

The same dilemma surfaced in Europe at the dark edge of the Middle Ages on a massive, collective scale during the horrendous persecution of witches and heretics. In this case the double-bind was created by the vision of life dictated by a Church dogma. The infernal fires of demonic hysteria were constantly stoked by an Inquisition far more diabolic than any poor wretch they condemned. But somehow we forget that the magnificent churches of the Renaissance, the sudden flowering of such artists as Botticelli, Leonardo da Vinci, and Michelangelo was contemporaneous with the infamous *Malleus Maleficarum*, the Inquisitors' manual of the witch hunts. The weird and ambivalent nature of the whole Renaissance lay in the fact that in one single moment humanism flowered in a world infested with demons. Later, under the Inquisition, that old world attempted to crush the newly found and originally unhampered intellectual development of man and Europe became as tormented as any of the worst scenes of the Inferno to be found on the church walls.

Equally schizophrenic was the stark contrast between the priests' condemnation of the sins of the flesh and the exuberant celebration of that very same flesh which appeared in the works of art commissioned by the clergy. Popular piety chose the new earthly and earthy imagery, most probably because of a healthy pagan spirit which permeates popular worship and which manages to save most of us from the effects of religious fanaticism.

The Medium is the Messenger

The Church had long controlled virtually all the popular visual media. In many respects the Church took the place, in terms of visual stimulation, of our modern cinemas and television. Today, it is difficult to imagine what a profound effect the fleshy, realistic, angels and demons had upon the collective imagination of Renaissance Florence, Siena, and Venice. Meanwhile in northern Europe the first printed pages were beginning to run off the new printing presses. Early books were liberally illustrated with woodblocks and engravings of the most lurid demonic goings on. And by the late Renaissance these images had multiplied a thousand-fold. And so, tragically, had the torments of the Inquisition.

At first glance it seems an unjustified leap of imagination to blame the passionate outpourings of the artists for the sufferings of innocent witches. But the fascination with the diabolic that was a raging torrent during the late Renaissance was maintained at fever pitch by many of the graphic images circulating at the time. Even in our century, a film like *The Exorcist* brings in its wake a whole series of reports of unaccountable demonic happenings and a wave of exorcisms. Consider what any image of hell fire and demonic nastiness, found hanging in any church of the time, might do to a less sophisticated mind.

So it is relevant to ask ourselves, today, to what extent do our present visions and ideas, of both the light and the dark angels, depend upon all the visual and literary imaginings of the past? To attempt an answer to this question, let's return to the original equation of "believing = seeing." We'll demonstrate the power of this equation by examining the unfolding visual evolution of the Angel from the 7th century until its culminating expression during the late Renaissance, which has come down to us almost untouched by the intervening five centuries. Interestingly enough, while the outward appearance of the whole angelic species has hardly changed since 1450, it was in this very epoch that they underwent their greatest inner transformation.

Angels in Perspective

The second council of Nicaea in the year 787 decreed that it was lawful to depict angels in both paintings and sculpture. This decision of the early Church altered the entire evolution of Christian imagery, leaving much of the responsibility for expressing angelic form in the hands of artists. This had an unexpected side effect. The calling of the artist at the time of the Renaissance was to quite literally explore the world through a new perspective. The painters and sculptors of this unique era were a vanguard who challenged all the time honored ways of perceiving life, time and space long before the philosophers and theologians ever got around to it. By the time the Church recognized that the earthy, solid and realistic images which had appeared on their walls were instrumental in bringing down the old traditional order, it was too late.

Previous page: **Adoration of the Magi,** *detail from a painting by Ghirlandaio, 1485.*
Above: **Virgin and Child** on the left by *Lorenzo Monaco,* 1416, and on the right by *Hans Memlinc* in 1490. Although only seven decades separate these two works, we can see how the infant Christ has been transformed from being a purely spiritual embodiment of the flesh, as sexless as any of the angelic host, to a realistic and male, human child.

Yet if we look back to the 8th century, when the original foundations of the angelic host were being laid down, we discover that the original inspirational sources were not Christian at all but Pagan. The two major and available images which caught the fancy of the artists of the time were the classic Greek examples of Nike, the Winged Victory, and the various renderings of the winged Eros. It is fitting that Eros as Love, or the later Roman version, Cupid, should form the image of the later angels of mercy and love. Curious, too, is the link between Venus with Cupid on her lap and the image of the Virgin Mary with Jesus on her lap. It took another six centuries before the Greek influence was again to find new winds for its flame in the Renaissance as angels lost much of their numinous and ethereal quality to become more fleshy and down-to-earth embodiments of the spirit.

The Renaissance was packed jam full of paradoxes. One which quickly becomes apparent is that the less substantial angels became in the eyes of the theologians and humanitarian thinkers the more solid and real they were when appearing on church walls. So much so that in Michelangelo's great masterpiece of the Last Judgment in the Sistine chapel their wings have disappeared altogether. But Michelangelo was far ahead of his times in convincingly clothing his angelic host in the flesh. The Church was unconvinced that angels were sexual and that the male phallus was redeemable. The clergy still hotly denied that angels had anything between their

---

The Annunciation, *detail from the painting by Leonardo da Vinci.* Inset: **Gabriel** *by Jacopo Bellini, Brescia.* Only twenty years separate these works yet the Leonardo is revolutionary by comparison with the earlier work. There is a new sense of spacious perspective.

Top: **Kairos of Tragir,** *300 B.C.* This winged God of Luck or Coincidence, who predates any Christian depiction by over one thousand years, holds the scales of chance on a razor's edge. Above: **Demon,** *an Etruscan tomb painting 500 B.C.* Long before the Christian Church decreed that it was lawful to depict images of angels, paintings such as this, were appearing on the walls of the tombs of Tuscany.

thighs at all. Playing safe, the Curia had all sex removed from the Sistine's naked figures by painting little bits of blue to conceal what was underneath. We can hardly blame them, for quite clearly these angels were revolutionary. They were of flesh and blood and real like us which should have made the authorities even more suspicious than they were.

But such ideas even find an echo in our our enlightened century. The novelist D.H. Lawrence was understandably outraged when his own exhibition of nude paintings was closed down by the police in England. He vented his frustration in verse.

"Fig trees don't grow in my native land,
There's never a fig leaf near at hand
when I want one. So I did without.
And that's what all the row's about."

The solution was as unacceptable to a rebel like Lawrence as it was to Michelangelo, and he wrily adds,

"A fig leaf, or if you cannot find it,
a wreath of English mist with nothing
behind it!"

Even so the ecclesiastic horror of the flesh was subtly being eroded by the new humanistic atmosphere of the 15th century. As the insubstantial angelic host and the complex hierarchies of heaven were seriously challenged by the new philosophers, even the infant Christ was assuming a very real human flesh on the canvases.

As Christ became more identified with the suffering of human beings in the midst of the Black Death, he became more a real Man. It took theologians another century to see that Christ needed no hierarchy of angels to back him up. He was enough unto himself as a human being. Artists had felt this more immediately and by the end of the plague were even giving him a real sex. Up until this point Christ had appeared as primly androgynous as any

of the angelic host. He now appears in portraits with the Virgin Mother, sporting a proud little penis. Only fifty years before such ideas would never have been permitted for the highest ideal in those times was to be as sexless as the angels. And that had included the Savior and the fanatic Christian saints and hermits.

Top: **Nemesis,** *votif relief at Brindisi, 300 A. D.* The Greeks understood this Queen of Heaven as Fate. Winged victories attend her.
Below: **Nike,** *450 B.C.* Victory makes all things obey her tune on the lyre and the sculpture from Samothrace on the right is one of the pagan images which had the greatest impact and influence upon the later painters of angels.

Eros Restored

During this extraordinary period in Europe, and especially in the courts of the new trading and banking Princes, as exemplified by the Medicis of Florence, the Church and the secular powers came to an uneasy truce over the new republican and humanitarian ideas. In works of art for the courts, interest in angels gave way to a fascination with classical heroes and Gods. The old pagans once again were restored to their place on the walls replacing the angelic host who had somehow got lost. Eros reappeared as if a cycle was complete. By then the form of the angel which had been based on these pagan originals was fixed in the popular imagination. Since the Renaissance the continuing evolution of the angel has simply and abruptly been arrested. It is as if specimens have been inadvertently sealed up forever at the peak of their power in an eternal golden age. Seldom has an entire species been wiped out at the height of its youthful glory. But perhaps only the good angels die beautiful. And that is a lot more than can be said of the bad ones who managed to live on, consuming the fearful attention of the whole of Europe for at least another two centuries.

Dark Shadows on the Wall

The fascination and belief in the devil and his hordes long outlasted any corresponding belief in angels. In the demonic atmosphere of Europe it was a matter of survival. There were too many instances of what could happen to anyone who claimed to have met with an angel. When even a national heroine like Joan of Arc was burnt at the stake by the Inqui-sition for having claimed that she had seen the Archangel Gabriel, what chance had any normal citizen. Even if someone actually encountered a Son of Light few would have had the courage or stupidity to admit it. No one could ever be quite sure that it wasn't a devil in disguise. However, you could be sure that the Inquisition would know. And who better equipped to recognize the Enemy? So it is hardly a wonder that angels got a very bad reputation. At least the devil you know is better than an angel you don't.

The early renderings of both the devil and his demons were meant to be expressions of the monstrous. Lucifer, who was once the most beautiful angel in heaven, had to become his own antithesis in hell. While good angels had been modeled upon the Greek Eros, or Love, the devil took his shape from Pan, the God of nature and the wilderness, of fertility and above all of lust. As we watch the evolution of the Devil's image, this wild goat God is never far from the surface. As soon as Pan had been re-established on the Renaissance palace walls, the shape of the devil correspondingly changed until he became the suave and urbane Mephistopheles in the drama of Faust.

Adoration of the Shepherds, *detail from a Triptych by H. Van der Goes, Uffizi.* This northern vision depicts the angels as being the "little people," who seem far more like the celtic faeries than their substantial Mediterranean counterparts. The northern el-f, like the ang-el, derives from the original root word meaning a shining one. The faerie Queen described her realm as "the land of the ever-living, a place where there is neither death, nor sin, nor transgression," which could equally describe Heaven. Celtic Christians claimed the fairies were offspring of the fallen angels.

1420   1432

These four images of the Archangel Gabriel span thirty-five years. The one above, on the left, is by *Lorenzo Monaco* and was completed in 1420. Here, Gabriel is seen to luminously float against a solid golden background. The figure is delicately modeled but seems ethereal and insubstantial. The decorative wings remain essentially two dimensional. Fifteen years later the Gabriel of *Fra' Angelico* is placed in an enclosed and almost cage-like setting. Both the figure and its robe have taken on a more substantial appearance, although the wings remain a little flat and awkward, as if belonging to the earlier epoch.

Masolino, painting around the same time (1435), gives a soft, full roundness to the figure by the use of a subtle play of light and shadow. In the last painting by *Piero della Francesca*, in 1455, we find Gabriel's transformation into a real being of flesh and blood, firmly kneeling on the ground, as if gravity has at last anchored the spirit. The luminous angel of light now has a face almost hidden in shadows. Clothed in the flesh, the angel obeys the laws of the material world. The inner illumination can no longer be seen for the angel has become like man.

1435   1455

The Angel comes to Ground

The persuasive visual fantasies of the Renaissance artists have largely shaped our internal ideas of what the devil or the angel looks like. For instance, in the early painting on this page, by Lorenzo Monaco, Gabriel is both luminous and numinous. The painting of the Archangel expresses an unearthly and mystical being. The original, solid gold background against which the angel floats, symbolizes the Light; the natural spiritual home of the angel. By the time Piero della Francesca created Gabriel, the Archangel has become a creature of flesh and blood, kneeling in a setting of solid and substantial architecture. Even the face is obscured and darkened by shadows cast by natural, earthly light. She is no longer illuminated from within by the supernatural light of the Divine flame and is a long way from being the original "fiery, flying serpent of Love." Likewise, in the last picture of the evolutionary sequence on

163

page 167, all the unique signs which symbolize angelic illumination, including the halo, are gone. We are left with a human being, essentially no different from the figure of the Virgin: that is save for the wings. Could it be that artists of that era instinctively felt the transformation of the angelic host long before philosophers, reformists and theologians began to challenge the old orthodox beliefs in the Heavenly Hierarchy? Or are we back to the original equation of seeing is believing? For it must be remembered that these images inspired an entirely new way of envisioning space, time and matter and the natural laws of the Cosmos. As this, of course, also included the angels, they had to become human-like in order to fit the new belief in a Supreme Law of Nature.

Yet if seeing is believing then what of believing is seeing? To understand how we begin to only see what we believe it is necessary to expose that what we all accept as real might be nothing more than the effect of an artistic device; perspective. Perspective is actually an illusory visual trick to make the observer believe he or she is looking through a window upon a scene which has an imaginary vanishing point on the horizon. It is cetainly one way of looking at the world but is very limiting. Most of our everyday world is made up of a mosaic of constantly changing and moving images. But the painters of the Renaissance offered a static and unchanging viewpoint which was a play of light and shadow giving the illusion of an arrested moment of time. Our present day cameras are no more than a mechanical version of this principle. We have been conditioned to this way of seeing by a constant barrage of images which surround us today, often forgetting that when we see a picture of a movie star or actually watch a movie the images are only light reflecting from a flat surface, giving an illusion of a live person. Many fresco painters of the late Renaissance attempted to trick the observer into thinking there were real windows with scenes behind them when in fact they were looking at a wall or a ceiling. Trompe l'oeil, or "deception of the eye," became a rage in many courts. The same principle holds with the images of angels which we collectively share today. As we look at a photograph of our beloved and she or he seems to be staring back at us, it is difficult to make the visual jump and just see the piece of photographic paper as just a collection of colors on a flat surface. Internally we all have the same problem when visualizing an angel. The Renaissance artist did us the questionable favor of making them "real" and bring the original fiery messengers of Light and Love, down to earth.

A Question of Wings

From the latter part of the Renaissance until today artists and their patrons gradually lost interest in angels, save for the chubby, little cherubs so useful to decorate the odd empty corner or ceiling. But during the 12th to the 15th centuries angels appeared everywhere. For those artists who were thrilled with the challenge of representing these powerful winged messengers of God the dilemma was to fit wings onto the bodies of human-like angels and yet still give the impression that the mechanics of actual flight were possible.

Largely speaking, the wings chosen to be most befitting for an angelic body were of course modeled upon the largest and most beautiful birds which were available to the artists for study. Thus it was that the wings of swans, eagles and geese that adorned the shoulders of the celestial bodies in the great masterpieces of Leonardo, Botticelli and Caravaggio. The hideous denizens of the abyss, by contrast,

Above: **Creation of Adam,** *detail from The Last Judgment by Michelangelo.* In many ways artists became God-like in their creation of angels. In the artistic evolution of the angelic form pictured below, we see the complete transformation from 1315 to 1515. While the 12th century angels appear plausible due to the symbolic nature of the paintings, the later, more realistic versions suffered, inevitably, from the awkward feeling that their tiny wings could never lift a real body to the sky. One of the drawbacks of the new perspective was that in order

were given the wings of reptiles or bats, these being associated with the dragon, the serpent or unknown and fearful creatures of the night.

The Renaissance artists, in their attempt to create a feasible connection between the human form and wings, used as their models the winged figures of Hellenic Greece. If we examine the anatomical reality of welding wings to the earthly form, we find that none of these renderings could possibly fly, yet somehow we have all suspended our disbelief in accepting their possible reality.

The visual trick which has been offered is that they *look* real and yet, without divine and supernatural intervention profoundly adjusting the laws of gravity, we all intuit that these beings could never lift off the ground.

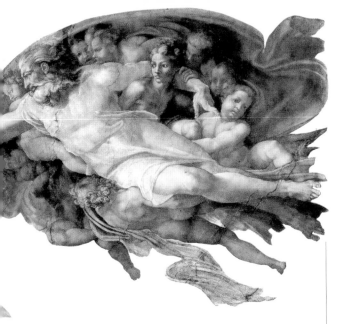

objects obeying natural and mathematical laws of space, light and gravity. Shadows are cast and color depends upon reflected light in contrast to the earlier paintings which seemed to have an internal light and color of their own. Angels who entered within the new framework had to abide by the very same laws. They cast shadows, they had weight and form and were illuminated by natural earthly light. In fact, they looked exactly the same as humans, except for their wings. Michelangelo even dispenses with these, preferring a whirlwind of figures and billowing drapes. This naturalism coincided with the rise of the new humanistic philosophies and the early proto-sciences. Belief in a universe which was moved by angels gave way to a cosmos which ran like a Divine clock mechanism. The Book of Nature supplanted the Book of the Angel. More than anything else, it was the paintings which anchored the celestial host so firmly to the ground; so firmly, that the tiny wings the artists gave them could no longer return them to the heavens.

for the scene to visually work, the artist had to suggest that the observer was looking through a window frame without being able to move his or her head. This "single view-pointed" vision of the world is the one we have inherited in the camera images which surround us today. However, in the mid 14th century this was a revolutionary step. It laid the ground for the later objective sciences and continued up until the middle of this century as our major perspective of the world. Such an image gives the impression of a moment, frozen in time, with

It'll never Fly!

Just suppose for a moment that the earthy-looking angel of Caravaggio on this page, which is one of the prototypes of the most popular versions appearing in our times, actually does manifest as a real being of flesh and bone with normal human reactions to the force of gravity. In fact, there is at least one incontrovertible reference in the Bible suggesting that angels do take on the full gravity of humans. Jacob wrestled with an angel all night in what seems to have been a close fight. When the angel saw "that he had not prevailed over him, then he touched the socket of his thigh joint; and the socket of Jacob's thigh got out of place during his grappling with him" (GEN 33:25). This is hardly the act of an insubstantial and weightless wimp pitted against a strong desert man!

So if angels did, on occasion, weigh in about 200lb., what would the size of their wings have to be in order to lift such a mass from the ground or allow them to hover in the air?

The largest birds on earth, like the white pelican or the mute swan, have a weight of about 25 to 30lb. They need a wingspan of about 13 feet to lift this bulk. The record for an efficient lift amongst the large birds is held by the Canadian goose which lifts about 4lb. for every square foot of wing. Most birds, however, manage little more than half a pound for every square foot of lifting feathers.

If we calculate an average lift power it will be found that a tall angel, having a full earthly weight of about 200 lb., would need a wing span of anything from 36 feet [12 meters] to 120 feet [40 meters]. This roughly corresponds to the size of a modern hang-glider, although those types of wings can only be used for gliding and soaring. It does indicate that the modest Renaissance wings have more than a flutter of poetic license.

Yet it is strangely such models as these which constitute our present-day hazy ideas of how an angel should be.

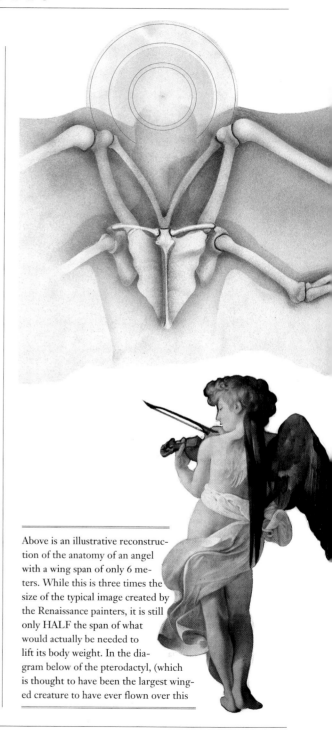

Above is an illustrative reconstruction of the anatomy of an angel with a wing span of only 6 meters. While this is three times the size of the typical image created by the Renaissance painters, it is still only HALF the span of what would actually be needed to lift its body weight. In the diagram below of the pterodactyl, (which is thought to have been the largest winged creature to have ever flown over this

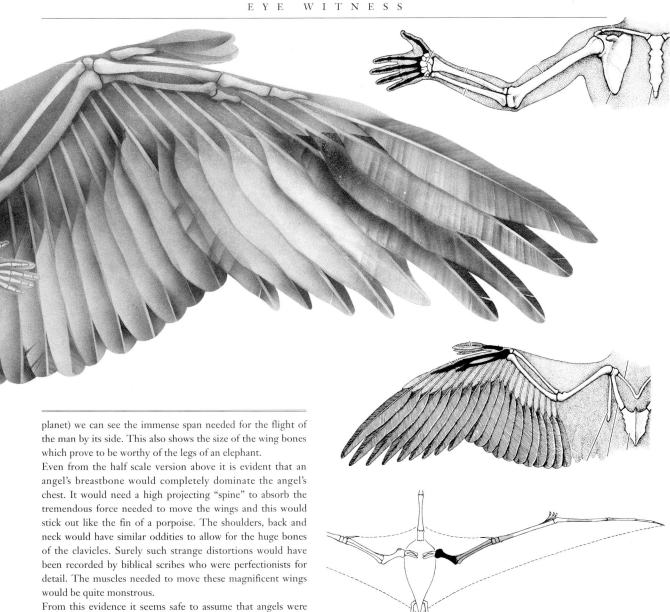

planet) we can see the immense span needed for the flight of the man by its side. This also shows the size of the wing bones which prove to be worthy of the legs of an elephant.

Even from the half scale version above it is evident that an angel's breastbone would completely dominate the angel's chest. It would need a high projecting "spine" to absorb the tremendous force needed to move the wings and this would stick out like the fin of a porpoise. The shoulders, back and neck would have similar oddities to allow for the huge bones of the clavicles. Surely such strange distortions would have been recorded by biblical scribes who were perfectionists for detail. The muscles needed to move these magnificent wings would be quite monstrous.

From this evidence it seems safe to assume that angels were either non-substantial or weightless or if not, had some unknown divine dispensation. If they actually obeyed the laws of gravity they would have been quite monstrous.

However beautiful, fascinating or real the images seem, like that on the left by *Caravaggio*, the angelic fictions by artists of the Renaissance must be considered amongst the most fanciful flights of imagination ever conceived.

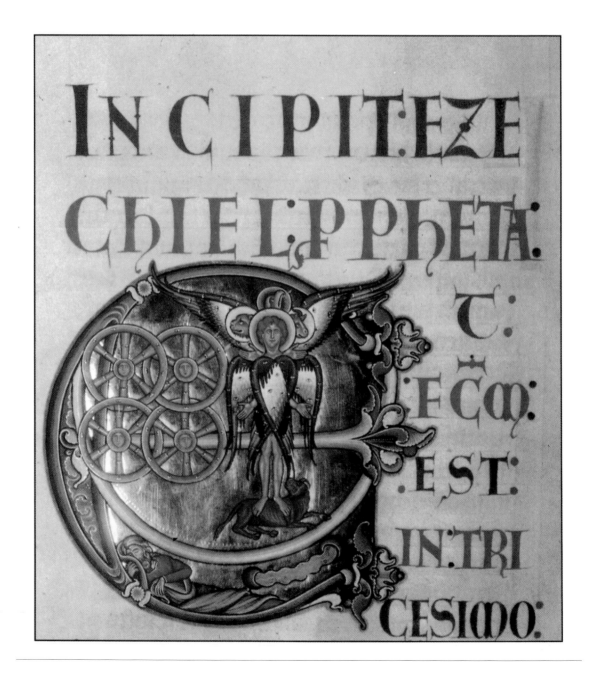

CHAPTER TWO

Ancient Encounters of a Luminous Kind

S O FAR WE STILL DON'T KNOW whether angels are ethereal beings of light without substance or if they take a solid human form with real wings which actually enable them to fly. Just how many people have actually had a close enough encounter with one to be able to tell us?

When my own grandmother was dying she became ecstatic on seeing angels awaiting her on the 'other shore.' Yet in that moment of supreme truth her detailed descriptions of the divine beings surrounding the deathbed had, even to my mind as a small child, a suspicious resemblance to one of her favorite Victorian Pre-Raphaelite paintings.

But who is in a position to judge whether her vision was real or not? Most visions of angels do seem to come when the witness is in a near death state or has an out of body experience on the so called astral plane. And who is to say that Gabriel or Michael don't resemble the sentimental renderings of a Burne-Jones or the earthiness of a Caravaggio? Maybe, in order not to alarm anyone by appearing in their true form (or formlessness), they assume the contemporary and fashionable ideals of the day. On the other hand artists could be privy to visions of worlds which are denied to the less sensitive among us.

In this century only the vaguest theories have been advanced as to the nature of angels. The official Church stance that angels are "insubstantial and spiritual" hardly constitutes a substantial theory. There are suggestions that angels might have something to do with electro-magnetism, collective hallucinations or morphological memory fields. When all else fails we can always fall back upon lumping the whole phenomenon under the heading, para-normal. Yet as we have seen in Part I, angels and devils have had, in earlier centuries, just as much a reality as the equally ethereal and invisible atoms and particles of our present technologies. Some prominent psychics and channellers of today go as far as to claim that it is we who are are the angels. It is both a comfortable and persuasive idea that we are beings of light and energy who have just forgotten our real identity. It is suggested that many of our dream images or near death experiences are actually glimpses of our true light nature when free of the restrictions of the body and of earth's gravitational forces. We will shortly explore such possibilities as angels being collective archetypes or reflections of our astral bodies of light, as the creators of the universe, messengers of God, spirit guides and even as extra-terrestrials. But before embarking on these delightful higher realms of speculation let us come to earth with some real hard facts and substantial evidence.

Witness for the Defense

Any cross-examination of witnesses who have claimed to have encountered an angel is impossible today because most of the most famous witnesses are dead. And as the entire case of whether angels exist or not rests with first hand accounts, the case for the reality of an angelic host rests on decidedly shaky foundations. It has already been seen that it is impossible to separate the witnessed from the witness. And even if it were feasible to establish the unimpeachable character of the observer, we are still left with the vague and confusing nature of the reports themselves. The dilemma facing any witness, and one common to all the records, is that the words used to describe the indescribable are obviously inadequate. Almost invariably the encounter is so overwhelming, being completely outside of any normal experience, that all the observer could do is to describe it in terms of *something else*. The phrase "has the appearance of..." all too frequently occurs. So, what might well have appeared as a radiating glow of light became "like wings of Fire." An unfamiliar style of boot is expressed as "feet like unto burnished gold." This poetic form of speaking and writing in symbols, metaphors and analogies, of course leaves a completely open field of speculation, which more often than not is exaggeratedly sensational in form.

As a demonstration of the pitfalls and difficulties likely to be encountered in building up a lucid image of what an angel might be, let us look at a classic encounter. We have already been introduced to part of the most spectacular account ever recorded of a meeting with an angelic presence in the Treasury. This is the one which has stirred the popular imagination the most. In it the ancient Hebrew prophet Ezekiel is transported from Chaldea to Jerusalem and back in an "aerial chariot of God," operated by angels.

Encounter with a Hebrew Angel

EZEKIEL 1:4

And I began to see, and look! There was a tempestuous wind coming from the north, a great cloud mass and quivering fire, and it had a brightness all around, and out of the midst of it there was something like the look of electrum, out of the midst of the fire.

5: And out of the midst of it there was a likeness of four living creatures, and this is how they looked: they had the likeness of earthling man.

6: And [each] one had four faces, and each one of them had four wings.

7: And their feet were straight feet, and the sole of their feet was like the sole of the foot of a calf; and they were gleaming as with the glow of burnished copper.

8: And there were the hands of a man under their wings on their four sides, and the four of them had their faces and their wings.

9: Their wings were joining one to the other. They would not turn when they went; they would go each one straight forward.

10: And as for the likeness of their faces, the four of them had a man's face with a lion's face to the right, and the four of them had a bull's face on the left; the four of them also had an eagle's face.

11: That is the way their faces were. And their wings were spreading out upward. Each one had two joining to each other, and two were covering their bodies.

12: And they would go each one straight forward. To wherever the spirit would incline to go, they would go. They would not turn as they went.

13: And as for the likeness of the living creatures, their appearance was like burning coals of fire. Something like the appearance of torches was moving back and forth between the living creatures, and the fire was bright, and out of the fire there was lightning going forth.

14: And on the part of the living creatures there was a going forth and a returning as with the appearance of the lightning.

15: As I kept seeing the living creatures, why look! There was one wheel on the earth beside the living creatures, by the four faces of each.

16: As for the appearance of the wheels and their structure, it was like the glow of chrysolite; and the four of them had one likeness. And their

appearance and their structure were just as when a wheel proved to be in the midst of a wheel.

17: When they went they would go on their four respective sides. They would not turn another way when they went.

18: And as for their rims, they had such height that they caused fearfulness; and their rims were full of eyes all around the four of them.

19: And when the living creatures went, the wheels would go beside them, and when the living creatures were lifted up from the earth, the wheels would be lifted up.

20: Wherever the spirit inclined to go, they would go, the spirit [inclining] to go there; and the wheels themselves would be lifted up close alongside them, for the spirit of the living creatures was in the wheels.

21: When they went, these would go; when they stood still, these would stand still; and when they were lifted up from the earth, the wheels would be lifted up close alongside them, for the spirit of the living creature was in those wheels.

22: And over the heads of the living creatures there was the likeness of an expanse like the sparkle of awesome ice, stretched out over their heads up above.

23: And under the expanse their wings were straight, one to the other. Each had two wings covering on this side and one had two covering on that side their bodies.

24: And I got to hear the sound of their wings, a sound like that of vast waters, like the sound of the Almighty one, when they went, the sound of a tumult, like the sound of an encampment. When they stood still, they would let their wings down.

25: And there came to be a voice above the expanse that was over their head.

26: And above the expanse that was over their head there was something in appearance like sapphire stone, the likeness of a throne. And upon the likeness of a throne there was a likeness of someone in appearance like an earthling man upon it, up above.

27: And I got to see something like the glow of electrum, like the appearance of fire all around inside thereof, from the appearance of his hips and upward; and from the appearance of his hips and

downward I saw something like the appearance of fire, and he had a brightness all around.

28: There was something like the appearance of the bow that occurs in a cloud mass on the day of pouring rain. That is how the appearance was of the brightness round about."

Ezekiel was not the only witness of the biblical world to meet such wheeled vehicles, with their accompanying pillars of cloud and light, with an angel at the helm. Elijah also ascended in a fiery chariot and was gathered up "in a windstorm to the hea-

vens" (2 KINGS 2:11). Enoch sees a luminous cloud: "and a mist summoned me, and the course of the stars and the lightning sped by me, and the winds caused me to fly and be lifted upward and bore me to heaven" (EN:XIV 8VB).

The Shining Serpents

There were other encounters like that of the prophet Isaiah which bear remarkable similarities to the experience of Ezekiel. In fact so closely do some of the descriptions tally that we might even be tempted to imagine there really were people living in the biblical lands who did exhibit bizarre differences in appearance to the indigenous peoples of the area. Perhaps there were beings who were definitely taller, and who possessed a strange luminosity about their faces, especially around their eyes. It is not such a wild speculation as one might at first think to suppose they

had access to technologies superior to those of the local tribes, or that they were a different human type. What is to be made of this description for instance? "...two very tall men different from any that I have seen in the Lowlands. Their faces shone like the sun and their eyes burned like lamps."

This quote is from the Chronicles of Enoch. This was a document copied or compiled from material believed to be some eight thousand years old. Even five thousand years after this meeting these mysterious peoples were still around if the account

by the prophet Daniel is anything to go by. (Dan 10:4-6) "A man dressed in linen, with a girdle of pure gold round his waist; his face shone like lightning, his eyes were like fiery torches, his arms and legs had the gleam of burnished bronze, the sound of his voice was like the noise of a crowd."

Left: The Vision of John, *from the Apocalypse of Liebana*. The four compass points correspond to the four flags of the tribes of Israel. The Bull, the Eagle, the Lion and the Man. Originally these were in the multiple form of the winged temple guardians of the Sumerians and Assyrians. They appear in the vision of Ezekiel as the four headed aspect of the Cherubim. Later these were to become the symbols of the four Evangelists; Matthew as Man, Mark as the Lion, Luke as the Bull and John as the Eagle. These can be seen on the following pages from the Irish, *Book of Kells* and in the Christ of the Apocalypse from *Chartres Cathedral*.

In Chapter Five we will find that some researchers have gone so far as to suggest that these were the first great cultivators who lived in the highlands of Lebanon, located to the east of the modern town of Ehdin (Eden?). In a number of Sumerian and Babylonian tablets these peoples were specifically described as Shining or Radiant Ones or, more curiously as Serpents. It would certainly explain the origins of the later Chaldean seraphs who were the fiery, flying, lightning serpents. Obviously there were some very mysterious angelic goings on in the Middle East at that time, and it is unwise to dismiss even the most outlandish proposals as to what they might have been.

Illuminating Speculations

Of course, such fascinating passages can be interpreted in some pretty bizarre ways. There have been claims that Ezekiel actually saw an Atlantean helicopter with an ancient luminous priest at the helm; that his was just one amongst many meetings with flying saucers whose glowing occupants were from another galaxy. More ingenuous is the 16th century illustration on this page which shows a literal bed of coals underneath a typical papal ceremonial throne. But perhaps higher technologies from Atlantis or the stars did exist six thousand years ago and the original angel was in fact an extra-terrestrial being. In any event, it might be instructive to imagine how

a primitive mind would attempt to describe the sight of an illuminated helicopter from our century. Any advanced technology need not have been that advanced to impress men like Enoch, Elijah or Ezekiel.

On examining the original Bible text, with its deeply evocative imagery, it is understandable that there have been so many seemingly plausible speculations as to what Ezekiel or other biblical witnesses actually saw. Some of these "scientific" explanations make those of the very unscientific world of esoteric symbolism and mysticism seem almost solid ground by comparison.

The alchemical symbolism of the Kabbalah and early Christian writing on the occult curiously offers a pragmatic interpretation of what the prophets really were indicating. According to such symbolism, the wheels supporting the throne represent the orbiting planets, while the whole chariot is the solar system. The four headed aspect of the angel is seen as the four directions of the compass. We find surprising historical evidence to support this view. When the twelve tribes of Israel encamped in the wilderness, the banners of Reuben (Man), Judah (Lion), Ephraim (Bull), and Dan (Eagle) were placed at the four corners. The encampment itself was a representation of the universe and this is clearly seen in the Rosicrucian illustration on this page.

Ezekiel himself would have been familiar with such concepts and would know that his readers knew the symbolism as well. And so his elaborate description of what at first appears to be an actual phenomenon could in reality have been a daring piece of symbolism which contained hidden meanings for the initiates. So in reconstructing the image of such an angel we have to be extremely wary of jumping to sensational conclusions too soon. The subject, as we have already seen, is spectacular enough in itself.

The Christian Angel

The preceding texts were of course Hebrew accounts of Jewish angels as recorded over two thousand years before Christ. Just over twelve hundred years after his death there is a new report. "On a certain morning about the feast of the Exaltation of the Cross, while Francis was praying on the mountainside, he saw a Seraph with six fiery and shining wings descend from the height of heaven. And when in swift flight the Seraph had reached the spot in the air near the man of God, there appeared between the wings the figure of a man crucified, with his hands and feet extended in the form of a cross and fastened to a cross." Here we have the highest angelic order, the seraphim, assuming the body of Christ rather than taking on normal human form. This signifies an entirely new angelic concept, for it implies that a man like Francis, who, at the time of this vision, receives the stigmata of Christ, can also be transformed into Christ Consciousness. St. Francis appears to have been one of the few enlightened beings who became a realized consciousness within the framework of Christianity. He would have probably felt far more at home in India where his liberation would have been instantly recognized. The Christian tradition, according to most Eastern mystics, stops short at the stage of the saint. But on a spiritual ladder the saint is at the fourth level with three rungs still to climb to being one with the Divine Source. According to the same seers, angels are disembodied spirits at the same level as the saint. So the great transformation of Francis is one which soars high above his angelic peers. This was actually the great turning point, when human-like angels became angel-like humans. This theme will be explored in the last chapter.

St. Teresa of Avila has a similar and parallel experience three centuries later. "It pleased the Lord that I should sometimes see the following vision. I would see beside me, on my left hand, an angel in bodily form – a type of vision which I am not in the habit of seeing, except very rarely. Though I often see representations of angels, my visions of them are of the type which I first mentioned. It pleased the Lord that I should see this angel in the following way. He was not tall, but short, and very beautiful, his face so aflame that he appeared to be one of the highest types of angel who seem to be all afire. They must be those who are called cherubim: they do not tell me their names but I am well aware that there is a great difference between certain angels and others, and between these and others still, of a kind that I could not possibly explain. In his hands I saw a long golden

Ecstasy of St. Teresa *by Bernini, 1650*

spear and at the end of the iron tip I seemed to see a point of fire. With this he seemed to pierce my heart several times so that it penetrated to my entrails. When he drew it out, I thought he was drawing them out with it, and he left me completely afire with a great love of God. The pain was so sharp that it made me utter several moans; and so excessive was the sweetness caused me by this intense pain that one can never wish to lose it, nor will one's soul be content with anything less than God. It is not bodily pain, but spiritual, though the body has a share in it – indeed a great share. So sweet are the colloquies of love which pass between the soul and God that if anyone thinks I am lying I beseech God, in His Goodness, to give him the same experience."

Amen!

Angels, Hot and Cold

For all of their power and poetry, it can be seen that few of these reports could claim to be the best of the witness accounts. It can be argued that this hardly amounts to evidence at all. One might reasonably wonder how on earth with such slim pickings as these that the whole galaxy of angels managed to remain a Christian corner stone. It is significant that, compared with the handful of first-hand glimpses, which might altogether fill a single small file, the volumes of theoretical treatises upon the heavenly agents could fill a library. The following expansive rhetoric from Gregory of Nazianus, a 4th century Church Father, typifies the theoretical genre. "The angel is then called spirit and fire: spirit, as being a creature of the intellectual sphere; fire, as being of a purifying nature; for I know that the same names belong to the first nature. But, relatively to us at least, we must reckon the angelic nature incorporeal, or at any rate as nearly so as possible. Do you see how we get dizzy over this subject, and cannot advance to any point, unless it be as far as this, that we know there are angels and archangels, thrones, dominions, princedoms, powers, splendors, ascents, intelligent powers or intelligences, pure nature and unalloyed, immovable to evil, or scarcely movable; ever circling in chorus around the first cause (or how should we sing their praises?), illuminated

thence with the purest illumination, or one in one degree and one in another proportionally to their nature and rank." Dizzy, yes, but any clearer? Hardly, for here is a classic example of the cool intellectual and *second-hand* knowledge so beloved by scholars. By contrast the first-hand accounts are passionately on fire with love. You can even feel the punch and the power of the episode of the seraph and St. Francis through the writings of his biographer, Bonaventure. A real first hand experience carries its own authentic ring of truth.

Forever Young in Amber

The golden age of angelology was more accurately the amber age of the church scholar. Like Gregory, these men of words created ever more complex yet empty hierarchies of heaven and hell. At the core of this vast kingdom of paper angels lay a dogmatic assumption: that human beings were to be the replacements in Heaven for the fallen angels and that the Church was a reflection of the heavenly hierarchies on earth. Few of these canonical ideas and even fewer angels survived the public exposure of a corrupt clergy. By the 15th century the writings of Dionysius, that ultimate

Ezekiel's Vision, *from the 17th century Bear Bible.* Kabbalists claim that the prophet's vision was a mystical experience of the hierarchy of the Worlds of Action, Formation, Creation and Emanation. What is now known as the Kabalah was once called the Work of the Chariot.

authority on the celestial hierarchies, were for the first time seriously challenged as being a fraud, while at the same time a deep rift appeared to cleave the Church as two opposing and equally infallible popes tried to lead the faithful flock, one from Rome and the other from Avignon in France. Any angels remaining in heaven after such a debacle of their "mirror-image" on earth were finally wiped out by the Black Death, which effectively also halved the human population of Europe. It was as if the plague struck at the very heart of these winged beings. Yet outwardly they were struck down at the very height of their powers in the golden age of the hierarchs. It was as if a cosmic pustule, a volcanic Vesuvius had erupted over a heavenly Pompei, encapsulating a whole age of angels under its black and deadly fallout. Angels never recovered from the blow of the plague. They were caught in an everlasting golden youth and have since then remained forever young. On the other hand the Dark, fallen angels and demons had acquired sturdy immune systems, doubtlessly due to their long association with corrupt humankind. Angels had no such resistance to the deadly virus.

The Aftermath

By the beginning of the 15th century when the worst ravages of the plague had passed, only art and popular piety with its strong pagan undercurrents really kept up the pretense that a host still existed in heaven. Theologians were already turning to the concept that Christ was enough and did not need vast legions of immaterial spirits behind him (who were for the most part Jewish anyway). The whole hierarchy of heaven had been so tainted with the corruption of the priesthood that when the apocalyptic plague descended few were surprised that ministering angels were nowhere to be found. But their absence and obvious impotence in the face of this terrible scourge was duly noted by the despondent survivors. The Church, in desperation, dropped any effort to defend their old winged allies. They quickly employed a diversionary tactic through the militant Inquisition and eagerly turned to attack the devil instead. And even if they couldn't actually tweak his tail they could destroy his fleshly handmaidens, the witches.

Where Did They Go?

But angels are supposed to be immortal, so even if the plague did claim them as victims they couldn't actually have died. So if they emptied the old mansions of Heaven where did they go? And where are they now?

Before answering this it will be helpful to examine the dossier of a modern encounter with a superior messenger from another world which might offer some clue as to their possible whereabouts.

CHAPTER THREE

Modern Encounters

SOME CHRISTIAN WRITERS have speculated that UFOs could well be a part of God's angelic host who preside over the physical affairs of universal creation...UFOs are astonishingly angel-like in some of their reported appearances."

Here is the voice of the popular evangelist Billy Graham in his book *Angels. God's Secret Agents* Although he may speak for many Americans it is not the only Christian view. Stuart Campbell, who seems to be of a more fundamentalist persuasion and who has the reputation of seeing fire and brimstone in the nakedness of a daisy, holds the opposite opinion. "The devil's angels...are calling themselves visitors from space today," he preaches, ominously adding: "The appearance of UFOs in our skies means the devil

is intensifying his satanic campaign against the good." We can all be grateful that he offers absolutely no evidence to support his claim. But neither does the more optimistic Billy Graham. Some writers even suggest that there are both angelic and satanic beings behind the helms of their flying chariots and that our skies will see the final apocalyptic battle between the forces of good and the hordes of evil by the end of this millennium. You can, of course, choose whichever scenario takes your fancy, but that germ, or seed

of an idea – that ETs are the new manifestations of angels or demons – is a very popular one. It fits very snugly with those who believe that earth has been visited by space travelers many times before throughout our history. It is equally acceptable to those who feel that angels assume the cultural or mythic form most acceptable for any particular era or milieu.

It becomes really fascinating, when comparing the angelic and the alien form, to find so many correspondences and similarities between the two phenomena.

The following list shows just a few of these.

1) Both angels and aliens are "Other Worldly" beings, whether they exist in inner or outer space.

2) They are superior entities who are either at a higher stage of development, being morally, spiritually or technologically superior, or are simply closer to the Deity.

3) The benevolent variety usually appear as the ultimate perfection of harmonious and youthful beauty. The vaguely androgynous nature of their appearance suggests a union of the male and female principles. However, it has to be admitted from the evidence of the ET reports that North American male witnesses tend to see more clearly defined and ravishing female aliens than their Russian, Euro-

pean and South American counterparts.

4) Both ETs and angels are clearly formidable linguists, speaking perfect English, German, French, Spanish, Russian, Dutch or Italian whenever necessary.

5) They all have a message to deliver. If there is any particular tendency to be observed, then angels do seem more inclined to the individual transfer of information, while the ET has a more global message. However, both usually have specifically chosen the witness in order to impart the word.

6) Both have remarkable means of aerial transportation, although there are very few reports of ETs with wings and these have to be filed away amongst the more suspect of accounts. However, both are known to use disks, wheels or saucers of light as their major mode of movement.

7) Both are beings of light. They seem to share a numinous, luminous essence which is most pronounced in their eyes which often glow with a brilliance that almost suggests rays; and in their faces which are said to shine.

8) They appear to radiate subtle auras of compassion, goodness, kindliness and a sense of peaceful harmony.

9) There is a remarkable similarity in their dress. Close fitting tunics or long flowing robes with a predominance of blue and white. Usually there is either a girdle of gold or bracelets, wristbands and rings of the same precious materials. It is actually a little curious that these beings always appear to the witnesses fully clothed. Surely only man, having sinned, found his nakedness evil. In this respect only the fallen angels would feel the need to wear clothes at all. Surely some ETs might

find their nakedness beautiful in the sight of whichever Almighty they believed in.

10) Their height is usually given as human-sized, although there are a few cases which give the height as much as 8 feet.

11) Both aliens and angels show considerable concern at the state of man and the planet upon which we live. Invariably the general direction in which the peoples of earth are heading appears to cause alarm and concern. Oddly this is often attributed, by ET and angel alike, to the devil's work which does suggest that the "Enemy" has a long galactic arm. Otherwise a New Age flavor creeps in, which lays the blame of our behavior on poor attunement to the subtle vibrations of natural harmony. Whatever the detail might be, humans are in great need of the message which the beings have brought.

12) Although both ET and angel alike are impressively superior to any of us, they often talk as if we are equals, brothers or fellow travelers through space and time. However, they are seldom seen as free agents but rather as messengers bound by higher cosmic laws or, in the case of angels, by God.

13) The witness and the witnessed are intimately and inseparably bound together. The evidence is subjective and relies upon our acceptance or rejection of the sincerity and credibility of the beholder. Both the phenomena of angels and ETs rests upon trust, faith and belief.

This list, although in no way comprehensive, gives more than a hint that angels and ETs have a lot in common. This suggests we should be very wary of dismissing the possibility that present day sightings of UFO's or contacts with ETs might be similar phenomena. A comparison of a modern encounter with that of the earlier account by Ezekiel may here be useful.

It is difficult, however, to select one contemporary example which combines most of the typical characteristics of the whole genre. In comparison with the relatively modest number of encounters that can be traced in our ancient portfolio there are, literally, thousands of often convincing, disturbing and inexplicable reports in our times. One account, however, does stand out as being a classic case which fits both the contactee and the more recent abduction phenomenon. While the narrative exemplifies the whole mysterious and bizarre genre of UFOs and Alien meetings it is, at the same time, the record of a unique mystical experience. It managed to catch the shrewd eye of the veteran psychologist, C.G. Jung, who included it within his book on UFOs.

But before embarking upon this account it must be said that, like many who have told such stories before, the witness tells of the whole meeting in good faith and obviously is convinced, even if a skeptic might feel mistakenly, that the whole episode actually occurred. The particular epic chosen to exemplify the whole phenomenon of contactee and abduction drama must surely rank alongside with the angelic encounters of Enoch, Ezekiel or Elijah in powerful imagery. The very similarities suggest an uncanny central source, as if all of them have tapped into the same mythic circuit or have actually encountered the real thing.

If they have encountered the real and substantial angel or ET – or a combination of the two – then there is little left to say except that we should examine the message that they bring with great care. If, however, they have triggered some collective or individual process within the mind, then perhaps we can glimpse a pattern which all of us share and which makes the significance of the phenomenon of

angelic sightings far more revealing.

Taking this second option allows an examination of this truly remarkable story in terms of what we know about myth and dreams. One could imagine what a treasure trove this tale would be for any psychologist who was listening to his patient recounting it. It is a veritable powerhouse of mythic and archetypical elements. The annotations within the narrative point to the gems, those glistening archetypal jewels which unconsciously we all respond to.

These interpretations are in no way offered as an explanation of the narrators experience. If Angelucci's experience was real, objective and verifiable as a substantial and material phenomenon, it still doesn't invalidate this interpretation as a guide to how we all tend to think and feel within a mythic or archetypal framework.

The Case Study of a Modern Encounter

To start with, the name of the witness comes as an unexpected treasure – *Orfeo Angelucci*. At the outset we are immediately plunged into a mythical world. Center stage stands the modern Orpheus, the legendary Greek hero-poet who enters the "other world" in order to make himself whole through regaining his female part, Eurydice. Angelucci means *Little Angel* but also has overtones of *Angel of Light*. Either way it is difficult for this witness to go wrong. Having established his substantial, magical credentials, we discover on a more pedestrian level that Angelucci was a mechanic, employed by Lockheed Aircraft Corporation at Burbank, California at the time of his early contacts with what became known as the Space Brothers.

Angel *by Sam Haskins.*

He had been working a night shift but had been feeling unwell, having a prickly sensation as if prior to an electrical storm.

Often psychics and mystics experience considerable discomfort before a visionary experience. It is not unusual; that this is expressed in terms of a restless electrical energy as if some static is running up and down the spine. In some cases this can even be the first stirrings of what Eastern Yogis have called the Kundalini or serpent power. Mystics attempt to awaken this through meditation but on occasion it arises spontaneously. If the recipient is unprepared or does not know of its import they can often experience its effect in very bizarre ways. The eastern mystic, Ramakrishna often experienced considerable discomfort before entering some of his ecstatic states.

As he drove home about 1 o'clock in the morning he saw a "red- glowing, oval-shaped object" flying in front of his car. "The object was now so close it seemed to be a master, commanding, almost breathing. There was not a sound from it."

This account is one of those which indicate that Jungs' firm and insistent belief that we use mandalic images to find our way around what seem to be complex or contradicting circumstances, does appear to have more than a grain of truth. The mandala is a circular cyclic and enclosed image which can manifest itself in a variety of images, one of which is of course the circular flying saucer or the flaming wheels described by Elijah or Ezekiel which were interpreted as the Ofarim, or the third order of angelic being. Even more interesting is the account by the modern yogi, Krishna Gopi, when he first awakened the kundalini current we have just mentioned. There were periods when he felt felt exhausted, drained

and depressed: "Whenever I closed my eyes I found myself looking into a weird circle of light, in which luminous currents swirled and eddied.

Orfeo felt impelled to follow the light as it led him off the main highway. It was as if he had become disconnected from the world and only associated with the ethereal object.

"Here we come to the classic moment of transition from one world to another. In Celtic myths the other world existed alongside our own. Yet it was a world of Other Time and to the denizens of that land our universe seemed a shadow world. But Orfeo was well prepared for this concept as he had written a book prior to his encounter entitled "The nature of Infinite Entities" in which he explored the nature of atomic evolution and involution. In myth and legend the hero cannot help but follow his destiny and often appears in a dazed or comatose state as he enters the quest.

Suddenly the red disk shot upwards at a colossal speed, releasing as it did so, two green balls of fire from which came the sound of a "most delightful masculine voice," which, in perfect English, reassured Orfeo that he was not to be afraid.

These cosmic brothers, like their angelic counterparts, do seem advanced enough to distinguish languages for they seldom seem to make any goofs over speaking Russian in California during the McCarthy era of communist witch hunts. For many observers this ability of angel and ET alike to converse in any tongue does stretch our credibility. The official language of angels is Hebrew yet few Americans find it odd that Gabriel or Michael can speak like a native when appearing in New York or Burbank, California.

The voice bade him to leave the car and told him that the lights were "instruments of transmission and reception,"

Immediately we are made aware of the tremendous extensions of the senses across space and time. This is the omnipresent, all seeing prerogative of the Gods alone.

and that he was "meeting friends from another world."

The "Other World" is an extraordinarily emotive archetypal image. It suggests a breakthrough from one set of laws of the universe into another. In the illustration" The Spiritual Pilgrim Discovering another World" we find a Rosicrucian Illumination where the pilgrim has broken through into another space/time continuum. We see the heavenly spheres reminiscent of Ezekiel's flying wheels or the rings of UFOs. Some of the strange and bizarre happenings claimed by other contactees or cases of abduction point to this other world as having an entirely different

sense of time. According to many different religious sources the gods don't live in our time. *"For a thousand years in thy sight are but as yesterday when it is past, and as a watch in the night." (Psalm XC:4)*

The voice, uncannily seemed to sense that Orfeo was thirsty and a crystal cup appeared on the fender of his car as if from nowhere. In it was the "most delicious nectar I had ever tasted."

The crystal goblet brings to mind the Holy Grail. The grail is Light; it is the Light connected to the Sun. There are many legends around this theme in which a magic goblet mysteriously fills with an ambrosia and yet no one can drink it unless they be pure. Even the Grail itself loses power if in the wrong hands. In folk lore fairies bring drinks to lost travelers appearing in lonely places. It is also the sign that Orpheus can enter the Underworld or the deeper levels of the unconscious.

A full luminous three-dimensional screen appeared in the space between the green disks.

This is a perfect example of the projection of a common cultural element. This was of course the period of novelty as far as a television screen was concerned. Television had only been in operation a few years so it is easy to see the context of the 1950's here. A later generation would surely have just "beamed" the space beings down in the style of Star Trek.

In it Orfeo saw the head and shoulders and the angel-like features of a man and woman "being near as possible the ultimate of perfection."

The extraordinary beings who seem so perfect and beautiful are simply off-the-shelf stereotypes which culturally we can all agree on. The attributes of compassion, love, care, harmony and higher spiritual lives which they exhibit are all qualities which have been agreed upon by popular consent. The images of the brothers correspond with 90% of all benign encounters in that they share our common cultural heritage. The fact that they would fit into the ranks of the angelic host, without raising the slightest suspicion, does indicate just how persuasive our stereotype is. It is small wonder that Jung suggests that Orfeo's cosmic friends, if not actual antique gods and heroes, are at least angels. Another cultural clue is that Angelucci only saw the head and shoulders of the two beings. This, of course, is perfectly in accord with what he had come to expect from watching television where announcers and personalities would be restricted to the size of the screen. It is unlikely that in the advanced technology of the space brothers such restrictions would apply.

They had huge shining eyes.

Angelucci was not the first to encounter beings from another planet. Helene Smith, the Swiss medium even created a Martian language assisted by her Guardian Angel, depicted above, as long ago as 1912. The imagery now would probably be more in the manner of the computer generated figure on the opposite page. Visionaries seldom depart from the contemporary images available even if the original phenomena might be totally outside their normal range of ideas.

This is an enduring image throughout the history of encounters. Its mythical content is of course an all knowing awareness, a bright penetrating look, the eye of Horus, the inner eye and higher consciousness. They seemed as if vaguely familiar.

"They conveyed kindness, understanding, experience, moderation, and a complete joy of the five senses. Life in full. All this and not a word spoken" They communicated telepathically.

This is a favorite theme of our own modern era for it seldom appears in myth and legend. However it does indicate a magical rather than technological achievement. It hints at a higher consciousness and a more advanced spiritual lifestyle.

They told Orfeo that Earth has been under surveyance for centuries.

This is the typical background of higher intelligences or cosmic guardians who are all seeing and omnipresent. Here we are introduced to the wise being, benevolently inclined to human beings and watchful over our destinies.

It seemed there was an especial interest in re-surveying the planet. The vital statistics of each and every person on earth, they told him, is recorded on their crystal recording disks.

The eastern concept of the akashic records or the idea of memory fields is now introduced. That we are all important enough to be recorded in some higher cosmic file is a very reassuring theme, as is the concept that there is an all seeing eye which does the recording in the first place.

They felt a deep sense of brotherhood with earth because of some undisclosed kinship with their own home, the planet *Lucifer.* They asked Orfeo to look upon them as "older brothers." Cosmic law forbade them any spectacular revelations on Earth but they had to act now as the planet was threatened by greater dangers now than had been realised. They specifically mentioned the "creeping menace of communism that threatened the world."

At this point contemporary cultural and personal preoccupations are creeping into the narrative. This encounter happened just prior to the Communist witch hunts of Senator McCarthy. There was a paranoid atmosphere as the new threat of the vast destructive capacity of the Soviet nuclear arsenals became known. It is small wonder that, if Commu-

nism wasn't at the top of the space brothers priorities, it certainly was at the top of Angelucci's.

All this heady stuff had an electrifying effect upon the witness. He felt exhilarated "as though, momentarily, I had transcended mortality and was somehow related to these superior beings."

This is a typical timeless moment in any mystic or spiritual happening. The hero has now experienced a type of timelessness which gives him a glimpse of the nature of the Other Worlders who exist in a different time continuum. He has become one of them, or at least shares some of their mystery.

Angelucci's next meeting with the beings occurred precisely two months after that first overwhelming contact. On July 23rd 1952 Orfeo again felt unwell and tense. He took a walk in the evening and in another lonely setting saw before him a "huge misty soap bubble." This he entered, finding himself in a vaulted room about twenty feet in diameter,

in the center of which stood a reclining chair. As he sat down on it the chair adjusted to his body form.

This is an individual journey. We can see how different the significance would have been if the room was filled with chairs and yet he was the only occupant.

The walls were lit mysteriously and looked like "ethereal mother-of-pearl stuff."

Light is fundamental to most encounter experiences. Generally the background lighting in most of the meetings is soft and unified. It seldom comes from an identifiable source. Many of the "other world" situations in legends and myth are bathed in a soft twilight.

The UFO, as this is what it turned out to be, took off and Orfeo seemed to fall into a trance like state of semi-dreaming.

Here we observe one of the important transitional points which occur in all myths. The witness moves from reality to dream and back. The hero finds it difficult to distinguish one state from another

Through an opening in the walls he could see Earth a thousand miles away and he started crying. He heard a voice saying "Orfeo weep...we weep with you for earth and her children. For all its apparent beauty Earth is a purgatorial world..."

A favorite theme amongst most quasi-religious groups. It suggests the battleground for the forces of Good and the forces of Darkness. Even Georges Gurdjieff said that "Earth is a very bad place from the cosmic view – it is like the most remote part of northern Siberia. But the idea of purgatory is a late Christian invention and did not appear as a concept until the late Middle Ages."

...among the planets evolving intelligent life. Hate, selfishness and cruelty rise from many parts of it like mist." The voice went on to say that while every being on earth was divinely created some naturally were good while some gravitated towards evil.

One wonders how the concept of a dualist universe, which appears to be quite a latecomer to human thought, *managed to permeate the rest of space. However, in terms of Earth myths, it is part of the hero's quest that he transcend all the polarities, that he unites the good and the evil, the earthly and the heavenly, the male and the female. This is the ultimate reward for his journey into the Other World.*

Above: **A UFO** snapped by an amateur photographer in the early 1970's, in Virginia, U.S.A.. Concrete evidence of the power of folk legends of UFOs is to be found in backyards throughout America, from rockets to flying saucers and highway signs.

"We know where you stand Orfeo," they tell him reassuringly, for he has been chosen by them for a mission.

The Quest is seemingly imposed by a superior or higher entity: it is the quest to find the true Self. This is one of the most persistent themes to be found in UFO material. Most contactees express genuine surprise that they should be the ones singled out as being worthy of the mission. Few can believe that they have any of the required qualifications (save that of being very ordinary – Mr. or Mrs. Average. Many of the heroes of legend have similar misgivings and blame fate for the seemingly arbitrary nature of the choosing. However, on closer examination of the intricate webs of the cosmos, the hero discovers a deeper pattern which remains essentially unknowable, but one that he has to follow. We find such forces in action in the Hebrew accounts of the legends of the tribes of Israel. Here it is not just an individual who finds himself chosen but an entire people.
The question arises "Chosen for what?" In this respect Orpheo is more fortunate than many of his contemporaries for he actually has a gospel to impart to us. Most witnesses are told that they are amongst the chosen few and yet are left dangling when it comes to the fine print of the message. "Don't call us, we'll call you." is a too frequent tale in UFO accounts.

As part of their general explanation of how the forces of good and evil interact, the cosmic guardians mention Christ but only as an allegorical Son of God. In reality he was the "Lord of the Flame" and not of earth at all.

Most contactees have something to say about Christ. Invariably they offer new accounts of who he really was, often emphasizing the new age character of the space savior. The illustration of Christ as spaceman is a familiar image of our times. Yet in this account Angelucci does add a touching and original note.

This "Infinite entity of the Sun" sacrificed himself for the children of woe and in doing so "has become part of the oversoul of mankind and the world spirit. In this he differs from all other cosmic teachers.

We have so few accounts of UFO sightings or contacts from the East that there seem to be no words of enlightenment concerning the cosmic nature of such spacemen as Gautama the Buddha, Mahavira, Lao Tzu, Chuang Tzu, Bodhidharma or Saraha. It does suggest a certain cultural bias exhibited by our cosmic watchers.

"Everyone on earth has a spiritual, unknown, self which transcends the material world and consciousness and dwells eternally outside of the Time dimension in spiritual perfection within the unity of the oversoul."

Orfeo is then baptized in the true light of the world eternal and undergoes a spiritual rite of passage. At that moment there is a lightning flash in which he sees into both past and future, understanding the mysteries of life. He thought he was going to die as he was wafted into "eternity, into a timeless sea of bliss."

This is the centerpiece of the drama. Here we have the typical rite of passage, the initiation to the mysteries and a landmark towards a final resolution of knowing the wholeness of Self. The description is remarkably similar, even though naively expressed, to many experiences of both Eastern and western mystics. Light is the most important element here. Literally, Orfeo saw the Light. We find a remarkable similarity of vision with the composer Jerry Neff,

who experienced the following during a trip on LSD." In front of my eyes, as if in a dream, I could only see a blazing pool of white or slightly golden light...I did not so much see it as feel it, and that feeling was one of absolute ecstasy, involving every 'good' sensation and every 'rightness' imaginable, and in a moral sense as well. This bliss included benevolence, joy, and reconciliation of opposites – literally everything all at once...the absolute certainty that what one is seeing is the real reality – a timeless source of all that exists."While this is a far more sophisticated expression than that of Orfeo the experience is uncannily alike.

At the end of this remarkable episode, on returning to his home, Orfeo discovers a clear stigmata

The hero always needs a symbol or sign which signifies the nature of his search.

...on the left side of his chest which was an inflamed circle with a dot in the center. He sees it as the "symbol of the hydrogen atom" which represents the circle whose center is everywhere and whose circumference nowhere.

This is the hero's personal, manifest sign of a search for the Unio Mystica, the totality of wholeness, Jung's individuation or the alchemical transmutation. It is the symbol which Orfeo has chosen as Self.

On August 2nd of the same year he, along with eight other witnesses, claimed to have seen a UFO. He went on alone to the lonely spot of the first encounter. Here he found a tall handsome man with unusually huge, luminously expressive eyes.

Christ as Spaceman: Spaceman as Christ, *from Angeles ayer, extraterretres hoy.*

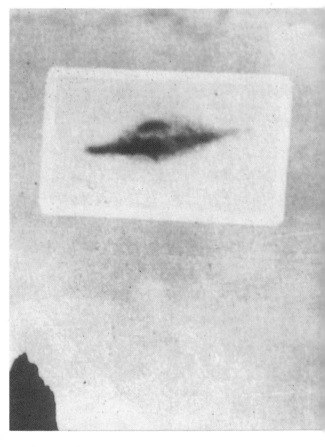

This is a persistent imagery, which can be found throughout history. Contemporary with the widespread religion of the Eye Goddess of Old Europe were those strange and enigmatic beings with luminous eyes which shone like the sun who appeared 12000 years ago in the Middle East and whose image gave rise to the stories of the angels.

This ethereal figure introduces himself as "Neptune."

This was the Roman god of the ocean deep. In Greece his name was Poseidon who arose from an even earlier deity Varuna. Varunas is the Sanskrit word for "The night firmament." All are emotive titles for the ruler of the ocean of the unconscious, the Other World or the vast firmament of the stars.

The edges of his majestic form seemed to ripple like wings or "water in the wind. *(Certainly an angelic characteristic)* He then tells Orfeo more of why earth was endangered and of its coming redemption.

Invariably in meetings in which some message is passed we find the same finger from the cosmic pulpit warning us about what we are doing wrong with ourselves and the planet. It is notable that these space or angelic emissaries don't sit down and laugh with the witnesses and cheerfully pass the bottle round congratulating the contactee on his good fortune to be a human being and making such a good job of it in the bargain. It is all so serious. Usually the message, the overall philosophy behind it, the pleas for humanity to give up its aggressiveness, to raise the low vibrations of our planetary consciousness to higher frequencies, is couched in such vague terms as to be virtually useless in practical ways of getting out of the mess they assure us we are in. It all sounds too much like a fundamentalist preacher wagging his finger and pointing towards Armageddon while getting his ecological facts all wrong. And so far the most damning evidence is that search as you might neither ETs nor Angels crack even one joke. If the accounts to date give some idea of the humor of our cosmic brothers or the laughter in heaven then we are in for a dull future.

In September of the following year Angelucci experienced a complete blankout for a week. In this time he was not consciously aware of his normal life on earth, although he still appeared to his friends and family as normal.

During this "absence" from Earth he somehow led a double life by appearing simultaneously on a planetoid which was a fragment of what had origi-

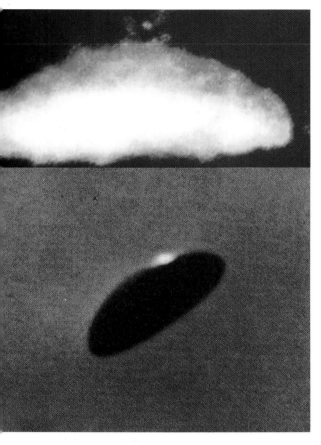

a glorious civilization, to Orfeo it was still seventh heaven. Without exception all the inhabitants were "statuesque and majestic." They moved through a world of colors, of flowers and delightful odors, delicious food, nectar and almost continual harmonious and celestial music.

Here the paradise garden is transported into space. However, from the descriptions given, it seems even this was a pale reflection of the golden Age on Lucifer itself.

Orfeo came to know that his true name was in fact Neptune while the being who posed as this was in fact called Orion.

The phenomenon of the UFO refuses to yield any really plausible explanation. Like angels, the occupants seldom leave any concrete evidence. But, at least, in our technological era they do leave a trace even though they seem pathologically camera shy. These three amateur snapshots have been judged genuine by experts. All three were confirmed by independent witnesses. The top, spectacular, glowing UFO was photographed from a Concorde jet in 1973 and the bottom one was seen in Peru. Below is a concrete sculpture by *Jene Highstein.*

nally been a planet Lucifer. All that remains of the planet is the ring of asteroids which orbit between Mars and Jupiter. It had once been been ruled by a prince, "Son of the Morning," who, through personal ambition and pride, had seceded from the other "etheric Hosts" of the cosmos and had managed to contrive the destruction of his planet.

This is almost a straight, biblical account of Lucifer, the son of the Morning, Bearer of Light who fell from the heavens through pride. Angelucci suggests that here is a simple explanation for this story of Satan but we have mistaken the real source up until now.

However, even if the facilities of the planetoid were meager by comparison to what once had been

In other words he finds that he is both the superior being and the dark ocean of the unconscious himself. Now Orion holds even more dark secrets. The Persians named the constellation Orion as Nimrod, linking him with the rebel angel Shemhazai which would certainly fit the story of Lucifer's fall. Nimrod was also the evil creator of the Tower of Babel which instigated God's ruse to have 70 languages spoken instead of one, thus creating confusion amongst the Tower builders and preventing it from ever reaching heaven. The Greek Orion was a mighty hunter who also rebelled and offended his God. Strange company that Orpheus keeps.

He is increasingly in the company of Lyra, a beautiful female with long golden hair, large eyes and wearing a long Grecian robe.

Here is the age old theme which we find in the Celtic stories of Iseult who has the most outrageous hair as fair as Gold or the Sun. Grainne, another mythical heroine means Sun and as Queen of the fairies lives in a crystal palace, in which all the rays of the sun converge. In Orfeo's descriptions we find crystal buildings full of sunlight and prismatic colors. The Sun Goddesses are all initiators, having a deeper wisdom than that of the hero. Here the mythic archetype appears to Angelucci as he is skillfully guided by Lyra.

Telepathic communications reveal that she arouses erotic feelings in poor Orfeo and the whole company is rather primly shocked.

When she stimulates some pretty earthy instincts in Orfeo it shocks the otherwise calm and superior brothers who see this aggressive male principle as something to be ashamed of and which must be controlled and channeled into higher, almost Tantric realms. Arousal and generalized sexual themes often

appear in encounter reports. Most of the contactee reports of the 1950's tended to be rather prudish and adolescent in their attitudes to female ETs. Invariably, when the ET is human and female the woman conforms remarkably to the fashions of the times. As one enthusiastic contactee, Truman Bethurum wrote of his cute little telepathic ET.
"Her flesh was real and plenty firm,
Her shape was like an expensive urn.
She was just over four feet tall,
And certainly entrancing, all in all."
In the later abductee events the pattern has a more sinister ring. It starts in 1957 when a Brazilian farmer, one Antonio Villas-Boas, was taken on a space ship and forced to have sexual intercourse with an ET. The 1950's still had a certain romantic naivete for the ET turns out to be a very beautiful spacewoman. By the 1960's the Ets had taken a definite turn for the worse. The new breed of space being were often remarkably ugly and sinister. They continued to experiment with willing or unwilling victims, either through artificial insemination or other sexually centered activities.

But all ends well as he masters his baser instincts and is drawn into a more spiritual union with her." I turned and looked into Lyra's wonderful eyes shining with sympathy, compassion and purest love. My own heart swiftly responded. Then suddenly, miraculously we were as one being, enfolded in an embrace of the spirit untouched by sensuality or carnality."

Here, at last, we find the transforming culmination of the Quest. Like that of the Grail it is a search for the identity of the whole being. It is the Unio Mystica, which in Orfeo's case is both a union of the male and female principles but also a merging with the Light of all worlds as in his baptism.

One of the first contactees of beings from space was George Adamski. Here he poses with a rather idealized painting of one of them. While it is likely that his story was an elaborate hoax many accounts of contacts and abductions have an incontestable ring of truth.

The outward transformation in Angelucci is that he drops his former existence and becomes a prophet of the message even if his gospel is met with scorn and ridicule. One wonders whether Ezekiel, Enoch or Elijah had similar receptions to their accounts. Perhaps their times were more sympathetic to belief.

The Quest

Even a man like C.G.Jung offered a very patronizing interpretation of Orfeo's experience. He tells us that, "Orfeo's book is an essentially naive production which for that very reason reveals all the more clearly the unconscious background of the Ufo phenomenon and therefore comes like a gift to the psychologist." He goes on to say that, "The Individuation process, the central problem of modern psychology, is plainly depicted in it in an unconscious, symbolic form which bears out our previous reflections, although the author with his somewhat primitive mentality has taken it quite literally as a concrete happening."

Now, personally, I am surprised at Jung letting that last statement slip by as though it is a normal event of life. Orfeo believed it had happened to him and has "taken it quite literally as a concrete happening." This man, naive or not, has seen something so transforming and powerful that he will endure the ridicule and scorn of his friends and family in speaking out for what he sees as truth. How many of us have the courage of any of our normal convictions to do the same? This man doesn't even have any substantial evidence, save for his own subjective memory, and yet he sallies forth to fight the ever eager detractors, armed with nothing that they will believe in – that is except the emotional charge behind the story. It is that massive charge of energy which was able to shake even the most cynical amongst his critics. What is it within his story which, against all odds, has an authentic ring of truth?

Orfeo seems to have tapped a core of myth much as the ancient story tellers must have done. Perhaps they too re-enacted the events in their minds as if they were actually happening. Maybe in order to do so they took a little help from some drug, an ambrosia in a crystal goblet, before they started the tale. With the aid of a sacred mushroom the whole episode would become an elaborate piece of shamanic theatre – a display for the benefit of an audience who needed to know something about themselves. A play does simulate reality and in it we identify with the Other World.

Maybe the individual mind can put on such a display, for itself, devising a simulated reality in some dramatic episode in which the witness seems to encounter an other worldly being. The incident must be lifelike, so it is presented to the top layer of the conscious mind in such a way that it will be accepted as reality. The otherworldly figure has the necessary authority and power and mystery to resolve the needs of the visionary.

Stripped of all the ET or angelic trappings such encounters are clearly akin to legends of heroes, mighty quests, spirit guides and descents into the under or overworld. But investigators of the phenomena insist that such a story is not an exception. Tales far more bizarre and outlandish are appearing every day. The latest rash of reports of abductions is really quite alarming. Many peoples lives are drastically being altered by the encounters and many of the witnesses are far from being cranks, millennium riders or charlatans. They are as convinced of the validity and substantial nature of the encounter as someone who is sure that he or she has seen the sun rise in the morning.

As can be seen from this account the witness cannot be separated from what he or she has witnessed. The angel, the ET or the UFO are inseparable from the individual who claims to have seen them. And if the stories are true and we are meeting beings who are not of this earth, then it surely is one of the most important events in the history of humankind. If it turns out that it's not true then we

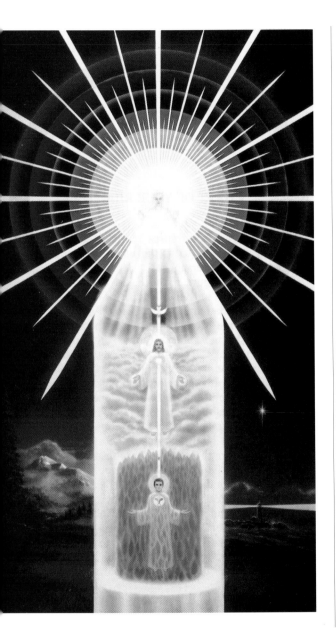

do have a situation which warrants our most careful scrutiny. If thousands upon thousands of people claim that they have seen angels or ETs, UFOs or aliens, and most seem genuine in their convictions that they have, then why on earth do they appear? What is the inner mechanism which triggers such concrete visions and what is the real message behind their appearances?

In order to explore at least one possible explanation it is necessary to turn to Jung's concept of the archetype.

The Image of the Real Self as envisioned by *Elizabeth Claire Prophet.* At the top is visualized the individual essence of God within each of us. Below that is the Mediator or Christ Consciousness which is the Inner teacher of the lower soul evolving through the body. On the left is the stained glass window at *Mare Island Naval Base, California,* showing the **Archangel Gabriel.** It is no accident that most modern representations of angels are to be found in military establishments. Some of the most notable angelic encounters of this century also come from sightings by the armed forces. The best known of these were the Angel of Mons in World War I and the stories from Air Chief Marshal Lord Dowding who tells of aircraft whose crews had been killed continuing to fight on in the Battle of Britain. Dowding was convinced that angels flew these planes. It was during World War II that sightings of alien, aerial craft were first reported. Pilots, at the time, on both Allied and Axis sides, believed their enemy had invented new and unknown craft.

CHAPTER FOUR
Archaic Memories

After All That Has Been Uncovered, still without any sign of concrete evidence, are we then to assume that angels are merely figments of a collective imagination? Are they, as many psychiatrists assert, projections of mysterious archaic memories which are somehow passed down from generation to generation in the form of archetypal images?

Carl Gustav Jung, in his introduction to *Man and his Symbols* tells of a patient, a theologian, who began to have visions. He had previously told Jung "that Ezekiel's visions were nothing more than morbid symptoms" and that when Moses and other prophets heard "voices" speaking to them, they were in fact suffering from hallucinations. You can imagine the panic that this religious scholar felt when something of a similar nature "spontaneously" happened to him.

We are so accustomed to the apparently rational nature of our world that it is scarcely imaginable that anything can happen which cannot be explained away by common sense. But the primitive man, confronted by a shock like that of the theologian, would not doubt his sanity; he would simply turn to his fetishes, his spirits, gods or angels.

Both Freud and Jung discovered exotic and bizarre elements occurring in their patients' dreams which seemed totally unconnected with the dreamer's personal experience. Freud called them archaic "remnants," or mental forms whose presence could not be explained by anything comparable in the everyday experience of that individual's life. They seemed to be aboriginal, innate and inherited shapes within the human mind. These he saw as biological leftovers from prehistoric and unconscious parts of the mind of archaic mankind.

Jung called these *archetypes* or primordial images. The archetype, in his view, was the tendency to build particular internal shapes and forms from more general over-images. He thought they were an instinctive trend, as the impulse for pigeons to "home" or termites to build huge towers. Such a thesis is clearly incompatible with the present conventional assumption that heredity depends upon information encoded within DNA molecules.

However, recent brain research does seem to confirm many of Jung's hunches and has uncovered some fascinating facts about the nature of phenomena which bear close resemblance to the archetypes. We have already been introduced to one model of how the brain functions which suggests that it is layered in three distinctive parts, each of which evolved at different stages of the human development. The oldest core of the brain is what has been popularly termed the "reptilian." The second layer which envelopes it is called the "neo-mammalian," while the third and very thin layer is a more recent acquisition. This thin shell which surrounds the other two brains is the "neo-cortex."

The core, or oldest, brain, in some way stores, or has access to, the archetype tendencies. These are ancient genetic memories, which can be stimulated by some outside situation or in the dream state. As they are evoked and struggle to the surface of consciousness they are inevitably colored and given form and detail by the other two more recent evolutionary layers. It would then seem that the final colorful and expressive form large-

ly depends upon the cultural background and conditioning which is programmed within the neo-cortex. But sometimes the image evoked is so powerful and emotionally charged that the neo-cortex doesn't have the time, or inclination, to interfere.

Jung divided the symbols to which we respond so fiercely and irrationally into "natural" and "cultural." The natural symbols are derived directly from the unconscious contents of the psyche, or in our more recent terms, the reptilian brain. Cultural symbols are collective representations of some of the more persistent and common archetypes which have surfaced enough times to be recognized as "eternal truths" for those societies which have adopted them. These particular archetypes depend upon the various cultural and religious pressures which gave them outward expression.

Angels can be seen as a perfect example of such a cultural symbol which has been embraced in the West. Four thousand years of belief in such creatures has created just such an "eternal truth." It matters not whether they appear a bit tar-

nished in the cold light of our scientific morning; they still exert considerable unconscious power, for they retain much of their original numinosity or magic. Such archetypes continue to be capable of evoking deep emotional charges which are often expressed as irrational prejudices and overwhelming feelings against all reasonable evidence.

Although we are still vulnerable to the archetype, generally speaking, modern humans do appear to have otherwise lost the capacity to respond directly to the numinous world. This is a tragic loss which is probably due to the over-emphasis on rational learning and scientific thinking. So we tend to read *about* the numinous and mysterious rather than actually live it. And just because it is not central to our own

The benevolent guardian angel of the 1940's was, of course, *Superman*. While a cloak replaced the wings, this expression of the all powerful guardian archetype, who battled the evil dragons of satanic violence, greed and injustice, replaced the Archangel Michael in the popular imagination. On the one hand he was timid Mr. Everyman of the city streets and offices and yet in the next instant he was transformed into the supernatural, righteous angel of mercy. Of course he was also one of the very first popular ETs who's home planet was Krypton.

experience we are in considerable danger when some of the wilder aspects of the psychic underworld erupt to the surface and threaten our sense of sanity. This means that we are especially prone to fanatical ideas and to some of the more bizarre expressions of the more powerful symbols which haunt that under-world.

When an 84 year-old woman with rhinestone flecks on her eyelids, orange sherbet hair, wearing a purple chiffon gown arrives in an electric blue Cadillac with a flying saucer on the roof and announces that she is the Archangel Uriel, we are no longer in

Above: **Alchemical images** are perhaps the purest form of archetypes and show their multi-dimensional character most clearly. *Hypnos*, the Greek god of sleep, was the brother of Death and the son of Night. Dreams were once considered to be Divine messages and angels the messengers. †Below left: **Ruth Norman,** known to her 400 Unariun followers as the Archangel Uriel, poses before her electric blue Cadillac. Howsoever whacky this 84 year old widow might appear to many of us, those who have met her are impressed by what they call her "awesome ability to command and influence people and their behavior." And who is in the position to say that she is not an archangel or a reincarnation of a supreme being?

any position to judge whether she is speaking truth or is having a ball at our expense.† Because our belief is second hand we no longer can rely our own gut feelings to tell us whether things are true or false. The original Archangel Uriel might well have such kinky tastes, but in our confusion we cannot tell for sure. On the one hand we yearn for that archetype of higher consciousness, – a Wise man or woman coming from the skies or space to solve all our problems. On the other there is the rational, skeptical, "belief programmed" neo-cortex, censoring all such information which doesn't fit its conditioning. The conflict of these two processes within us all has become chronic.

The "Ancient Wise One" is the common archetype to which we are particularly prone. Children love the image of a guardian angel. However, as adults we are supposed to be able to distinguish between an encounter with an angel and the projections of our unconscious yearning for the comforting security of a father or mother figure to watch over us and guide our actions. From what can be seen of the general state of the world, it is all too obvious that most of us can't. So when someone like Brad Steiger recently writes a book like *The Star People* in which he goes as far as to propose that extra-terrestrial beings of "higher intelligence" may enter the bodies of common pets, there will be plenty of us who credulously accept that "in a sense these animals become guardian angels for a time." For where can we draw the line distinguishing

The photograph by *Joyce Tenneson*, below, shows the dreamlike visions we all share which are particular forms arising from an archetype over-image.

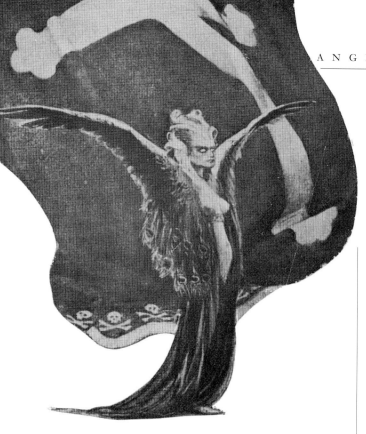

reality, fantasy or plain, unadulterated rubbish, if we are always in a triple-bind with our squabbling three brains?

Having lost contact with our emotional and unconscious centers many of us feel increasingly disquieted and alienated as scientific knowledge continues to proliferate. No longer do rivers contain "the spirit of the waters" otherwise we couldn't pollute them as we do. No voice speaks from the skies, otherwise we could not destroy the ozone layer, and no Pan or great Earth Goddess inhabits the soil to stay our hands from raping the lands. And no angel watches over every blade of grass, encouraging it to grow any more. This terrible loss of the numinous and the mysterious finds its desperate compensations through the archetypes which appear in our dreams, our nightmares and our irrational fears. Modern humans are a curious mixture of scientific convictions and ancient demons. We are so stuffed full of beliefs and outmoded habits of thought that we

cannot deal with the emotional charge behind those dreams.

The angel archetype is the messenger of the higher self. It is the wise being, the advanced soul, the Shaman, the Enlightened master, Superman, or the saint. Our present fascination with highly evolved extra-terrestrial beings who have come to guide humanity, or the galactic messengers of peace and love who contact the chosen few (who will form the new Ark of earth when we blow ourselves up), appears to arise from this extraordinarily potent interior archetype.

Such symbols may represent an individual who is striving towards a full realization of his or her cosmic self. The whole episode in chapter 3, which we have already encountered, of Orfeo Angelucci, would seem to fit this theme.

So it is hardly surprising that the major characteristic of this archetypal image is one of flight. The wild and erratic flight of insects, the soaring flight of birds, the slow wheeling of an eagle, or the flight of the soul as it leaves the restrictions of the body, are images which give an immense sense of freedom and deep satisfaction to the dreamer. But in certain special circumstances, a crisis or an impossible situation, the consciousness of an individual divides. Then that self-same dream image can appear as real to the observer who literally has no way of telling whether the experience is internal or external. It is common for small children to find it difficult to distinguish between events which occur in their dreams and happenings when awake. Even the writer Carlos Castaneda was never quite sure whether the

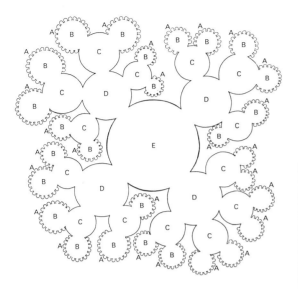

Although Jung felt the collective unconscious was planet-wide, he did suggest that different social conditionings would create different collective psyches as well. The diagram above, showing the overview of the collective unconscious, is by Marie-Louise von Franz. A = Individual ego consciousness; B = Personal unconscious; C = Group unconscious; D = National group unconscious; E = Unconscious which is common to all human beings containing the universal archetypes. Of course this could apply to smaller units like religious groups of those who believed in angels and those who don't.

impossible antics of his sorcerer teachers, Don Genaro or Don Juan, were real flights, or an illusion induced by drugs or a dream state. Yet weird accounts of sages who are able to fly or walk on water are common in many cultures.

It would appear that one doesn't have to look far beyond the projected archetype to see a possible origin of the encounters with angels. In this century Jung has given us a plausible explanation for the phantoms which can materialize so convincingly. In more ancient days witnesses were not armed with such knowledge and may have accepted their own

If anyone imagines that the old Superman image of the 1940's has lost its emotive charge then they should be directed to the Batman film of 1989 which was the all time box office hit. In this we have the age-old conflict of the good angel and the bad. Not so surprising is that Batman's Adversary is the Joker. This corresponds to perhaps the oldest archetype in the book which Jung identified as the Trickster. The Trickster has two faces; one is the Prince of Deception and Lies and the other is the Wise Man.

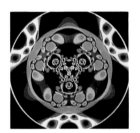

projections of angels at face value. And in a case like that of Angelucci, today, the experience was so powerful that it does not ever seem to have crossed the witness's mind that one part of him might have created the whole episode to in order to communicate to the other part.

An archetype appears to surface when something needs to be communicated. The angel only seems to appear when it has a message to impart.

These twin characteristics of communication and flight are significant. Flight is the hallmark on the sterling silver of the higher self, just as ang-els have "el" tacked firmly on the end of their tails. And the open communication of essential information throughout a whole organism is the hallmark of a healthy being. The appearance of an angel archetype can signify the first step on an individual's journey to become whole; to unify the divided consciousness. If sufficient numbers experience phenomena like angels or ETs then it would appear that the collective unconscious seeks to be healed in the same way.

Left: **Angels turning the Wheels of the Universe,** *14th century French Miniature.* The entire workings of the cosmos were once seen as being caused by a vast world of angels and spirits. The medieval mind loved a sense of the universe as having circular and fixed boundaries with simple divisions like the four compass points. The two mandalas, on the right, painted by one of Jung's patients exhibit the self-same archetypal spirit. Jung suggested that such mandalic symbols correspond most clearly to a psychological expression of the totality of the self and as such have a universal appeal. The modern computer generated image is a mathematical equation which has been transformed into a similar visual form.

CHAPTER FIVE
Elohim The Shining Ones

THERE IS A CERTAIN LAZY ARROGANCE in our modern assumptions of who we are and where we came from. We smile indulgently when we learn of the Anglican Archbishop of Armagh, Dr. James Ussher, who calculated the Creation of the World to have been at precisely 8 p.m. on the 22nd of October 4004 B.C.. We remain amused to learn that the Vice Chancellor of Cambridge University insisted that Adam was not actually created until 9 a.m. on the following day (Greenwich mean time of course).

Most 20th century citizens have Darwin's theory of evolution, with its vastly expanded time scale, firmly established in their minds when rea-

ding of such childish inventions. It is now acknowledged that any hypothesis which gives the age of the universe as less than ten billion years old is absurd. Virtually all the authorities from the various disciplines which examine pre-history, present a comforting assurance that Homo Sapiens Sapiens appeared simultaneously with the last of the Neanderthalers around 32,000 years ago. It was these new humans who created the awesome drawings and paintings to be found in the caves of Lascaux. Orthodox theory then seems to lose track of these superbly gifted and visionary peoples until they turn up twenty thousand years later in Jerico, the Indus valley, Sumer, Crete and Egypt. But by then our ancestors had mysteriously, as if overnight, acquired the most miraculous skills in cutting building blocks, harvesting, storing grain, making long ocean trips in large seaworthy vessels and working metals.

Every year new discoveries in all parts of the world push this historical horizon further and further into the past. But, although there is concrete evidence that our old pre-historical view is wrong, outdated chronologies live on in our minds. The problem seems to be that the sheer weight and mass of archaeological opinion is about as movable as the Pyramids. Too much painstaking labor has gone into the whole theoretical framework for a few curious anomalies to make any dent in the superstructure. However, there are a number of unorthodox views as to how

primitive, foraging, cavemen so abruptly acquired a superb civilization in the Middle and Near East as if from nowhere. Theories of how this could have come about range from the plausible to the outrageous. Van Daniken proposes that we are the experimental product of visitors from outer space. Charles Berlitz suggests that the legendary island of Atlantis once had a thriving and advanced culture even before the painters of Lascaux had found their caves, and that about 12,000 years ago it suffered devastating collapse. He maintains there were survivors who escaped to both the old and the new world with remnants of their once advanced technology. James Churchward spent his whole life searching for concrete evidence of a lost continent in the pacific which he called Mu, supposedly contemporaneous with Atlantis and almost as technologically advanced. He also believed that this great civilization was drowned by some terrible volcanic upheaval which caused the land mass to sink into the ocean. The survivors spread to the South Americas in the east and to China and India in the west, reaching as far as the coast of the Mediterranean. In a more sober account Christien O'Brien would have us believe that there was a small band of luminous individuals who appeared out of nowhere, yet had such a profound

effect upon our ancestors that they remain in our memories, and in our myths and legends, as angels. It is easy to dismiss those writers whose academic or

Far left: Completely recognizable prehistoric animals are seen in this scene from an incised stone of *Ica, Peru (3500 B.C.)*. Even if such creatures were existing in the Peruvian highlands over 100 million years *after* they were supposed to have died out, it is even more remarkable that the hunters who seem to have domesticated these 50 ton pets have also invented the telescope. If a single image can collapse the orthodox historical palace of cards then it is surely this one. The clay statuette from the Julsrud Collection of Acambaro, Mexico appears to depict an allosaurus and the lively scenes of women with huge reptiles suggests that "dragons" still existed 5000 years ago in Mexico. Many so called legends may be far more factual than we have believed. Also from *Ica* the pictograms above can be compared with those immediately beneath from India. 10,000 miles separates these two sites and the pictograms are dated as being 7000 years old.

Below: A reconstructed map of the **Lost Continent of Mu,** with the position of Atlantis. This picture neatly fits the theory of continental drift and of the recently discovered Pacific plate although James Churchward forwarded his theory half a century before these discoveries.

scientific backgrounds do not correspond to what an archaeological expert is supposed to be, but they do us the valuable service of questioning the holy cows of orthodoxy. O'Brien is of especial interest as he offers a closely argued case giving a plausible and very down-to-earth explanation of the origins of the angelic host. And it is an explanation we just cannot afford to ignore. It is a classic within the genre usually labeled "alternative history."

His action centers in the Lebanon and the Mesopotamian basin. Sumer has long been considered the crucible of civilization and about 5,500 years ago it had suddenly blazed forth in a number of closely connected centers within the valley of the Tigris and Euphrates. There was a prodigious explosion of art and artifacts which appeared with seemingly no transitional era between cavemen and the priest-kings who seemed to be the focus of all this activity. The archaeologist and writer, André Parrot, has suggested this sudden flowering could only be attributed to "the genius of the few."

Who these brilliant innovators could have been or where they came from formed the basis of O'Brien's speculation. He suggests that they were a group of advanced agriculturalists who physically appeared to be very different from the indigenous natives of the area. It was these great Lords of Cultivation who created a settlement in the region of present day Lebanon. It was this cultivated area, with its extensive irrigation schemes and rich orchards, which became the model upon which later scholars and priests based the various myths of paradise. It was within the boundaries of this garden of Eden, located in the highlands near Mount Hermon, that we first encounter the seven archangels, their Lord and the infamous Watchers who became the fallen angels.

This is hardly a timid theme. Its very boldness becomes all the more attractive when we discover that there are at least two factual and relatively unadorned accounts describing this settlement and those who lived and worked there. It is a story of the building of a community which might well have been very like a modern Israeli Kibbutz. Between the two records we can build up a picture of its creation, its golden age and the steady decline when the so called angels dispersed and left the area.

What is fascinating about the whole epic is how the Sumerians, the Babylonians and the Hebrews, all of them incontinent "God Makers," managed to so embellish the original story that by the 4th century B. C. the leader of the settlement had

Right: **Anu,** *from the Temple of Abu at Tell Asmar, 2,700 B.C.* This figure and the one of Ninkharsag below, are part of a group of figures who, O'Brien suggests , could have been the original inspiration for the Hebrew Yahweh and His seven Archangels. In this case the female figure is the first representation of the Archangel Gabriel. The huge, staring eyes remind us of the descriptions of the Annanage,"and their eyes burned like lamps," or " his eyes were like fiery torches." We can see the continuing tradition in the 13th century carving of Christ from Madrid.

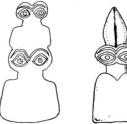

such a process has probably been in action for over five millennia. Religious ideas were plastered over secular events creating legendary stories. Over the years these stories became "truths", which avidly fed upon themselves within whichever closed or "chosen" community they were found. In such greenhouse conditions even the most patently absurd ideas can become stronger and more incontroversial with each ritual and act of worship. In this way two very ordinary, secular events could have become "deified" and given a religious significance which they didn't originally warrant. One is the legend of the Garden of Eden and the other is that this Paradise was peopled by supernatural beings called Angels.

Origins of Heaven

According to eleven clay tablets from Sumer, backed by later Hebraic texts attributed to Enoch the scribe, a small band of mysterious but very much embodied beings arrived in what is now the Lebanon, about ten to twelve thousand years ago. From what we know they were physically unlike the local tribes, being considerably taller, having strangely shining faces with large and brilliant eyes. It is difficult to judge whether this was due to a cosmetic with some glowing property or whether they really were quite alien beings. Whatever the cause of this luminosity these peoples were known as the "Shining Ones." There are many descriptions of these peoples from early sources. Enoch describes them as being very tall and different from any that he had seen in the lowlands. "Their faces shone like the Sun, and their eyes burned like lamps." They were

become God, His lieutenants had been transformed into the archangels and their working assistants were now flying around as angels.

The early Hebrews, in keeping with their wandering nature, were habitual exiles and thus a highly eclectic people. Their scholar-priests freely borrowed from whichever culture they happened to find themselves in, whether it was Egyptian, Sumerian, Babylonian, Assyrian or later Persian, Greek or Roman. Scholarship by its very nature, whether religious or secular, anthropological or archaeological, is notoriously inventive when describing the artifacts of ordinary life. The temptation to spice up an otherwise dull subject often has led to attributing great events to little happenings and creating supernatural phenomena where none actually existed. Thus a chair is transformed into the sacred throne of a priest-king, and a toothpick acquires the aura of a holy relic. In the following account we see how

still around five millennia later when the Old Testament prophet, Daniel, sees one with a girdle of gold round his waist and the same shining characteristic: "His face shone like lightning, His eyes were like fiery torches."

We have already examined a description of an offspring born as a mixture of these peoples and the local inhabitants. This is the biblical Noah, whose supposed father, Lamech, was terrified of his weird baby who filled a darkened room with light. Lamech realizes that he is more likely to come from the loins of the "Sons of the Lord in Eden" than from his own. He complains to Methuselah that Noah "is not like you and me – his eyes are like the rays of the Sun and his face shines. It seems to me that he is not born of my stock, but that of the Angels" (En CVI:1-8).

It would seem that whoever these "angels" were, they were not restricted to the Middle East, for the Tibetan *Book of Dzyan* speaks of "luminous sons" who are the "producers of the form from no-form." One leader "shines forth as the Sun; he is the blazing divine dragon-serpent of wisdom." Thousands of miles away, in Sumeria, these same luminous

Above left: **The Kharsag Epic,** *2700 B.C. from the original baked clay cylinder.* Above: **Eye Goddess** statuettes from Old Europe. During the seventh to the fifth millennium B.C. early peoples of southeastern Europe developed a unique civilization which owed nothing to the developments of the Near East and in fact pre-dated them. What is fascinating is that these peoples independently discovered how to work copper and gold and even evolved a rudimentary script. Their extensive worship of the Eye Goddess does suggest that another group of "Shining Ones" had sown the seeds of civilization two thousand miles from Eden at roughly the same time the first settlement appeared in the Lebanon. The two Egyptian eyes of Horus suggest a similar source of inspiration although these did not appear until five thousand years later.

gar — sag
Kharsag

an — ki — bi — da — ge
heaven earth

erim — an — ni
and assembly heavenly

dingir anu — a — nun — na — ge
lord Anu sons great (of)

im — tu — ne
entered they

es — a — zu
many wise ones

peoples were called the One-eyed and Two-eyed serpents. "Listen ye Sons of Earth, to your instructors, the Sons of Fire" could as well be said in the Lebanon as in Tibet. Whichever part of earth they settled in, the newcomers set about teaching the local inhabitants the cornerstones of civilization such as writing, metal working, planting, cultivating and harvesting grain. Such knowledge would have been overwhelmingly impressive to the indigenous cave dwelling and foraging peoples. In the Sumerian tablet we are about to examine it says that before the coming of the shining dragon-serpents of fire, "Man had not yet learned how to make clothes, or permanent dwellings. People crawled into their dwellings on all fours; they ate grass with their mouths like sheep; they drank storm-water from the streams."

There are other Sumerian tablets which speak of "luminous beings" who drove through the sky in barks and disc-shaped ships of fire. In these epics they descended from the stars to teach and impregnate the daughters of Man in order to create a new kind of conscious being. Having completed their work they then flew back to the stars.

Kharsag Epic

The particular epic which concerns us is a very early version of this story and one which was recorded on eleven clay tablets which were copied sometime in the third millennium B.C. This so-called Kharsag epic actually described a period which dates back almost twelve millennia. The story is told in simple and secular terms with no religious or supernatural overtones at all.

A group of wise sages (it depends upon one's taste whether these are seen as aristocratic invaders, aliens, extra terrestrials, survivors from Atlantis or

Mu, or just tall agricultural tribesmen) arrived near Mt. Hermon in the highlands near the present border of the Lebanon and settled in one of the high valleys. They called the whole area Eden and their major settlement Kharsag. They appeared very dif-

Left: **Stile of Naram-sin.** Christian O'Brien suggests that this could be a commemoration of the descent of the Annanage upon Mt. Hermon. His interpretation of the original Kharsag text reads, "At Kharsag, where Heaven and Earth met, the heavenly assembly, the Great Sons of Anu, descended – the many Wise Ones." The two brilliant disks do appear to be a mystery although the seemingly dismembered figure beneath the foot of the leading figure does suggest other interpretations. So many Sumerian artifacts are open to so many conjectures it is as well to remember most of what we know of these extraordinary peoples is just theory.
Above: **The scribe Dudu** (*Sumer 2,500 B.C.*) or as is believed by some, Enoch, the "writer of truth."

ferent from the indigenous tribes of the area who mostly inhabited the lowlands.

With the help of a separate group, who are later identified as the "Watchers" in a parallel version of the epic by Enoch (En VI:6): And they were in all two hundred, who descended in the days of Jared on the summit of Mount Hermon," these settlers ploughed the land, created enclosed fields, sowed grain of at least three different varieties, planted orchards and trees. They bred herds of cattle and sheep and housed them in pens and buildings which were well watered. In a relatively short space of time the settlement prospered and there was a surplus of food. But all this had required a tremendous physical effort. The Watchers, who seemed to bear the main burden of the manual labor, became restless and finally rebelled against their overlords. If these epics are anything to go by these lords then hit upon a solution which has affected us all. On later tablets, copied about 1635 B. C., called *Atrahasis*, we hear the lords agreeing to the workers' demands. "Their work was very heavy and caused them much distress...while Belet-ili is present let her create a 'lullu' – a man, and let the man do the work." And such a man was created from the "blood" of a Lord mixed with a mysterious "clay." We shall shortly return to this fascinating theme.

Building recommenced and a reservoir was con-structed above the settlement to provide round-the-year water for a complex irrigation scheme. When all this was done the sages had residences built, especially one large principal house which was brightly lit by strange and unconventional means.

Now this, in very abbreviated terms, is the story of the golden age of Kharsag as told in the second of the eleven clay tablets and cylinders. This whole program was accomplished in seven clearly separated parts which could have contributed to the later Judaic and Christian version of the creation myth, also in seven parts.

When Enoch the scribe first visited the self-same settlement about nine thousand years ago, he had first been summoned by two very tall men whose faces shone like the sun, with burning and radiant eyes. Our attention is drawn to the next description: "Their clothes were remarkable – being purplish with the appearance of feathers; and on their shoulders were things which I can only describe as 'like golden wings'."

Enoch then attended a meeting in which a selection was to be made of those who were to receive an extension of their life span. This was supposedly granted by imbibing the life-extending fruits of the Tree of Life which grew within the settlement. Enoch attended this meeting seven millennia before the birth of Christianity and yet even by this time

he was referring to the original Annanage or Shining Ones as Angels. It is difficult to tell when the transformation happened, as the accounts which have come down to us are copies made by later Hebrew scribes from other copies. There is no guarantee that the scribes have not translated El-ohim into angels in order to be comprehensible to their new readers.

Anyway, Enoch asks his angel companion who the four outstanding presences were who greeted the Lord of Spirits. (Enoch XL:1-10) "And he said, The first was Michael, the kindly and patient one; the second was Raphael who is responsible for treating illnesses and wounds among the people, here; the third was Gabriel, and the fourth was Phanuel (Uriel) who is responsible for dealing with those who are selected to receive an extension to their normal life-span."

From the general tone of Enoch's account it seems that even if there has been a change of name these angels remain very down-to-earth and even the reference to life extension is not necessarily supernatural. There has never been a shortage of life enhancing recipes throughout the ages including the daily advertisements in our own times.

So we now see how the Lords of cultivation, who were once identified with the original El-ohim or Shining Ones, became the angels. In the legends

following Enoch's account, the Lord of Spirits, is deified and is transformed into the Hebrew God, Yahweh. The ordinary chair has become a throne in heaven.

Even without the addition of supernatural powers these peoples were obviously alien to the area. Whether they were alien to earth is one of those questions best left to more courageous investigators. For my money I would look towards either the Atlantic or the Pacific.

The settlement of Eden prospered for a while and then something went seriously wrong. First there was a sickness which seems to have been caused by eating contaminated food. This particular episode took on a more supernatural nature in a later and

Above left: **Assyrian Winged Genie,** *885-860 B.C.* Above: **The Assyrian Tree of Immortality,** *850 B.C.* This magical tree is to be found in legends as far apart as Polynesia, where a maiden is tricked into eating the fruit of a paradise tree by a serpent and so loses her immortality; in Iceland, where it is guarded by the goddess *Iduna* or in China where it becomes the Peach Tree of Immortality guarded by the serpent witch *Hsi Wang Kui.* In the Islamic version of the temptation of Adam and Eve the evil serpent tells them that "your Lord forbade you from this tree only lest you should become angels." In the Assyrian relief we see a mysterious winged chariot hovering above.

well known version of the Sumerian Paradise. In this we are told of a number of Lords who arose from the sea. (Atlantis, Mu?). Their leader was Anu who was accompanied by Enki, Enlil and Nammu (Ninlil or Ninkarsag). They created a garden in the heavens and Ninlil fashioned a new creature who could be a servant to the Gods – man. At first it was a golden age of harmony and accord. The gardens flourished under the watchful eye of many goddesses of vegetation. Many new plants were created. But, so the story unfolds, Enki ate eight plants created by the Goddess Uttu before she had time to name them. This seemingly innocent act threw Uttu into a such a rage that she laid a terrible curse on Enki and he became ill. The other Gods were helpless as the gardens turned to desert and man had to go out into the wilderness.

In the earlier, secular, Kharsag epic the reason given was far more within our own experience. The food had been badly prepared. After, what appeared to have been a disastrous case of salmonella poisoning, the leader "established these wise precautions…In Eden, thy cooked food must be better cooked. In Eden thy cleaned food must be much cleaner… eating meat is the great enemy." This is hardly supernatural stuff, and these are the angels and archangels who had fallen ill.

Shortly after this, according to the *Atra-hasis*, another later Akkadian text of the same story, the Lady Ninlil appeared to conduct a genetic experiment with the local tribes. "She separated fourteen sections of the culture. She put seven sections on the right, and seven on the left, separating them by a partition. Fourteen experienced foster-mothers had been assembled. Seven were impregnated with the male cultures, and seven with the female cultures. The Birth-Lady, creatress of destiny, had them

impregnated in pairs in her presence. So Ma-mi (Ninlil) laid the foundations of the human race." Two of the fourteen were, as you might have guessed, Adam and Chawwah (Eve) and thus the first generation of the great patriarchal line of the Jews.

Now, according to the epic, this had been a controlled experiment which supposedly had been designed to combine some of the qualities of the Lords with those of the peoples of the lowland. And we are to find in the later story that the Annanage Lords were at considerable pains to keep the patriarchal line of what became the Jewish peoples an uncontaminated stock. Perhaps they just enjoyed Jewish humor. There are a number of current theories which have curious links with this story. The anthropologist, Stan Gooch, suggests that Jews are the direct descendants of a rare breed of half Cro-Magnon and half-Neanderthal stock which has been found to have lived in the area 20,000 years ago. Certainly there is no argument that the Hebrews have the greatest claim to be linked with the angels. As we have seen angels can be viewed as very much a Jewish invention. Is it possible that in their turn the Jews were very much an angelic creation?

The second calamity to disturb the peace of the paradise gardens happened when the socially lower artisan angels, who we now know of as the Watchers, or in Hebrew, as the *Eyrim*, dispensed with the artificial procedures altogether, finding the time-honored and sensual methods far more to their fancy.

This legend has already been introduced in the Treasury. They developed an insatiable lust for the daughters of men and begat many children by them.

The results were disastrous; the offspring were monstrous and aggressive. The Watchers were described as gigantic but their progeny were even larger. The whole lowland area was ravaged by these mutants, so much so that the Lords in Eden, albeit with much regret, decided to destroy them. This destruction coincided with the flood, or as one theory goes, the massive reservoir of water at the settlement was opened to devastate the valley below and drown the terrible brood. .

The settlement itself seemed to have suffered from some natural disaster around 5000 B. C. and the various leaders resettled in the Mesopotamian Valley eventually founding the early Sumerian City-States. The "angels" eventually dispersed over the whole of the Near and Middle East, eventually moving into Europe and reaching as far as Britain. They left in their wake images of shining peoples, eleven folk, Valkyries, and Giants. But, of course, their greatest legacy of all was the myth of angelic lore.

So far there is nothing to suggest for what reason, apart from being excellent farmers who, on occasions appeared with an oddly mysterious

A Shining One, *from Sumer, 2600 B.C..* The gold leaf on the face and hands heightens the effect and reminds us of the "face of burnished gold."

luminosity, these people attained the status of God and angel by the second millennium B.C. Certainly they did manage to teach the locals a thing or two and possibly they meddled a bit with their genes, but even so this would hardly generate the sort of worship and awe that later texts exhibit. The reason is both simple and yet difficult to swallow. It is recorded that they had two mysterious powers which were really awesome in those days: that of *flight* and that of *light*. These are the two major attributes they share with the angels.

Enoch is very specific here "They (the angels) lifted me up and placed me on what seemed to be a cloud, and this cloud moved, and going upwards I could see the sky around and, still higher, I seemed to be in Space." (Secrets of Enoch III:1)

Again in the Book of Enoch we find (XIV:8) : "Behold, in the vision a cloud invited me and a mist summoned me, and the course of the stars and the lightnings sped by me, and the winds in the vision caused me to fly and lifted me upward and bore me to heaven." This is almost word for word the description given by Orfeo Angelucci in the 1950's when he was irresistibly drawn towards the UFO belonging to the space brothers of Lucifer. His first impression, before stepping inside it was of a "huge, misty soap bubble...The walls were lit mysteriously and looked like ethereal mother-of-pearl stuff." It is at this point in the narrative that our credulity can be stretched in one of two ways. Either these Shining Ones really were substantial beings who had supernatural powers, or they were in possession of a technology which put them ten thousand years in advance of their lowland competitors. Whichever way, where is the evidence to support either claim? This is of course the point at which any serious researcher finds it difficult to meet the eyes of the

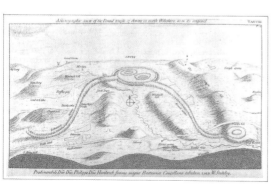

funding committees and when any reader starts to put the book down. Yet if half the citizens of the United States of America can accept the existence of a supernatural host of angels then surely our mind could be open to the possibility that there have been civilizations before us which had technologies equal or even superior to our own.

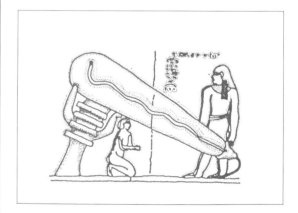

Above: **An electric light bulb** *from a carving 2,500 B.C. at Dendra, Egypt.* It is known that the ancient world used electric current generated by efficient little batteries which were probably used for electroplating metals with gold or silver. Reconstructions of these primitive batteries reveal they could produce about 2.5 volts each. Connected in series they might have lit the six foot light bulb shown in the carving. The serpent-like filament held up by high-tension insulators, from which run braided cables, connected to what is clearly a transformer of some kind, could have had a brilliance equal to the headlamp of a modern car. *Left:* An 18th century engraving of the great stone serpent at Avebury in England, seen, as if from the air. Compare it with the winged serpent from Egypt or the flying vehicle above. The Avebury stones are thought to be contemporary with the Pyramids and are claimed to store powerful earth currents called the Dragon.

As it happens, there are many intriguing examples throughout the world of ancient images of flying machines, from Egyptian toy gliders over four thousand years old to models of delta-winged jet aircraft found in Peru or mysterious rocket-like space vehicles found on the walls of temples deep in the jungles of South America.

But so far, it is true, an actual working example has not been unearthed or dragged up in a deep sea fishing net off the Azores.

So, not only are we understandably skeptical, but also, we still possess a mindset of civilization which is linear rather than cyclic. Yet Plato could be right when he insists, in his two books on Atlantis, that periodic catastrophes have left the few survivors "destitute of letters and education to begin all over again as children." In Plato's account, an Egyptian priest informs him of the many times that humankind has reached golden era's of knowledge and wisdom, only to lose everything in some calamity which erases all the evidence of those times. Yet those periods live on in myths of supernatural beings with legendary powers. With some justification the phenomenon of angels appears to fit this pattern.

Evidence of earlier epochs, when humans could have flown does exist. The Sumerians, Akkadians, Babylonians and Persians, all have records and pictures of flying machines and winged beings. Ahura Mazda, the Lord of Light, was supposed to fly in a disc and this was a very popular subject in bas reliefs. There are even the well known accounts in the Sanskrit texts of India which describe "an apparatus which moves by inner strength like a bird." That "...can move in the sky from place to place...The secret of building flying machines... that do not break, cannot be divided, do not catch fire... and cannot be destroyed. The secret of making flying machines stand still...invisible...overhearing con-

versations in enemy flying machines... of taking pictures of the interiors of enemy flying machines...of making beings in enemy flying machines unconscious and destroying them." These brief extracts are from a text by Maharishi Bharadvaya, an Indian seer who lived thousands of years ago, who is almost offhand in giving details of aircraft. Similar details are to be found within the *Vedas* and the *Mahabharata* which supposedly dates back to 7016 B. C. This precise dating is valid if we are to reconstruct the time span required for the specific constellations described within the text to have appeared in the ancient skies. Add to these curiosities the little models of airplanes found within the Peruvian Highlands, or those winged toys of Egypt, and we begin to accumulate a modest, yet nonetheless solid body of evidence which clearly points to the possibility that silvery flying machines were probably climbing into the skies long before the two Wright brothers reinvented the device.

Friar Joseph, the Flying Monk

There is an alternative, yet no less startling explanation: these mysterious peoples could have learnt to fly without mechanical means. This is not so far fetched as at first may appear. Throughout history there have been a number of authenticated, although inexplicable cases of men and women who could sail into the air. One of the most famous of these cases was that of St. Joseph of Copertino whose miraculous flights in the 17th century were attested to by many influential and respected witnesses.

Except for this strange talent, Joseph was in no way remarkable. On the contrary, one Bishop even described him as *idiota*, which could be interpreted as innocent, although brother Joseph was also nicknamed "open mouth" as his lower jaw always hung open. Feeble-minded or not, Joseph could fly. It first occurred in the middle of mass: the monk could not restrain his ecstatic mood and drifted up from his seat to land on the high altar twenty feet away. Such zeal did not escape the Pope who ordered him to Rome. Joseph was so ecstatic in the Pontiff's presence that he floated off the ground for all to see. So high did he go that it was commented that he even showed due propriety by having on underwear for the occasion. In Assisi he was so overcome by the enthusiastic reception of the crowd that he sailed over the onlookers to land on the altar and embrace the statue of the Virgin. Once he flew into the topmost branches of a tree on overhearing a fellow monk remark on the beauties of the day. He demonstrated his bizarre power too many times for it to be dismissed as a mass hallucination. He could even help others to fly, as he demonstrated when he healed a demented aristocrat by seizing him by the hair and taking off. This time he flew for a record fifteen minutes. The Church is often a little embarrassed by such miraculous displays. But before they decided to canonize this rather awkward saint, the authorities examined the sworn testimonies of hundreds of witnesses including a Pope, two Kings, the Duke of Brunswick and his philosopher friend Leibnitz, who was certainly no credulous fool. Even when the doctor was cauterizing Joseph's leg just before he died, the surgeon was shocked to find that the friar was floating six inches above the chair.

It is certainly difficult to know quite what to make of this story. The sworn depositions of so many intelligent people suggest that Joseph could, indeed, fly. If a simpleton like this monk could do so, then surely it is not beyond others to use a human capacity which, for some reason or another, apparently lies idle. The Shining Ones of the Middle East could have discovered the magical secret by stumbling on one of our inherent potentials.

Illumination

If it is difficult to unearth concrete evidence as far as flight is concerned, what of the second "advanced" technology? In the case of electric light there is at last real and substantial evidence of its use as far back as five thousand years ago. There are, for instance, actual examples of efficient electrical batteries which have been unearthed in Egypt and Baghdad. Many of these devices were actually used to electro-plate metals with gold and silver. There is, however, one example of a huge device depicted in a wall carving in Egypt, dating from 2500 B.C. which clearly resembles an electric light bulb.

Returning to the settlement for a moment we read in the earliest tablet:

"At the House of Joy and Life, the bright dwelling, Where the destiny of Man was established; The splendid place of Flaming Brightness.".

Another reference was to a "Brilliant, glowing House" which was obviously very different from the mud walled dwellings of the lowlands lit by either oil lamps or rush torches.

In Enoch's later account of the same house it is difficult to know whether his awed description is the genuine response of a simple country man who lived at the edge of pre-history and who had never seen brilliant light at night time, or a case of the "chair transformed to a throne." But Enoch was known as a writer of truth and most of his descriptions are remarkably free of religious or supernatural trappings. He enters a building with glistening white stone walls which was brilliantly lit. The floor was white marble and illuminated fountains seemed to be playing ("fiery sentinels and heavenly rain").

"In every respect, the inside was so magnificent, and spacious, that I cannot describe it to you. Its floor was brilliantly lit, and above that were bright lights like planets, and its ceiling, too, was brilliant.

"I looked and saw a high Chair, there, with the appearance of crystal, shining like the courses of the Sun; and I saw Cherubim. And from under the Chair came a blaze of light such that I could not bear to look at it.

"And on it was a stately Being – his clothes shone more brightly than the Sun, and were whiter than any snow."

This is a description, written over 9000 years ago, of a room which quite plausibly could have been lit by the electric power produced from the simple chemical batteries which have been unearthed in the region. So the dark pre-history of the cave dwellers might not have been quite so dark as our history books so solidly proclaim.

This tentative scenario of the origins of real, down to earth angels could explain how a group of beings, with far less miraculous powers than gods or angels, but having, nonetheless, an awesome technology compared with the primitive peoples in the area, could have been operating in the Bible lands over ten millennia ago. But where could they have picked up such a technology and where did these proto-angels come from in the first place? There are a number of plausible explanations without resorting, as many authors have done, to extra-terrestrial intervention.

Angels over the Oceans

There have been various theories as to the location and fate of the legendary island of Atlantis or of the pacific continent of Mu. For the sake of brevity and following the meticulous Mayan calendar, the destruction and sinking of Atlantis was recorded as taking place in the year 8498 B. C. It is suspected that a small asteroid penetrated the Earth's atmosphere and crashed into what is now the Azores. Equally plausible was that overzealous Atlantaean scientists managed to blow themselves up, causing a similar catastrophe on the other side of the world. Whatever the reason, there is evidence to suggest that small parties of survivors from both Atlantis and Lemuria fanned out into their old colonies on the remaining continents. Some entered Southern Europe, North Africa, Egypt and the Middle East. It is surmised that some of these belonged to an elite scientific priesthood or aristocracy, who had advanced technologies and in some cases considerable wisdom. It was these who appeared with shining faces. Enoch did actually specifically state that these beings could, if they wanted, appear as normal, although exceptionally tall men, without this brilliant aura.

With such a background it is entirely feasible that such a group arrived in the Bible lands 12,000 years ago. It was they who transformed the myths and legends of the peoples who lived there. Of all the fabulous, supernatural, extra-terrestrial, psychic and psychological possibilities open to us, this explanation of how the whole phenomenon of angels suddenly appeared is one of the most persuasive and certainly one of the least suspect. It would also explain the powerful link between angels and the chosen peoples. For howsoever complex the later Christian heavenly hierarchy became, angels are at heart a Jewish creation. It must be remembered that the official language of angels was Hebrew long before they ever had to learn Greek or Latin.

CHAPTER SIX
Heavenly Hypotheses

S O FAR, IN THE SEARCH for what angels might really be, we have examined some of the most plausible explanations. But these in no way exhaust the hypothetical field.

In this chapter we will widen our vision and extend the horizons of speculation. It is regretted that space doesn't permit any "in depth" study of any of the various themes, but it does highlight the richness of the subject matter. We are beginning to appreciate that Angels can appear as all things to all men.

Creating What We Think

Modern day physicists and psychologists would agree that we tend to see what we expect to see. The moment a scientist attempts to observe atomic sub-particles, the very method he uses appears to influence the behavior of the particles. In fact his very presence, his mind frame and expectancies seem to basically alter their microscopic patterns. In quantum physics the observer becomes part of his observed world and can no longer be sure that so-called objective phenomena aren't just a thought cast in emptiness, or, at best, a shifting stream of thought-fields of possible worlds. The universe is no longer the solid substantive place as understood by the Victorians only a century ago. "You create what you think" has become one of the most fashionable idioms of our New Age.

We are familiar with the extremes of this concept. Psychiatric patients are known to sometimes live in interior worlds which they experience as being external and real. Their universe in no way corresponds to the one the rest of us collectively agree upon. But who is the final arbiter of what is real and what is dream? The visions of the schizophrenic are often closer to those of the mystic or the quantum physicist, than to those of the normal man in the street. Chuang Tzu once dreamt that he was a butterfly, but then asked his disciples whether it might be that the butterfly was actually dreaming he was Chuang Tzu.

Normalcy is a relative term which can only be supported by a mass composed of sheer numbers. What 99 out of every 100 people *agree* to witness is what we call both normalcy and reality. But normalcy is not necessarily reality. Truth has usually been found to be a lonely business and has seldom followed the majority.

So we cannot discount the possibility that witnesses of angels and other non-human beings could be the lonely one percent who see a reality which is denied to the rest of us.

Multiple Image

While most people could claim to be relatively sane, or at least normal in relation to those who are institutionalized, few can be said to be a whole and integrated entity. We are, what might be considered, a collection of fragments, a cluster of disparate parts. A schizophrenic is one extreme example of a personality which is divided in some way.

In an entirely different disorder of the brain, in which the bridge across its two hemispheres has in some way been damaged, the subject can be doing up the buttons of his coat with the right hand while the left hand is undoing them. Neither actions are being recognized by its the opposite compartment.

In some degree we all make unconsciously conflicting decisions most of the time. On one conscious level we are smiling at the wife or the boss, whilst on another "island" there is a volcano of resentment or anger which could explode any minute. A drunken state can suddenly bring back remembrances of similar occasions which have been totally forgotten when sober. Under deep hypnosis memories are uncovered of events which have otherwise been suppressed and therefore completely unavailable to the conscious part of the mind.

In a way everyone suffers from a weird kind of waking amnesia. Human beings are sleepwalkers who keep bumping into unrecognized chunks of their own drifting personalities. These fragments appear to retain memory stores which are lost or inaccessible to the rest of the conscious personality.

In attempting to show that such a mechanism could underlie encounters or visions of angels, it is instructive to briefly examine two of the most famous and well documented cases of fragmented or multiple personalities. These are those of Doris Fischer and Christine Beauchamp. These two, or more accurately nine, personalities enthralled psychiatrists and para-psychologists around the turn of this century and still are cited as classic cases.[†]

Stand Up the Real Me

By the time Doris Fischer was eighteen she had no less than *five* clearly separate personalities sharing her body. Doris herself was an intelligent, likable, conventional girl who blanked out every now and then. During these "blank outs", comas or sleep, the other four characters emerged unbeknown to her.

The first was Margaret, who seemed in every way Doris's polar opposite. Margaret was noisy where Doris basically was quiet and amusing where Doris was serious. Margaret was a feisty, mischievous ten year old tomboy. She was aware of Doris and could "go in and out" apparently at will. Margaret was also aware of the third personality which she called "sick Doris". This one, called Mary Anne, appeared suddenly at the moment of the death of Doris's mother. She had no memory whatever and had to be taught how to speak by Margaret. Mary Anne remained a timid, shy and rather wooden personality who was often unwell, hysterical and generally nervous. Her major occupation was knitting. The lowest entity in the hierarchy was named Jane, who was little more than a tape recorder for the conversations of the others, which she could "replay" verbatim even if the original event had been years before. The most mature self of all was called Ariel, who appeared only when Doris was asleep. She was the wisest amongst the hierarchy and the only one who had an overview of all the other characters.

However, she claimed to be a separate spirit who had been summoned to help. Each personality profoundly changed Doris's whole physical form. Photographs taken when each of the characters was in command seem to show different persons who had a certain family likeness. Doris had no sense of smell or taste and was often unaware of her bladder through some form of anesthesia, so she often wet herself. Mary Anne appeared to have no sensitivity in her nerves especially below her waist. Margaret was the only one who was acutely aware of her body and could even see in the dark.

Christine 1, Christine 2, Sally and B-4

Equally famous at the time and as well documented was the case of Christine Beauchamp. She had fragmented into four main characters. Christine One was in poor health, nervous and suffered from uncontrolled movements of the body. When under light hypnosis Christine Two emerged was very relaxed, open and intelligent. The third of the company was Sally who, like Doris's Margaret was a mischievous and high spirited opposite to Christine One. She contemptuously referred to Christine as a "goody fool." As Christine had no idea of the existence of Sally she was often the butt of her "twin's" pranks, suddenly awakening to find Sally's cigarette still in her mouth and a glass of unlady-like wine in her hand. Physically Sally was as full of life and energy as Christine was depleted. Sally would take off for long walks, knowing well that poor Christine would suddenly find herself miles from home totally exhausted. The last personality that the Pittsburg psychoanalyst, Dr. Prince, discovered was labeled B-4: she seems much like Ariel in the case of Doris. B-4 was more mature, responsible and self possessed, but had a high opinion of herself.

Colin Wilson, to whom I am indebted for bringing these particular cases to my attention, neatly sums up, in his very perceptive *Mysteries*, a bewildering interaction between three characters locked in one body. "Sally and B-4 loathed one another. Christine accepted Sally's practical jokes with passive fatalism; B-4 hated them and often repaid in kind. On one occasion, Christine set out for New York to find a job. Sally got off the train at New Haven and took

a job as a waitress. Christine found the work exhausting; B-4 hated it as being below her dignity. One day B-4 walked out of the job, pawned Christine's watch and returned to Boston. Sally took over and decided to spite B-4 by refusing to return to her old lodging; instead she took a new one. Christine 'came to' in a strange bed, having no idea of where she was or how she got there."

Eventually we discover that both Doris and Christine were able to integrate, albeit a little uneasily, all their fragments into a single character. This was done at a cost. Doris's Mary Anne eventually regressed and knowing she was about to "die" wrote a letter to Margaret disposing of her things. Margaret herself became younger and younger until one day she appeared laughing and then left for good. In the case of Christine, Dr. Prince decided to suppress Sally who resisted the sentence. "I won't! I won't be dead," she screamed, "I have as much right to live as she has!" As it happened she did make an occasional appearance even when Christine was far more integrated, managing to play a few practical jokes on her more conventional counterpart.

Multiple Personality Disorder, (MPD), is now known to be far more widespread than was once believed. The recent case of a woman in Massachusetts called M. M.George (an amalgam of her three major personalities; Mary, Monica and George) is as extreme as that of Christine, eighty years before. She tells us, "My core personality went out at age six, and my host personality, Mary, took over. Only one person in my family knows. That's the case with most multiple personalities. You just don't see it if you are not looking for it. My first husband, poor dear, never knew what hit him. See, part of my personality went to sleep for a year and woke up married to Eddie – that's my ex-husband – and I could not tolerate him. Monica was the one who married him." Mary didn't know Monica even existed.

These two cases have been cited as extremes, but milder forms of multiple personality are not at all uncommon. Most of us exhibit less bizarre versions. Simultaneously driving a car, talking idly with a passenger and thinking about what you will do when you get home, effectively involves three minds which are operating independently of one another. It might be an unconscious robot which steers the wheel, a semi-conscious robot which politely exchanges smiling niceties and a raging jealous lover who is prepared to shoot his wife. If there is an emergency like a near collision with another car there is suddenly a total response of yet another vibrant consciousness which sweeps away all the others in a split second.

I have gone to some lengths to demonstrate that we are not the single entity most of us fondly imagine. Actually we are a crowd.

In order to know how this fact could generate an encounter with an angel or an ET, consider what Elias Canetti perceptively says of crowds. He distinguishes two sorts of crowd. One is an *open* crowd which is the universal phenomenon we all know. As soon as it begins to exist it wants to consist of more and more people. It is unbounded and continues to exist just so long as it continues to grow. The moment it reaches its goal or stops growing it disperses.

The *closed* crowd, by comparison, stops growth and opts for permanence. It defines clear boundaries which limit growth but also postpones dissolution. Both types exist so long as they have "*an unattained goal.*" The implication is that this is true of our inner crowd as well, which only continue to exist while the goal of integration is unattainable. As soon as an individual gains some degree of individuation the crowds disperse. This happens as much with multiple personalities as with cases of abductions by ETs, or messages from angels.

This tendency to divide the self into separate parts which have separate memories and which are blocked from those of other "fragments" could form the basis of the encounter incident. Some powerful stimulus blocks the memory of an experience while at the same time leaving tantalizing and emotionally charged remnants within one or more of the other "fragments". We have already seen that the brain is composed of three evolutionary layers which have a degree of autonomy and independence, and that the archetypes seem to be triggered from or by the cerebellum. Any division of consciousness means that archetypal images which surface from the more primitive parts of the brain can actually manifest themselves to other less critical parts of our minds as if they were concrete reality. Under stress or unusual circumstances the likelihood of powerful exchanges, in the form of *waking dreams*, could occur between fragments. One fragment is the actor while the other becomes the audience.

As Jung suggests, the psychological and spiritual preoccupation of our times appears to be a striving towards unity, wholeness and individuation. This takes the form of a conscious or unconscious quest for a holy or *whole* answer to our increasing sense of feeling divided within ourselves and separated from the world about us. We all seem to be frantically trying to arrest the diaspora of our various parts which seem to be drifting off in every direction.

These drifting fragments are also trying to communicate with one another and will use any means to do so, including the images of ETs and angels. After experiencing a powerful encounter with an extra-terrestrial, one witness remarked with considerable insight: "I think the entire thing was a fantastic, beautifully executed theatre…a display solely for my benefit to convey something that right now is unbeknown to me".

Gregory Bateson, in describing a schizophrenic patient, has this to say: "It would appear that once precipitated into psychosis, the patient has a course to run. He is, as it were, embarked upon a voyage of discovery which is only completed by his return to the normal world, to which he comes back with insights different from those of the inhabitants who never embarked on such a voyage. Once begun, a schizophrenic episode would appear to have as definite a course as an initiation ceremony – a death and rebirth."

This must remind us forcibly of the experiences of the prophet, Ezekiel[†] and Orfeo Angelucci along with most of the abductee cases, like that of Whitley Striber who records his experiences in *Communion*. Both ETs and angels are the rare stuff of the "transformation myth."

This is the myth in which the plot hinges around the theme of *communication*. Angels are symbolic messengers of the Divine, just as ETs are the messengers of higher beings. In such myths of communication these messengers of the gods bring about a higher transformation in the chosen individual. Could it be that we are observing the drama which surrounds an individual who is restoring all the fragmented parts of his or her being into one whole? The magic of the story can only work, however, if the hero or heroine is unaware that they are stepping inside their own myth.

The science fiction writer Philip Dick went beyond both angel and alien, for he went to the source. He experienced an encounter with God. The Almighty "fired a beam of pink light at my head." His own mind was then invaded "by a transcendentally rational mind, as if I had been insane all my life and had suddenly become sane." His ensuing confusion arose from the fact that "this rational mind was not human. It was more like an artificial intelligence. On Thursdays and Saturdays I would think it was God, on Tuesdays and Wednesdays I would think it was extra-terrestrial, sometimes I would think it was the Soviet Union Academy of Sciences trying out their psychotronic, microwave, telepathic transmitter." Dick didn't once consider the possibility that the whole phenomenon was born within himself, but insisted that it was an external happening. The conditions of the cure are that the hero doesn't know the real nature of his quest. Even a highly perceptive and imaginative writer like Dick could miss this option. It does suggest that even above average intelligence is no match for a division of the mind which makes one part so alien to another.

This would suggest a tentative explanation for the phenomena of cosmic guardians, archangels, spirit guides, ETs and demons. If the whole heavenly host and the diabolic citizens of the Infernal regions are of this order of reality then we know that the whole of heaven and hell fits neatly within the caverns of our skulls.

The Acid Test

In this New Age era the term "fragmentation" is almost a dirty word. And yet, if an individual is seen as a hierarchy of many possible beings, it implies that we are actually far vaster than we ever imagined. Many gurus, mystics and psychologists insist that the words "in your Father's house there are many mansions" should read "in *your* house"; yet for some unaccountable reason we all chose to live in the woodshed. Once the consciousness can be coaxed out of its cramped quarters the vision widens dramatically. Those who wrote of their experiences with LSD and other hallucinogens in the 1960's and early 70's were afforded glimpses which had, until then, been the exclusive territory of the sages and mages. Those on trips began to experience just how many halls these mansions contained. One of the best known experimenters, Dr. John Lilly, wrote in *The Center of the Cyclone*, of one occasion when he "became a focused center of consciousnesses and traveled into other spaces and met other beings, entities or consciousness's. "In a golden light which seemed to permeate in all directions," he met, what appeared to be, two guardian angels: "They say they are always with me, but that I am not usually in a state to perceive them. I am in a state to perceive them when I am close to the death of the body. In this state there is no time." One is reminded of Christ's description of Heaven: "There shall be time no longer", or the painter William Blake, on his death bed, "gloriously" singing of the sights of angels in heaven.

On a later trip the two guardian angels appear again and this time he is told: "You still have some evasions to explore before you can progress to the level at which you are existing at the moment. You can come and permanently be in this state. However, it is advisable that you achieve this through your own efforts while still in the body."

After extensive experimentation with LSD, hypnosis and meditation, Lilly became convinced that there were four levels above our normal consciousness and four levels below. This roughly corresponds to the Eastern concept according to which there is a level of superconsciousness above the normal range of awareness which then leads to a cosmic consciousness above that. The two balancing levels below are the unconscious and the collective unconscious. The phenomenon of angels appears within the realm of the superconscious and the devils within the unconscious.

Lilly's own proposition suggests a rich layered territory which could account for the "Guided Tours of Heaven and Hell" which have been experienced by saints and mystics.

In visiting the bottomless hell of one bad trip, Lilly describes what he maintains was the most punishing experience of his life. In it he seems to be a very small program in a huge and alien computer (Lilly was a computer expert so would find it a useful analogy). "The whole computer was the result of a senseless dance of certain kinds of atoms …stimulated and pushed by organized but meaningless energies". In a total terror and panic he everywhere "found entities like myself who were slave programs in this huge cosmic conspiracy, this cosmic dance of energy and matter which had absolutely no meaning, no love, no human value."

From my own personal experience I have known a similar "bottomless pit" without the benefit of LSD.

This happened on waking from a lucid dream in which I knew I was dreaming and had attempted to find out just who was directing the dream. There was the same totally alien space filled with what appeared to be black stars like so many thousands of acupuncture points or galaxies of molecules which were completely devoid of all such human qualities as love, life, laughter or light.

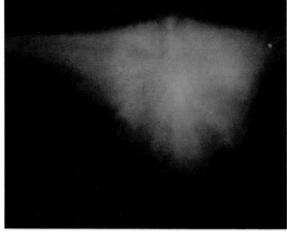

which does have velocity, that is light, and then slowing it down, it creates the manifest universe. The hierarchies of the angels found in the Treasury have identical principles. Lilly met the guardian angels on the second upper level, while on the highest level there was only a sense of being one with the Divinity. At last we have a clear location where beings who fit the description of angels appear to live.

Later I discovered that there is a long mystic tradition which describes this state as falling into "God's dark night". Supposedly there are times when God sleeps and in doing so vacates the void which is usually filled with Light. If a mystic is unfortunate enough to "flower" in meditation at the wrong point in the cycle he falls into this apparent hell. It is claimed that for some the experience is enough to put them off meditation forever. Equally, a glimpse of the upper layers has quite the opposite effect.

It will be recalled that we found a very similar layered hierarchy in the heavenly model in the Treasury. The contemporary channeled entity, Ramtha, has an interesting description of such layers. He says that, "when thought contemplated itself in your beginning, what it expanded itself into was the principle of thought called light. Light was created first, because whenever thought is contemplated and expanded, it always lowers into a vibratory frequency that emits light. Light is thus the first lowered form of contemplated expanded thought."

So all things are created by a thought which has no speed at all. By expanding it into something

Angelic locations

Many psychics and parapsychologists claim that Lilly's various layers of altered consciousness correspond to astral, ethereal and causal territories. According to the esoteric sciences we do not possess just one body but four, and each of these exists in a separate location. When someone experiences an out-of-body event, the *astral body*, for instance, moves in a world that is parallel to our own normal material universe.

Above: **Angel on Television** This image supposedly appeared during a Harmonic Convergence in Mt. Shasta, California. Postcards of the picture have an inscription, "Yes dear ones let it be known that the angels are truly here on Earth." This is certainly the first case of an angel who isn't camera shy. Opposite: **Angel appearing to the King in a dream**, *Lorenzo Monaco, 14th century, Firenze*. One possible explanation given for angelic phenomena is that some of us recall entering astral and ethereal territories and seeing wing-like auras surrounding other dream travelers.

There are many recorded and well documented instances of such phenomena. One of the classic cases is that of Robert Monroe who wrote of his experiences in *Out of the Body*. This otherwise very pragmatic American businessman discovered that he had the strange talent of being able to leave his physical body and travel in other realms or planes. He managed to explore three distinct localities with what he believes is his astral body. The first locale is our own physical world, but Monroe experienced that moving within this realm with an astral body feels very unnatural and the traveler is easily disorientated and exhausted. The second locality is a non-material, boundless immensity, which has very different laws of time and space, motion and matter to those found in locality one. In this world, as Monroe puts it, "as you think so you are". It is the natural abode of the astral body, the individual consciousness after death and the astral bodies of dreamers. Monroe's own theory is that there are "an infinity of worlds all operating at different frequencies". Just as wave vibrations can simultaneously occupy the same space, "with the minimum of interaction, so might the worlds of Locale II be interspersed in our physical matter world." A characteristic already observed in Dr. Lilly's account is that this corresponding level is a timeless zone. The past and the future co-exist with the here and now. However, the traveler can perceive what appears as solid matter as well as artifacts common to the physical world.

This locality is, "composed of deepest desires and most frantic fears", which are completely unshielded from others traveling in the same place. The zones nearest to the physical world are peopled by insane, emotionally driven beings who are still identified with their desires and fears. Passing through this region was like venturing into hell. There are precise descriptions in the ancient Tibetan Book of the Dead which closely correspond to Monroe's independent findings. His descriptions would also fit some of those Medieval visions of Heaven and Hell which we have already encountered. It will be recalled that at the borders of those heavens closest to our physical earth, demented and demonic creatures haunt the pathways and one of the specific duties of the angels of the order of Powers is to act as border patrols. The mystic Swedenburg would leave his body much in the same way as Monroe, and meet with angels and beings from the "Other World". In Celtic myths the "Other World" is parallel to our own and can be reached by crossing a stream, walking around a burial mound or meeting with the magical folk. But the hero is always warned that there is no sense of time in that nether region and he might re-

Above left: **The Silver Shield of the Mental Body,** *illustration by M. from "Dayspring of Youth."* The radiant field of energy currents which surround our mental, astral or ethereal bodies are remarkably suggestive of the wings of an angel. It is very possible that we experience seeing such images when moving in the astral or ethereal planes during sleep but do not remember in our waking hours. However the memory continues to haunt us at the edge of consciousness so that when we see a picture of an angel we feel some sense of recognition.
Above right: **Phane's Birth of the World Egg,** *117-138 A.D.*. Phanes is known as "The Shining One," and in almost all respects shadows the image on the left, as if the artist has remembered more than most of us.

turn to the physical world hundreds of years older.

If we examine any descriptions or drawings of auras or of ethereal, astral or psychic bodies, then there is an uncanny resemblance to the wings of angels. Anyone who has experienced astral traveling or an out of the body experience will tell of the sheer exhilaration of flight. The forces around the astral body fan out behind the traveler like the electromagnetic fields around the planets and this could account for the angelic archetype. In similar modes to that of sleep we are able to leave the body. In this state we might see other astral travelers, but on returning to the substantive world forget the experience entirely, much as we forget most of our dreams. And somewhere we keep a memory, although the conscious mind seldom has access to it.

Monroe once "projected" himself into the study of a well known parapsychologist, Dr. Andrija Puharich. He had a long talk with him but when verifying the visit later Puharich had no recollection of the discussion at all. However, Monroe was able to describe the study in perfect detail and confirmed exactly what the psychologist was doing at the time. It does suggest that we might be able to communicate with other astral entities but that our physical memories retain no record of the transaction. Which also suggests that the phenomenon of multiple-entities might extend even into parallel worlds.

One ingenious explanation for the appearance of angels is that the astral bodies of those who sleep on the nightside of the planet can manifest to those awake on the dayside. There may be more to this seemingly wacky idea than first meets the eye. There are many cases of dreamers who pick up what is happening in other parts of the world. Earthquakes, plane disasters and wars are experienced in dreams. Millions of dreamers may forget actually experiencing a particularly awful flood on the other side of the globe or just put it down to a nightmare. But the frequency of those who pick up the newspaper or watch the television the next morning to see their nightmare in the flesh is too great to ignore. Unfortunately little respectable or serious research has been done in this area. But imagine a dreamer in Europe who tries to warn the occupants of a house of a coming earthquake. At first the physical occupants are oblivious of her existence and the dreamer feels impotent to avert disaster. Making a supreme effort she somehow manages to get through to them and they rush out of the building to see it collapse in rubble a few moments later. To the dreamer it is a satisfying conclusion to a nightmare, to the substantial Colombians it is hailed as a miracle and the dreamer as an unknown angel.

Having examined some of the more elaborate angelic speculations it is well to be reminded of William of Occam. He was the first Western thinker to expound the notion of *Notitia Intuitiva* or Intuitive Cognition. He believed that we are capable of perceiving things without the need of words or concepts. He insisted that, in the presence of any theory, parsimony was best. Occam's miserly "razor" prunes all unnecessary elaborations from any hypothesis and heads for the simplest and most obvious solution. With this in mind and armed with Samuel Butler's adage that "all reason is against it, and all healthy instinct is for it," we can turn to the Last Judgment.

CHAPTER SEVEN
The Last Judgment

The Last Judgment *by Hans Memlinc, Brussels*

Having Examined Some Of The More Exotic Speculations as to who and what the angelic host might be and why they persist in our collective unconscious, it is clear that each hypothesis has had both its own peculiar merits and particular drawbacks. It remains largely a matter of individual taste which one seems to fit the facts. This is one of the problems fundamental to theorizing. If you are blind and have never seen the sun rise it doesn't matter how many hypotheses you can array, you still don't *know*. Belief is simply the adoption of someone else's idea. Once you have seen the sun you don't *believe* in it, you *know* it. But as far as angels are concerned, few have ever seen one, or if anyone has during some astral tour, he or she have managed to forget the whole episode. It is also surely evident by now that angels don't leave footprints so all that is left of their traces is a complex jumble of hypotheses. So this seems a perfect time to apply the sharp blade of Occam's "razor" to cut away all the excess ideas.

William of Occam is exactly the man for the job. He was the last great theologian of the Middle Ages who also helped to open up an entirely new vein of Christianity. As the brilliant pupil of Duns Scotus and a "theoretical" follower of St. Francis, he proposed the possibility of an immediate grasp and perception of singular objects, without any need for intermediary thoughts. This he called intuitive cognition. While, on the surface this doesn't seem to be an idea which could shake the foundations of the whole heavenly hierarchy, nevertheless it did. And his maxims are as relevant to our understanding of angels as they were seven centuries ago.

Occam argued that all concepts, like those to be found in our Treasury of Angelic Lore, were symbols devoid of reality, they were empty shells. This being the case the process of abstract reasoning is useless. The vast theoretical hierarchy of angels is actually constructed of concept, built upon concept or emptiness upon emptiness. In Occam's eyes the path to God could never be found through the intellect and of course what was known of angels at that time was almost entirely channeled through the minds of the scholars. The implications of Occam's principles were not lost on the brighter minds of the Establishment. For if one can perceive a thing

without an intermediary thought, then it is not a very long road to travel before one can see God or Christ face to face without the mediation and interpretation of a priest or a Church.

Before being able to apply Occam's sword to the angelic theories of today, it is necessary to see how they affected those of the golden age of the host at the time of the great schism which split the Church of the 14th century. The true cause of this split was not that two politically hungry Popes faced off in France and Italy, but rather, that two completely irreconcilable paths suddenly appeared in one religion. The intellectual, Aristotelian reasoning of Thomas Aquinas clashed with the Mystical, Intuitive experience of St. Francis. A line up of the two sides might be helpful at this point.

Thomas Aquinas	St. Francis
Angelic Host	Christ as a Man
Scholasticism	Direct Experience
Male	Female
Intellect	Mysticism
Reason	Intuition
Knowledge	Love
Communication	Communion
Dionysius the Aeropagite	William of Occam
Albertus Magnus	Duns scotus
Aristotle	Plotinus
Via Antiqua	Via Moderna
The Dominicans	Franciscans
The Curia	Spirituals
Dante	Bonaventura
Human-like angel	Angel-like human

Above: **The Entrance to Heaven,** and Right: **The Last Judgment** by *Hieronymus Bosch, Venice, 1500*

Up until this point in history, the right wing of the intellect, the orthodox Church, had never been seriously challenged since the wild days of the Gnostics a thousand years before. But now a new type of Christian arose, exemplified by St. Francis of Assisi, the mystic who inadvertently and simply by his presence, toppled the whole angelic hierarchy.

Human-like Angels meet Angel-like Humans

About a century before the outbreak of the plague two minor monastic orders had been created within a few years of each other. They were at opposite ends of the Christian spectrum, like the two hemispheres of the human brain. The Dominicans were established in 1216 to combat heresy and defend the hierarchic authority. By 1231 this was transformed into the dreaded order of the Inquisition. In complete contrast were the Franciscans who, forming around Francis of Assisi, desired to reimbue the Church with the original Christian spirit. Their self-appointed task was to re-awaken popular piety and engage in scientific work. These two orders represented the polar extremes of intellectual and mystical worship. The Franciscans believed that the soul's eventual union with God could be attained, not by "imitating" angels, but quite literally by "becoming" angels. This was a monastic order which sought to know God or Christ directly, dispensing with the traditional clergy as intermediaries, which of course hardly pleased that clergy.

When the orthodox authority of the Church, with its legions of angels, had manifestly failed to halt the plague in any way, there was a turning towards the simple and direct mystic faith which Francis represen-

ted. As his order was dedicated to the road of poverty, it was a welcome change to what was seen as a grasping and greedy priesthood. The gentle and almost feminine receptivity of the Franciscans also appealed to a people worn out with the ravages of the period.

These Franciscan monks, with the exemplary life of Francis himself to guide them, were there to offer a new vision. They believed that only the "fire of Love" could renew the world and cure its wounds. Remember, that the highest order of angels in the old hierarchical system were the Seraphim, those "fiery serpents *burning with love*." It was no coincidence that it was a seraph who appeared to Francis to communicate the Stigmata of Christ. This was a transmission beyond the scriptures. "The seraphic ardor" of Francis had simply made him a seraph on earth. But the stigmata transmitted by the figure of Christ which appeared superimposed upon the angel was the mark which showed that Francis had become *more than an angel*. He had become a Christ.

So in looking back at those battle-lines and the last champions who opposed one another it was the human-like angel of the scholar who was simply loved to death by the angel-like mystic.

Tale of Two Cities

The great flying buttress of the Medieval Church was built upon the dogma of the twin cities of God. As already seen, one was held to be the Holy City, the New Jerusalem and the Heavenly abode of the angels. The other was the City of Earth. Within this lower City, in which we mortal sinners live, was the Mother Church. This was the only part which modeled itself upon the Holy City above and upon its equally holy inhabitants, the angels. So the hierarchy of the Church was supposed to be a mirror

Above: **The Earthly City of the Serpent**
Right: **The Holy City or the New Jerusalem**
Both images are from the *Apocalypse of Liebana*,
11th century, Paris, National Library
Here are the twin cities, one of Man and the other of the Angels. The Black Death decimated the City of Man but it left the City of the Angels completely deserted.

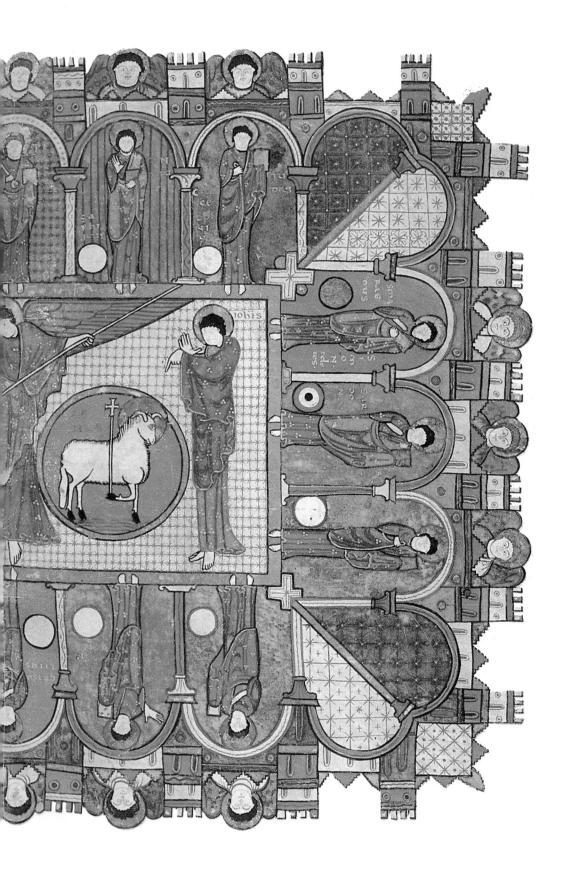

reflection of that superstructure of the heavens.

By the 14th century it was all too clear that something had gone terribly wrong with this model. All that the overtaxed and persecuted populace could see was the gross corruption of the clergy. Disenchantment with the ecclesiastical authorities boiled over when a deep schism appeared to split the Church of Peter, exposing its rotten and very earthly core. At this time the Holy vessel had two papal helmsmen: Clement VII elected in Avignon and Urban VI elected in Rome. After fifty years of stalemate, cardinals of both factions elected a third Pope. But just as the Church mirrored the Holy City with its complex angelic hierarchies, the reflection worked both ways, so the Heavenly abode must mirror the Church. Thus the entire celestial structure was seen to have also split and crumbled. The crash wiped out most of the angels who were supporting its pillars.

Simultaneous with the religious crisis, the horrified population of Europe of the 14th century had to face the terrible scourge of the plague. For most Christians the Black Death was the dreaded apocalypse come true, and was seen as the last trump and the end of the world. As half of Europe was dying, the Church vainly tried to rally its saints and its legions of angels to combat the menace.

Both saint and angel were supposed to be able to turn back such horrors, but neither did. Everyone could plainly see the emptiness and impotence of the Church's brave vanguard. Few angels escaped the effects of that plague in the memories of the masses.

Another significant Medieval dogma was that when a third of the rebel angels fell they were supposed to have left a vast gap in heaven. Humans were to have filled this gap by becoming "like unto the angels." We find many Christian ascetics stri-

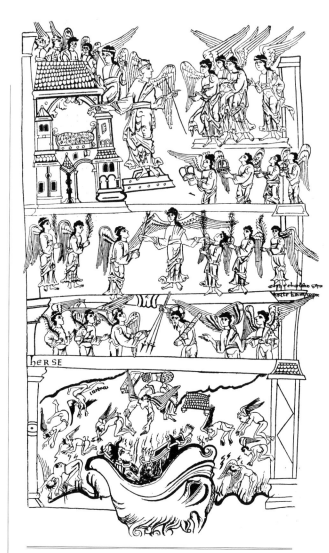

The Expulsion of Lucifer and the Rebel Angels from Heaven *Caedmon paraphrase.* When Lucifer fell he took with him one-third of the heavenly host. The empty places left in the Holy City were supposed to be filled by humans who became "like the Angels." By the middle of the 15th century this foundational concept of the Church was successfully challenged by the newly arising Humanism. In retrospect, it seems that quite the reverse actually happened. Angels came to Earth.

ving to rid themselves of the temptations of the flesh in order to meet that ideal. The corruption and desires of the flesh were seen to be the problem. Sex was obviously the real enemy, for of course angels were not supposed to have any. Taking pleasure in food was another hurdle to overcome, as it was generally acknowledged that angels didn't eat anything more substantial than God's Word. As we will shortly learn, a saint like Catherine of Siena most likely suffered from an acute eating disorder, probably anorexia, in her attempt to emulate this impossible angelic ideal.

Christ was only Human

In the aftermath of the plague a depression settled over Europe and with it a widespread distrust of all the Church's excessive religious ornamentation, its myriad spirits and impotent saints and holy martyrs. The new Humanist ideas which challenged the angelic hierarchies, the indulgences and the veneration of saints also perceived Christ in a new way. Since Christ was recognized as the real mediator between God the Father and humankind, or as one aspect of the Divine Trinity, why should anyone bother with an entire host of angels as well?

The very fact that Christ came to earth to share the sufferings of human beings makes him very human. Consequently it also makes him far removed from the angels who cannot share the experience of those self-same sufferings, without taking on the flesh themselves. And Christians knew all about angels who take on the corruption of the flesh – they're bad.

Yet another cherished concept was dealt a mortal blow as the early sciences began to gain respectability. In the harsh light of the new realities of astronomy, the whole concept of the seven heavens and the seven earths began to appear absurd. The old belief that it was the spirits and angels who kept the universe turning was replaced by a new belief in "natural forces" like gravity. As those proto-sciences expanded the horizons of their knowledge, so the whole angelic firmament of stars began to fade in the light of the new dawn. And as the old universe slowly crumbled, so too did the host of angels who had supported its existence for so long. The Heavenly City became deserted and was replaced on earth by the Book of Nature.

The mystical marriage of Christ and the Holy Jerusalem in Revelations, which once represented the pure female soul (and thus all saintly women were Christ's bride) , gave way to a new marriage in heaven. This was the union of man and nature.

The immediate effect of the scientific approach was an acquisition of new knowledge, which further weakened an already wobbly house of angelic cards. Through the printing press that knowledge was disseminated in ways unthinkable in the 14th century. Knowledge up until that point, had been the prerogative of the Church and of the angels who were supposed to govern the workings of the cosmos. With the birth of scientific methodology that active angelic intelligence had either been superseded by humans or it had really come down to earth.

While, later on, the Reformation was to successfully challenge the Church's virtue (which anyone could see was a particularly weak spot) the Age of Reason challenged its intelligence. On most subjects its priests and scholars were shown to be ignorant and credulous. And these experts were the very champions of the angelic cause. Surely if the clergy were shown to be fools it was necessary to question the intelligence of the heavenly host itself. In the ensuing battle the angelic shocktroops were the first casualties.

Just like the Angels

So now man was no longer a replacement angel for the Holy City of God in Heaven, but a living example of the Redeemer within the City of Earth. The man-like angel became the angel-like man who could reach out, beyond the angels, to Christ Consciousness.

Francis's successor, Bonaventure, says of the Saint, "by the Seraphic ardor of his desires, he was born aloft unto God; and by his sweet compassion he was transformed into him who chose to be crucified because of the excess of his love." The transformation into more than an angel happens "not through martyrdom of the flesh but through the fire of his love consuming his soul."

Bonaventure goes on to tell us that Francis "was joined in a bond of inseparable love to the angels who burn with a marvelous fire." It was these Seraphim who would then "inflame the souls of the elect."

Whatever one's personal spiritual persuasions might be it, is difficult to remain unmoved by the story of Francis. But if he is the new angelic prototype then, at first glance, the species is likely to remain rare. At the same time, whatever remains of a living Christ within the boundaries of that religion must surely come from St. Francis. It is also no coincidence that his direct heirs are actually heiresses. For to be an angel on earth requires a receptive and female attitude. The virile angel of Thomas Aquinas, who remains, in essence, an intellectual, incorporeal, spirit has given way to the Seraphs of the "Fire of Love."

Strangely enough, a figure who appears to be one of Francis's spiritual daughters, Catherine of Siena, was a Dominican and therefore in the opposite camp. She would have been more familiar with

the intellectual teachings of Thomas Aquinas than those of Francis. Yet, while Aquinas, the "doctor of angels," was known to have a prodigious appetite, Catherine herself was anorexic and died at the age of thirty three having nourishment only from communion wafers. Like Francis, her overwhelming passion was to become what she called "an earthly angel".

Her approach was extreme, for in trying to imitate the angel she accepted a vision that the soul only becomes angelic by eating the right kind of food. And this is simply the Word of God. Her typical admonitions to her fellow sisters read: "Dearest daughter, contemplate the marvelous state of the soul who receives this bread of life, this food of angels, as she ought." In one of her visions God tells her that the Church has become a temple of the devil: "I appointed you to be earthly angels in this life, but you are devils who have taken up devils' work. "This is a very different message from that of before the Black Death. But by then even God had been forced to recognize that His servants on earth had found Satan's company more congenial.

With Francis the angel took on the flesh and experienced the divine in the same way as the mystic. The intellectual host of immaterial angels of Thomas Aquinas and the orthodox Church have descended to earth, but in taking on the flesh they have become receptive, like a female.

St. Francis receives the Stigmata, *by Giotto, Basilica S. Croce, Florence.* The six-winged, fiery Seraph of Love takes on the form of Christ. The Seraph was the highest expression of angelic consciousness and thus the perfect vehicle to communicate the stigmata. But the transformation of the angel into Christ meant a *communion* with Francis which went far beyond the angel, for in this supreme moment Francis became Christ Consciousness.

Even the stigmata of Francis, and those of Christ before him, show the signs of a vagina. The wound in the side of Christ has often been likened to a lactating breast. Perhaps nowhere is this image of the femininity of the seeker more poignantly expressed as in the rapturous vision of St. Teresa of Avila which we have already seen in Chapter Two. As the angel pierces her body with a long golden spear, it causes her a "pain so sharp that it made me utter several moans; and so excessive was the sweetness caused me by this intense pain that one can never wish to lose it, nor will one's soul be content with anything less than God."

The fanatic mystic, Bernard of Clairvaux, had already written of the Virgin: "A polished arrow too is that special love of Christ, which not only pierced Mary's soul but penetrated through and through, so that even the tiniest space of her virginal breast was permeated by love." A chaste virgin, according to Bernard, "Adores and worships one God, *just like the angels*; she loves Christ above all things, *just like the angels*; she is chaste, *just like the angels*, and that in the flesh of a fallen race, in a frail body that the angels do not have. But she seeks and savors the things that they enjoy, not the things that are on the earth…that as an exile on earth she enjoys the glory of celibate life, than that she lives like an angel in an animal body."

It was the pure Virgin of Siena who carried Bernard's image to a logical extreme by renouncing worldly foods in order to savor the food of angels. It is difficult to tell whether Catherine's visions were the hysterical outpourings of an anorexic or whether they were genuine religious experiences, but her obvious ecstatic states equal those of the angels. In talking of her soul she has this to say: "Her desire knows no pain nor her satisfaction any boredom…she often attains such union that she hardly knows whether she is in the body or out of it." Just like the Angels.

Evolutionary Feathers

So, one might inquire, is this the end product of applying Occam's pruning knife to the elaborations from the earlier theoretical explanations of what angels really might be and why they persist in our times? Are we to surmise that in the Middle Ages angels had come down to earth and suffered from anorexia? Perhaps we might conclude that this is why someone like Catherine can fly and the fat Aquinas could never leave the ground?

The argument that angels have indeed come to ground is more far reaching than it might at first appear. It might imply that the phenomenon of the angel is a very particular, evolutionary, stage in the development of human spirituality. But it would be more precise to suggest that angels are an essential stage along western man's path to enlightenment.

In the East the major religious and spiritual path is through meditation. In the West the union with the Divine Source is usually sought through prayer. In meditation a witness needs no intermediator, although mystics can experience some very bizarre encounters with the deities of their particular background. The 19th century mystic, Ramakrishna, was totally absorbed with the Goddess Kali. She appeared to him as a completely substantial

Melancholia *by Albrecht Dürer.* With the rise of Humanism and the new proto-sciences, during the 15th century, much of the numinous and imaginative universe of the earlier centuries faded from the collective consciousness. Inevitably this cool intellectual and objective way of viewing the world brought with it a certain severing of the magical links with reality. Angels were amongst the first casualties.

being and he became obsessively stuck at that point simply because she was so beautiful and he loved her so much. Eventually it required a violent intervention by his Guru, to force him to destroy the image. Once accomplished, this destruction allowed Ramakrishna to move into a more comprehensive stage of consciousness. Likewise in our century the charismatic master Da Free John experienced both a real and substantial Virgin Mary, as well as a full and fleshy Goddess, before both faded and he moved to the final stage of his realization. Many mystics and spiritual seekers experience just such bizarre apparitions at certain times.

In a number of traditions there are particular experiences that help the seeker's progress along the so called spiritual paths and these have been carefully documented. For instance, there are certain meditations in which the seeker can explore the mysterious inner workings of the brain pathways. During this certain images and sounds seem to separate themselves from the observer and appear real and exterior. It is possible that on consciously entering the cerebellum or the brain core the observer actually triggers the archetypes hidden within its interior.

There is an equally powerful route to the Divine through devotion and prayer. In India this is exemplified by the *Bhakti*, or the Devotee. There have been many mystics who have worshipped the deity Krishna as if he was actually before them, in the flesh. Both men and women devotees accept that Krishna is the bridegroom and they are the brides. The process can be seen to be virtually identical to the one experienced by St. Francis. Whether in the form of Christ or Krishna, the ecstatic meeting with the Beloved is a meeting of the "fire of

Love." The devotee in essence becomes one of the Seraphim, one of the innermost intelligences which surround the Divine Source as seen in the Heavenly Hierarchies. But now, instead of the process being an intellectual idea, the mystic lives the experience of that ecstatic vibration of Love. It recalls the experience of the composer Jerry Neff. "I could only see what seemed like a blazing pool of white or slightly golden light – what you might see if it were possible to look straight into the sun. But I did not see it so much as *feel* it, and that feeling was one of absolute ecstasy, involving every 'good' sensation and every 'rightness' imaginable, and in a moral sense as well. This bliss included benevolence, joy and reconciliation of opposites – literally *everything* at once." Just like the angels. But now the angel has come to earth and the human has arrived in Heaven.

Contacting the Higher Self

This New Age has brought to the surface many spiritual ideas which are odd combinations of the teachings of the East, of Western esotericism, of the occult and North American shamanism. One concept, which has its corresponding reality for those who practice it, is the belief in a Higher Self. This is the Inner Teacher of Claire Prophet or can even be seen as the "link" personality of those with MPD. It is the consciousness which has an overview of the

Angels of the Crucifixion *by Raphael, National Gallery, London.* The very fact that the Church was forced by the new Humanism to recognize that the Divine had come to Earth as a flesh and blood human being, who experienced the dualities of joy and suffering just as we do, meant that the angels, who could not (without falling), gradually faded from the picture.

individual. This Higher Self can be consciously contacted and sometimes it acts as a channeling entity. It has already been observed in the cases of multiple personalities that one of the "selves" is usually wiser and more mature than the others. Some even see this as the active angelic intelligence which is a hidden part living within one of the many mansions of our whole being. This higher self often tries to communicate with the normal everyday consciousness and sometimes does so in outlandish and bizarre ways such as creating an abduction episode or a contact with Other Worldly beings.

Now just suppose that this projection, which seems so real to the subject, can be seen by others who are in some way in a sympathetic space. Were the marks of the crucifixion on the body of Francis, those marks which supposedly were made by an angel, a mass hallucination on the part of his brother monks? This is the eye-witness report of the corpse of the saint: "His limbs were so soft and supple to the touch that they seemed to have regained the tenderness of childhood and to be adorned with clear signs of his innocence. The *nails appeared black against his shining skin, and the wound in his side was red like a rose in springtime.*" (Bonaventure). It was no wonder that the onlookers were amazed at the "miracle" and were confounded at how it was possible.

Equally miraculous is the Eastern concept that our normal consciousness is like the tip of an iceberg, or like Dr. Lilly's nine layers: we don't see the rest of a vast consciousness which is available to us. "Above us there is superconsciousness which is nine times as great as consciousness, while still higher there is cosmic consciousness which is ninefold that of super-consciousness. If that isn't enough the sages tell us: 'below', there is the unconscious, nine times as vast as our consciousness and below that there is the ninefold collective unconscious." At this point it might be wondered whatever happened to the Devil? Examining the model of the various layers of consciousness it is easy to infer an up and a down, an overworld of Heaven and an underworld of Hell. It does suggest that, just as angels can be seen as a stage in the development of awareness, so can devils. We are all perfectly capable of delighting or terrifying ourselves with visions from these ninefold layers, and we do.

The City *by Gustave Doré.* The Heavenly City or the New Jerusalem envisioned by John of Patmos remained empty of both angels and human-like angels. The reality of the paradise garden is most beautifully expressed in an old Zen saying. "This Very Place the Lotus Paradise, This Very Body the Buddha." For the Angels reside within us all and we are already standing in the Garden.

The Last Judgment

The Seraph which appeared to St. Francis could be seen as the last great visitation of the Angels. It was the turning point of a magnificent transformation and the last snip of Occam's razor. This glimpse was of the highest expression of angelic consciousness, burning with the fire of love. The image transformed into Christ who communicated the physical marks of the flesh to Francis. At that moment the spiritual man of the West made a great quantum leap. Man and angel merged in a consciousness higher than both. The essence of the higher angelic self, that higher vibration of Love became integrated with that of the lower vibration of the material world. All the multiple "personalities" became one whole. In the East such an integrity is known as enlightenment.

Eastern mystics have often commented, one might feel rather smugly, that the holy men and women of the West stop too long at a certain stage on the so-called spiritual path. That stage Meher Baba calls the "saintly" level. It corresponds to the opening of the third eye. It does appear that the experience is so ecstatic and literally miraculous that many mystics do get stuck there. Some maintain that this stage corresponds to the highest point of active angelic intelligence. It is said, that to pass beyond

this point, is the whole reason that the soul must take on the flesh. It might be added that the same is true for the angel. Many religious traditions maintain that Enlightenment can only be realized for those who are in the body. That final release, the Liberation, needs something to be liberated from. If you have to transcend possessiveness it's no good having nothing to give up. A great hoarder or miser who can suddenly walk away from all his wealth without a backward glance is free.

In looking back over this whole survey it can be seen that our images of angels were just too perfect, perhaps just too good. They simply lacked contrast. Even when some rebelled they then merely became just too bad. Both good and bad were polarities. It requires the encapsulation of both principles within the boundaries of one body to really effect a true union of such poles. Humans live within the constant war of the dualities of the body and the spirit, good and evil, love and hate. While in the body no one can escape the responsibility which that entails. Only through enlightenment can a union emerge and a true flight of freedom happen. And those particular wings leave the angelic host far behind. In this respect St. Paul was right. Man is a higher form of life than the angel. But he didn't mention that such a human had to be *whole*.

Epilogue

In the course of this volume we have covered a great deal of territory in our quest to discover the real angels and why we all seem to care so much about them. Although it would have been tempting, at the outset, to accept that their nature is one of those inexplicable and unknowable mysteries of existence, we have chosen, instead, to examine both long established ideas as well as some often outlandish possibilities.

However, sooner or later, all such concepts reveal limitations, beyond which our normal minds cannot travel. Beyond this point we enter the realm of Grace or one's particular faith or belief. Ultimately we arrive at each person's own first hand mystical experience. For, even after all this exploration, angels still appear as inseparable from their witnesses as they did at the outset. When all is analysed and written, the hidden meaning of angels remains that they are an *inseparable part of each one of us*. We are One; the angel is one of our inner and most magical aspects; the angel is an integral part of *ourselves*. This is also William of Occam's gift to us. Our intuitive cognition, our direct knowing of that angelic aspect of our many selves is worth all someone else's paper angels of the intellect, howsoever beautiful and awe-inspiring they might at first appear. It is a far greater message than any separate and external archangel could ever bring.

If you really want to see an angel don't look for one outside: they reside within, and so long as human beings seek their own totality and wholeness, the angelic species cannot be endangered.

"But as for me, if thou wouldst know
What I was;
In a word
I am the Word who did dance all things
and was not shamed at all.
'Twas I who leapt and danced...Amen"
The Hymn of Jesus (The Leucian Acts)

Dedicated to One who danced all these things,
with Love and Light and Laughter.

The publishers wish to thank the following for their kind permission to use images found in this volume.

Scala, Italy: pages 14, 38, 50, 100, 129, 152, 156, 160, 236

– British Museum, London
– Museum of Art, Brussels
– Campo Santo, Pisa
– Sam Haskins
– Johfra
– Museum of Art, Madrid
– Historical Museum, Moscow
– Paris National Library
– National Gallery, London
– Uffizi Gallery, Firenze

ACKNOWLEDGMENTS

This book was compiled during the winter of 1989 and 1990 in a remote and exquisite part of Tuscany, between Florence and Siena. These Renaissance cities have more angels and demons gracing their walls than anywhere else on Earth. However this splendid isolation had its drawbacks and many of those I wish to thank for their help do not even know they gave it, for I only met them in the pages of their books. All the same my thanks to Colin Wilson, whose *Mysteries* (Grafton 1979) gave the necessary spark to the chapter on multiple personalities; to Christian and Barbara O'Brien for their thought provoking *The Chosen Few* (Turnstone Press 1985) which provided the theme for the chapter called The Shining Ones; to Gustav Davidson whose *Dictionary of Angels* (Free Press 1967) remains the most extensive compendium of Angelic Lore with a marvellous bibliography which cannot be bettered, and to Stuart Schneiderman for simply penning such a delightful *An Angel Passes* (N.Y. University Press 1988).

My very particular thanks to Deborah Bergman who, as consulting editor, was a transitional angel who I have only encountered in the extensive footnotes and deletions all over the first draft of the original manuscript. Any coherence the reader finds in the text can only be due to her labors. My heartfelt thanks to Philip Dunn of Labyrinth Publishing, for his ever optimistic attitude when visiting Hell, firmly believing Heaven to be just around the corner; to Simonetta Castelli for managing to fit text around so many feathers and membranes; to beloved Navyo who keeps me laughing and who was the original model for Lilith, and to the "Old Boy", who celebrated All and Everything and was the fieriest seraph of Love and the most devilish rogue I was ever fortunate enough to know.